MAKERS OF THE NINETEENTH CENTURY
Edited by Basil Williams

LIFE OF ABDUL HAMID

BY

SIR EDWIN PEARS

LONDON
CONSTABLE & COMPANY LTD
1917

GENERAL EDITOR'S PREFACE

For, in a world where cruel deeds abound,
The merely damned are legion; with such souls
Is not each hollow and cranny of Tophet crammed?
Thou with the brightest of Hell's aureoles
Dost shine supreme, incomparably crowned,
Immortally, beyond all mortals, damned.

THUS wrote Mr. William Watson in a sonnet apologising to the late Sultan for having once called him simply "Abdul the Damned."

A word of apology on my part may, perhaps, be expected for having included this sorry creature, Abdul Hamid, among the *Makers of the Nineteenth Century*. It will be seen by those who read this volume, written by one who has spent most of the working years of his life among the Turks, who saw and made others see what was good in them, and who has always lifted up his voice against the cowardly oppression of their rulers, that, far from gaining as a personality from intimate knowledge, Abdul Hamid loses even the little credit he had with those who judged him from afar as, at any rate, an astute and able ruler. All this is true enough, and yet as an influence on the political thought and action of Europe in the last quarter of the nineteenth century, as one who has handed down that evil influence to the Europe of this century, Abdul Hamid may justly lay claim to be included among those who have helped in large measure to make or mar the world into which we were born.

During his reign Abdul Hamid was an evil nightmare

brooding over Europe, the kind of nightmare which a sleeper could shake off at any moment, did he but choose to move, but he cannot choose and still remains fixed and motionless: and so the nightmare abides. Abdul Hamid traded on his own weakness and on the weakness of his country; for he knew that though all abhorred him, no country would take the lead against him in retribution for his most outrageous crimes, lest instead of abasing him it should be set upon by the others and itself abased. Thus it could be said of Europe during Abdul Hamid's reign that she

> must hearken to the wail
> Of women martyred by the turbaned crew,
> Whose tenderest mercy was the sword that slew:—

and all the time

> She sees, she hears, with soul unstirred
> And lifts no hand and speaks no word,
> But vaunts a brow like theirs who deem
> Men's wrongs a phrase, men's rights a dream.

This apathy of Europe, and Abdul Hamid's crafty calculations on this apathy explain his success in crime: his treacherous murders, his policy of Armenian massacres, and all the corrupting methods of government, which he has handed down to those who turned him out and succeeded him. How empty was his appearance of strength may be seen from his immediate surrender to England, Russia or France, or any power that momentarily chose to insist on a point that concerned their interests, and from his collapse like a pricked bladder on the first assault by a few determined subjects.

He fell. But he still lives, and perchance, if he be allowed in his prison to hear news of the world, where he played so ignominious a part, he may still have a melancholy satisfaction in knowing that his ignominy is being perpetuated by his successors. They were men who rebelled against a hateful rule and a hateful tyrant, but by their hideous massacres in Armenia they have almost washed out the remembrance of the less complete massacres, of which he set the example, and have erected into a policy of extermination the scheme of secret and spasmodic outrages, at which he connived. He saw more of the Turkish Empire disappear than any one of his ancestors since the Turks came to Europe : since his deposition his successors have not only lost provinces, including the Holy Places, the very basis of the Sultan's power and prestige, but, whereas Abdul Hamid played one power against another so well that he never gave up a tittle of national independence, they have placed their country completely under the tutelage of one too-powerful neighbour. In all this they are carrying out and indeed improving on the methods of Abdul, whose title to fame is that he was the maker of ruin for his country and the man, to whose action and example Europe may be able to trace back her redemption from a cruel and oppressive burden, since the better part of her has at last risen to redress those and other wrongs.

BASIL WILLIAMS.

CHELSEA,
January, 1917.

CONTENTS

LIFE OF ABDUL HAMID

PRELIMINARY

In what sense can Abdul Hamid be considered as one of the Makers of the Nineteenth Century? His work was destructive rather than constructive, but destruction must often precede construction.

At the beginning of the last century Turkey still remained an armed camp. The Moslem population treated the Christians as *rayahs*, or cattle, who were not and never could be entitled to the privileges of Believers. Turkey's rulers knew little of and cared little for Western public opinion. The only opinion which they regarded was that of the Moslems of the Empire, and especially of the Capital. Nevertheless there were already signs of improvement in the public administration. There were fewer of the grosser forms of oppression and less brutality during the first half of the nineteenth century than in any period of the same length since the conquest of Constantinople in 1453.

The history of the internal development of Turkey records changes during that period which were in the direction of progress. The destruction of the Janissaries by Mahmud II. in 1826 was the elimination of an element of disorder which had prevented any kind of reform during at least a century. The efforts of our Ambassador, Mr. Canning, afterwards Lord Stratford de Redcliffe, which continued during nearly forty years, were largely directed to the regeneration of the Empire. A man of clear insight, great pertinacity and statesman-like mind, he saw that the great object to be accomplished for making a homogeneous people of the various races under Turkish rule was the substitution of religious equality for the dominancy of the Turkish Moslems. After long and quite extraordinary persistency he extorted from the Sultan the Hatti-huma-yun which has often been described as the Magna Carta of the Turkish people. Its provisions regarding religious liberty were constantly violated throughout the Empire and even in the Capital itself, but the placing of such a document on the Statute Book led slowly but certainly in the direction of obedience to its provisions. It was as sure a sign of progress as the granting of the Great Charter had been to England. It was mainly due to Canning's influence that, always with the idea of regenerating Turkey, the Empire after the Crimean War was allowed to take rank among the Great European Powers. In the years which immediately followed, a series of able Ministers, of whom Ali, Reshad, and Fuad Pashas were the most notable, seemed to justify Canning's efforts and hopes. The country was governed with a fair amount of success on what may be called reformed Asiatic lines. The Sultans rarely interfered with their Ministers so long as their wants and those of their harems were complied with. The Ministers were the real rulers of the country. Life and property were fairly safe. Turkey was indeed blundering her way out of barbarism. Certain well-marked steps towards improvement in Turkish administration had been taken during the first seventy years of the nineteenth century. Reform was in every one's thoughts.

Even in reference to foreign affairs progress had been made. When John Sobieski in 1683 relieved Vienna, the Turkish Empire had reached its zenith. Every succeeding generation from that date had seen a loss of territory, and such diminution continued steadily down to the accession of Abdul Hamid in 1876. It must be noted, however, that during this period it was the Moslem population, every member of which was a soldier, which was the element which counted most and indeed was the only element which counted in what the world spoke of as the Turkish Empire. That element had been even strengthened by its loss of territory, by the elimination of what to the Turkish military party were sources of weakness. A dissatisfied Greece had become independent. After the events in Bulgaria in 1876, for which of course Abdul Hamid is not responsible, Mr. Disraeli, speaking of them and of the Turkish Provinces which were separated from the rule of the Sultan by the Congress of Berlin, boldly claimed that Turkey had gained an advantage by this "consolidation." Naturally the word itself was much criticised at the time and was often taken to have been used satirically; but it had an element of truth. Rumanians, Bulgarians, Serbians, and other Christians were always, and justly, a dissatisfied portion of the population. The Turkish population, then and now, was inferior in education and intelligence to the Christian. It was inevitable that such inferiority would bring about revolt and ultimately independence. One could well understand therefore a friend of the Turkish people being satisfied with the lopping off of the disaffected Provinces. It was by the Moslems, and the Moslems alone—including in the term the Janissaries who, though of Christian birth, had become Moslems—that the Empire had come to its greatest extent in 1683. The Moslem population after 1876 was larger in proportion to the total number of Turkish subjects than before. Moslem rulers were therefore in a better situation to work out the salvation of the country upon their own lines.

Then came Abdul Hamid, the greatest of the destroyers of the Turkish Empire. One of the earliest evils which he inflicted upon his country and race was the destruction of government by Ministers. Under him the rule of the country became personal. He aimed at making himself the sole ruler of the Empire. From the first he was jealous of any Minister who was either eager in making reforms, or, indeed, taking any steps which had not previously met with his approval. Yet in comparison with him many of his Ministers were educated men according to the standard of European culture. According to such standard Abdul Hamid himself was an uneducated man. He endeavoured to govern the country on what he considered were the lines of the greatest of his predecessors and succeeded in copying only their barbarism. In one of the worst periods of his reign, one of the ablest of his Ministers remarked that if Abdul Hamid could be removed better government could be secured for the Empire. In reply to the question whether such a change would be anything more than the substitution of one Sultan for another the answer of the Minister was to claim that the Ministers were superior in knowledge, experience and intelligence to their master, and would probably get back the government by Ministers instead of personal government. The contention could not be rightly disputed.

Even in the early portion of his reign Abdul Hamid's attitude of suspicion made him distrust his own Ministers. To hold different opinions from the Minister was a recommendation in the Sultan's eyes for the appointment of a man to the post of Assistant Minister. Each of the two would act as a check, that is as a spy, upon the other. In the later portion of his reign he sought throughout to appoint creatures who had proved their subserviency. Independent Ministers like Edhem, Kiamil, and Kutchuk Said never held office long. He indeed commenced his reign by destroying the remarkable party of reformers who were headed by Midhat Pasha, and, as will hereafter be shown, he pursued the great reformer himself to death. By destroying government by Ministers and crushing out all attempts at reform, he was weakening the strength of the Empire.

The Turks have never succeeded in the art of ruling subject races. But no man less understood the statesmanlike way of treating them than did Abdul Hamid. Greeks and Armenians with occasionally Bulgarians had sometimes risen previous to his reign to the highest offices in the State, but at all times during the two centuries previous to his accession Armenians and Greeks had been largely employed in subordinate offices. Turkish foreign affairs usually having to deal with European, that is Christian, countries, the chief employees under the Foreign Secretary had nearly always been Greeks or Armenians. Abdul Hamid endeavoured to supply their places with Moslems. Some of these were good men of respectable ability and even exceptional knowledge, but no one, who knows the country, would venture to dispute the statement that the mass of such employees could not compare in intelligence and education with Christians in the same position.

When we pass from the official class to the treatment of the masses of his Christian subjects, we meet with Abdul Hamid's strange and almost inexplicable dislike for all of them, which showed itself at times in a readiness to deprive them of their liberty or even of their lives, and at all times in an inaptitude to render them justice. Such an attitude of mind was not altogether wanting in some of his predecessors. Cantimer tells an interesting story of an ignorant Sultan who wished to take from the Christians of the Capital all the churches which they had built after 1453, and to force upon them the alternative of Islam or death. The Grand Vizier at the time and the Sheik-ul-Islam recognised that such act would be hugely detrimental to the interest of the country. They called the Orthodox Patriarch and with him concocted a plan by which in presence of the Sultan they declared that such acts were in violation of the "Sacred Law," and thus prevented the execution of the Sultan's foolish designs. Abdul Hamid, however, though he showed hostility enough to the Christians to have entertained a like design, had arrayed against him the common sense and religious principles of the Ulema class. That class could not save the Greeks and Armenians from persecution, but they recognised the mischief of such persecution and gradually ceased to support his designs, and finally hailed the party of the Young Turks as delivering the country from the rule of an unjust and incompetent Sultan, under whom Turkey had lost all moral power amongst the nations of the world, and had seen the Empire which they inhabited largely diminished in extent. Probably it is safe to say that he had actually destroyed the Turkish Empire in Europe and had greatly imperilled its existence even in Asia Minor.

CHAPTER I

BIRTH, PARENTAGE, ETC., OF ABDUL HAMID—TURKISH LAW OF SUCCESSION

Birth of Abdul Hamid; his youth, early influences and education; digression on the Government of the Turks; the growth of the rule of succession to the Ottoman throne; child murder in Imperial family; illustration of its results; advantages and disadvantages of such rule.

ABDUL HAMID II. was born on September 22, 1842, and was the second son of Abdul Mejid, who commenced his reign in 1839, and died in 1861. Abdul Hamid succeeded his elder brother Murad, who was dethroned on account of mental incapacity after a short reign of a few weeks. Abdul Hamid's mother was an Armenian who had become a Moslem and had been a professional dancer in the service of Esme Sultana, sister of Abdul Mejid. By Ottoman law as applicable to the Imperial family the son of any woman by the reigning Sultan is regarded as legitimately born and entitled to be in the line of succession. The popular scandal amongst a section of the Turks that Abdul Hamid's father was an Armenian in Abdul Mejid's palace and other stories relating to his birth, may be dismissed as probably apocryphal and largely due to the fact that Abdul Hamid had an Armenian type of face. It is fair also to add that Abdul Hamid himself always denied that his mother was of Armenian origin, and that nothing offended him more than the suggestion that he had Armenian blood in his veins. The story was told of fourteen young men in the military school who were exiled in 1906 or 1907 for having composed or joined in a song in which the Sultan was spoken of as Bedros, the Armenian form of Petros or Peter. When

Abdul Hamid's mother died in 1849, he was entrusted to an elderly slave woman of the Imperial harem. Upon her death shortly afterwards Peresto Hanum, the fourth wife of Abdul Mejid, who had no child of her own, undertook the charge of Abdul Hamid as the second son of her husband. From all accounts she was an excellent mother, and when Abdul Aziz was girt with the sword of Osman in succession to her husband Abdul Mejid, the widow devoted herself to the education of Prince Hamid.

Peresto Hanum bore the title of Valida Sultana (the Sultan Mother). Though of course never appearing in society or visible to European men, she had a good reputation both in and out of the palace. It was currently reported that this lady and her adopted son, adoption being a practice legally recognised in Turkish law, failed after a few months to get on well together. We may disregard the court scandals on the subject with the remark that before long she lost her influence over Abdul Hamid and preferred to live at Nishantash rather than at Yildiz, his favourite residence. Abdul Hamid has quite enough to answer for as a Sultan without credence being given to this kind of palace scandal.

Little is known of Abdul Hamid's childhood. His father Abdul Mejid, who was of a kindly disposition, is said to have stated that while he was at ease in reference to his other children he saw little traces of anything good in Abdul Hamid. Armenius Vambéry, the famous Hungarian traveller who knew him in the period of his youth, describes him as pale, silent and melancholy, having the appearance of being distrustful and cunning. Little importance can be attached to the stories of an Oriental palace, but such as exist suggest that he was not fond of the companionship of other boys, and that as he grew older his tendency to care nothing for companions increased until it developed into sulkiness and largely estranged him from the other members of his family, including his father. He had various teachers, amongst whom probably Kemal Pasha was the most important. His elder brother Murad was a diligent scholar and eager to learn. Abdul Hamid was too self-willed to learn. His teachers of French, Edhem Pasha, afterwards Grand Vizier, Namyk Pasha and M. Gardet, are said to have complained constantly of their pupil, and an ex-employee at Yildiz, who writes as Georges Dorys, says it is well known that Abdul Hamid remained ignorant of his own language, which he never acquired with anything like accuracy. The same writer says that the Valida Sultana of Abdul Aziz, named Pertevalla Kadina, a fanatical old lady who was superstitious, ambitious and an *intriguante*, liked the boy because of his tendency to superstition, and because he already showed himself as the bitter enemy of the Christians with whom his father and his elder brother Murad liked to surround themselves. This lady was fond of witches and soothsayers and initiated Abdul Hamid into the mysteries of magic and of astrology. One may readily believe the story that their predictions that he would come to the throne of the Padishahs and would have a long reign had an influence in the formation of his character. When in 1867 Sultan Abdul Aziz went to Paris he took with him his two nephews and prospective successors Murad and Abdul Hamid. The Sultan was always accompanied by an interpreter, and Abdul Hamid pretended to be entirely ignorant of French, while Murad joined in the conversation as far as his knowledge of that language would allow him. It is said that Napoleon the Third was much impressed by the difference between the two brothers, that he was charmed by the affable manners of Murad, and remarked upon the difference to Fuad Pasha, the Grand Vizier, one of the most intelligent Turkish Ministers of his generation.

Abdul Hamid during the lifetime of Abdul Aziz had an allowance of £840 per month, and offended him by piteously begging for a larger sum. The Sultan granted his request, but expressed himself with something like disgust at the appeal. The love of money, however, and with it the tendency to extravagance, were always characteristic of Abdul Hamid. On the other hand, he was orderly and methodical in his payments and for a prince made his money go far. Before he came to the throne he carefully examined the accounts of expenditure, sought out the best investments, and checked all tendency to waste in his gardens and farms. It is known also that he speculated on the Exchange in Galata, but although he had the means of knowing something of what was going on in the Turkish financial world his speculations were not large, though usually successful. This was largely due to a well-known broker in Galata who, after Abdul came to the throne, was often invited to the official dinners at Yildiz, to the disgust of foreign ambassadors who would not have extended such an honour to him in their own embassies.

The natural character of Abdul Hamid in his youth did not give much promise that if he ever came to the throne he would make a successful ruler. Never given to study, distrustful of those around him, self-willed, caring nothing for sport or anything else which required out-of-door exercise, he went his own way. Such education as he received was of little value. He was unfortunate in his training, but that was largely the fault of the Turkish law of succession. He was never permitted to take any part in public functions. He never had the opportunity of royal princes in Christian countries of becoming acquainted with public men. It has rarely been the fashion in Turkey for those near the throne to make themselves acquainted with the history and politics of foreign countries. Even the knowledge of Turkish history so far as it can be acquired from Turkish books is fragmentary and often misleading, and Abdul Hamid had intelligence enough if he read them to recognise their practical worthlessness. While still a young man he appears to have looked forward to occupying the throne. Only one life, that of his elder brother Murad, stood between him and its possession after the death of Abdul Aziz, and without attaching importance to the many stories of intrigue by him to be appointed Sultan, he probably recognised that the health and habits of his elder brother would in the natural course of events soon render the throne vacant.

Before continuing the story of Abdul Hamid's life it is expedient to speak of the government of the Turks and of the rule of succession to the Turkish throne. The government of the Ottomans has always been a military despotism. Upon their entry into Asia Minor they formed groups under military leaders. Even if their previous history had not led these groups to assume a military character, their situation in Asia Minor compelled them to such organisation. The Ottoman groups were in the midst of enemies. They were struggling for pasturage and settlement amongst peoples who were quiet agriculturists or occupied in commerce, and the new-comers were constantly engaged in the attempt to seize the property of their neighbours. Whether such groups are spoken of as bands of robbers or as the founders of a nation matters little. In either case necessity required that they should have a strong chieftain, or perish. It is true that in their earlier stages the members of the group elected their chieftain, but as the group grew larger the practice became common to establish or accept a rule of succession to the chieftainship. As for military purposes the group could not tolerate that the succession should pass to a child or a woman, the rule of succession became established among the Ottomans, as indeed amongst most other Eastern races, that the eldest male member of the family of the founder chieftain should be the chief, or, as he soon came to be called, the Sultan. That rule prevails to the present day. It is easy to see that among a primitive fighting race it has much to recommend it. But from its first establishment there were many disadvantages attending it. The Ottomans having accepted the religion of Mahomet, polygamy became lawful even if the practice had not existed before the adoption of Islam. The natural instinct of each wife led her to desire that her son should occupy the throne of his father. It led her to intrigue in order to remove out of the way of his succession all who had right by reason of priority of birth. Hence child murder in the Imperial family became a common occurrence.

Even before 1453, when Mahomet II. captured Constantinople, the practice in the Imperial family of killing off younger brothers had become general. But Mahomet the Conqueror himself legalised the practice. It continued during the next two centuries. Turkish history from that day to a period within living memory is full of palace intrigues whose object was to get rid of claimants to the throne, of struggles between brothers, of younger brothers hidden away by their mothers, of cold-blooded murders when they were caught, and of infanticide. Infanticide indeed in the Imperial family was regarded as a necessity. By Turkish law all sons inherit equally, and all sons of Moslem fathers, no matter what the condition of the mother, are legitimate. Every mother whose child was living resented the birth of possible competitors by other mothers. The result was that infanticide in Turkish families where the husband was a polygamist was general. The fewer the children of the father, the larger the amount to be divided amongst his children. Even now in Moslem Turkey the practice of infanticide is appallingly common. It was in consequence of popular opinion on the subject that the law of Mahomet II. legalising infanticide in the Imperial family was regarded with favour or with indifference.

One or two examples will serve as illustrations. On the south side of Saint Sophia are three large mausoleums. In the middle one lies Sultan Murad III., who died in 1594. He left eighteen sons. The eldest ascended the throne as Mahomet III. At his accession all his seventeen brothers were bowstrung. Their bodies lie in the same mausoleum.

In 1617 Sultan Ahmed died leaving several young children. Thereupon the Council of State formulated the law of succession as it now exists. Up to that time, though the practice was much as it is at the present, more attention appears to have been paid to the wishes of the deceased. The brother of Ahmed was proclaimed Sultan under the name of Mustafa. From that time to the present only two Sultans have succeeded their fathers, one being Mahomet IV. and the other Abdul Mejid, the father of Abdul Hamid and of the present reigning Sultan, Mahomet V. The practice of killing off younger brothers ceased within the memory of living man. Colonel White, the author of an excellent book on Turkey called "Three Years in Constantinople," notes that it was still in force during 1844, one of his years of residence in that capital. The incident which led Abdul Mejid to put an end to the practice is pathetic. Mahmud II., spoken of as the "Reformer," and one of the ablest Sultans who was ever girt with the sword of Osman, was strongly attached to his daughter named Mihr. She, knowing the existence of the terrible rule by which her child would be killed, submitted herself to an improper operation from which both she and her unborn child died. Mahmud understood why she had so submitted herself and was not only deeply grieved but determined to make an end of the cruel practice. Nevertheless the law remained unchanged. He died in 1839 and was succeeded by Abdul Mejid. The incident of the death of the Princess Mihr and of the grief of Mahmud had become known in western Europe and to all the various ambassadors in Constantinople. Then another incident occurred which ended in the abolition of the almost inexorable rule to kill off younger sons. One of the sons of Abdul Mejid's sister, Ateya Sultana, had been killed in conformity with the palace law. When she was again pregnant her husband spent large sums to buy off the hostility of the mothers of other princes. But when a son was born the jealousy of the mothers of other princes of the new arrival was too strong to be resisted. Abdul Mejid's permission was obtained, and the child was killed. The poor mother went mad and in less than three months was buried near her child. The incident created considerable interest in England and France, and though rumour, probably correct, speaks of other Imperial children who have been murdered, their deaths have generally been concealed.

The tendency to keep the Sultan of Turkey absolute

was probably intensified by the institution of the Janissaries. Formed about the year 1355 by Sultan Orchan, they had carried the Turkish flag to victory in a hundred fights. They had become the great striking force, the spear head of the Turkish Army. They soon constituted an "*Imperium in Imperio.*" They made and unmade Sultans. Though every man amongst them was the son of Christian parents and though from first to last they rigorously excluded Moslems from their ranks, their allegiance was always due to their Commander-in-Chief, the Sultan himself. They deposed such commander when they found him incompetent, but they would never allow any other body in the State to do so. They and he were absolute. They were an army almost constantly in the field with the Commander at their head. A child Sultan would not have suited them, and therefore when by tradition the succession had to remain in a certain family the rule of succession was as good as any that could have been formulated. As soldiers they of course knew nothing of election, and would not have tolerated it unless the election of their Chief was left exclusively to them.

Whatever may have been the merits during an almost constant period of warfare of the rule of Turkish succession, the demerits of such a system stand conspicuously forward in time of peace and are well illustrated in the case of Abdul Hamid. It is not too much to say that during the whole of the nineteenth century the treatment by the reigning Sultan of the immediate or second heir in succession to the throne was of a character to prevent such successors from becoming good rulers.

The influence of Western public opinion after 1800 was not without a salutary effect on the Imperial family. In former centuries the mistrusted heir would probably have been killed. Respect for European opinion and for that of the Ulema class had condemned this mode of treating dangerous aspirants. Instead of murder, more or less strict internment was substituted. Murad was kept secluded by Sultan Abdul Aziz. He had no education in the Western sense of the word, nor any intellectual interest or even amusement, and fell a prey to habits of idleness and sensual luxury. Two months after his accession he was deposed, and Abdul Hamid, his brother, became Sultan. Murad was kept a prisoner by him in the Cheragan Palace on the Bosporus, almost adjoining the residence of his brother. He continued to live in obscurity during the reign of Abdul Hamid until 1904. The heir to the throne on Hamid's death was Reshad Effendi, the present Sultan. All the three had been debarred from intercourse with the outside world, and their intelligence was in consequence cramped. Murad was never allowed to leave his palace, was never permitted to receive visitors, and his residence was strictly guarded on all sides by soldiers and spies. Reshad experienced virtually similar treatment, and Abdul Hamid had suffered from the same limitations.

If such treatment be compared with that which is accorded to the heir to the throne of any European country the contrast will show the folly of the Turkish method and how inadequate it is to modern requirements. The education of Edward VII. and of George V. when each was Prince of Wales and of the present Prince of Wales is one which tended to fit them as much as human training can fit a man to occupy the highest position in the realm. Nor does the corresponding training of the heirs to the throne of Russia, Germany, Austria and other European countries differ. Edward VII. had relieved the Royal Mother at many public functions for many years before her death. In others he had been associated with her. He, like his successor, had been at the universities. Both had constantly met with statesmen, foreign ambassadors, and the best literary society that the empire afforded. Both travelled far from England and had had opportunities of seeing foreign peoples and institutions. The most careful preparation had been made by the reigning Sovereign in question to give the most suitable education to the heir to the throne. Under such a system, the longer the reigning Sovereign lived the better capacitated did the heir become for the succession. In Turkey, on the contrary, the longer the reigning Sovereign lived the more incapacitated was the Crown Prince.

It was under such a system that Abdul Hamid had been trained. In earlier days it had led to much child murder. But it produced and continues to produce other evil results. It is probably the worst plan which could be devised for securing a competent Sultan. It inspires and nourishes suspicion. The Sultan suspects the Crown Prince, and is regarded as an enemy by the heir to the throne. When Sultan Abdul Aziz visited England in 1867 he brought with him, as we have seen, both Murad and Abdul Hamid. They were possible enemies who were not to be trusted to remain in Turkey during his absence. The story told by a Turkish prince was that while in England Abdul Hamid made two or three attempts to conceal himself so that he should not be compelled to return to Turkey. His attitude was constantly one of fear, fear that he would be made away with.

CHAPTER II

CONDITION OF TURKEY ON ACCESSION OF ABDUL HAMID

Empire in course of disintegration; its extent; internal organisation; almost purely military; influence of Janissaries; their destruction in 1826; improvements in Army; introduction of foreign officers; Bashi Bazuks; Military and Naval Schools established; civil organisation; condition of Turkish finances; corruption in administration; administration of justice; Courts of the Patriarchates; Commercial and other Codes and Courts of Law; Land Court; public education; more advanced among non-Moslem than Moslem communities; railways and roads; relations between Moslems and Christians; industries.

In endeavouring to sketch the condition of the Turkish Empire on Abdul Hamid's accession it is convenient to consider (1) Its extent, and (2) Its internal organisation.

(1) In reference to its extent, the reader should never forget that the Empire was in course of disintegration. Its growth after the capture of Constantinople in 1453 had been steady. The whole of the Balkan Peninsula had passed under Ottoman rule. The Empire continued to enlarge its territory until 1683. After 1453 Belgrade, Mohacz and Buda had witnessed the triumph of the Crescent; the Crimea and another large district in Southern Russia owned the sway of the Sultan. Every country on the southern shore of the Mediterranean, from Egypt to the Atlantic, recognised him as Sovereign. Until 1683, when John Sobieski, King of Poland, compelled the Turks to raise the siege of Vienna, Turkish progress had continued almost unchecked. Readers will recall Macaulay's statement in the chapter on the condition

of England in 1685, that the first question asked of a traveller from the Continent was, what was the progress made by the Grand Turk? for Turkish advance had become a serious menace to the States of Germany, and created alarm among the peoples of France and England. The relief of Vienna marked, however, the zenith of Turkish rule. From that time to the present it has been on the down grade. Two statements may be made about its decline after that year. First, that each succeeding generation saw a steady diminution of the Empire; second,—that with few exceptions, Turkey rarely regained any portion of territory once lost. It had indeed not seldom happened that portions of territory were re-captured by the Turks, but without exception they were taken from her within a few years. Without attempting to give the history of the disintegration of the Empire down to the end of the eighteenth century, the successful struggle of the Greeks for independence in its first thirty years of last century, the semi-independence gained by Serbia and by the Principalities of Moldavia and Wallachia will show how strong the force of disintegration had become between 1800 and 1850. Roughly speaking, Russia was the only Power which was then regarded as persistently and constantly hostile to Turkey. Great Britain and France had arrived at the conclusion that the existence of the Turkish Empire was necessary to preserve the European balance of power, and the doctrine loudly proclaimed in both these countries previous to, and during, the Crimean War was that the integrity and independence of Turkey were necessary for the preservation of European peace. Indeed, that war may be regarded as an attempt to prevent the further disintegration of the Ottoman Empire. Even the battle of Navarino, in which England and France took part with Russia in destroying the Turkish fleet and thus largely contributing to the loss of Greece, was spoken of officially by the British Government as "an untoward event." But the historical movement could not be long arrested. The Conference of the representatives of the European

Powers held at Constantinople in January, 1877, had for its immediate object the devising of means for the better government of Serbia, Bulgaria, and other European dominions of the Sultan, and of thus preventing atrocities like those which had been committed in Bulgaria in the spring of the previous year. The desire of every European Power was to prevent war, and that which the representatives of all the Powers recognised as its probable result, a further diminution of the Empire. "We tried," said Lord Salisbury, the British delegate, "to save Turkey" (and the word "we" applied to all the members of the Conference), "but she would not allow herself to be saved." War ensued, the Principality of Bulgaria ceased to belong to the Empire; Serbia became an independent kingdom; Wallachia and Moldavia became the Kingdom of Rumania; the independence of Montenegro was recognised; Bosnia and Herzegovina were handed over for administrative purposes to Austria. Cyprus was surrendered to Great Britain for the same purpose. Batum, Kars, and a portion of Turkish territory in Asia Minor fell to Russia.

Thus, the disintegration of the Turkish Empire had continued to go on steadily up to the second year of Abdul Hamid's reign. The Turkish Empire had become a smaller one than any over which any of his predecessors had ruled during four hundred years.

(2) The internal organisation of the Empire had undergone curiously little change up to the accession of Abdul Hamid. It was based altogether and always upon military lines. The Turks, meaning thereby the Moslem element, for the Christians had nothing to do with warfare, constituted a nation in arms, where every man formed part of a Militia. In times of war a levy *en masse* could be called in which every man had to render military service. We have elaborate and careful descriptions of the organisation of the army and of Turkish Civil Administration as they existed in the seventeenth century and subsequently. Amongst English writers Paul Rycaut gives the most careful and

elaborate account of the organisation of the Turkish Army and people. He went to Turkey in 1661 as secretary to Lord Winchelsea, Ambassador in Constantinople, and after five years became British Consul at Smyrna where he remained eleven years. His three works on Turkey indicate him as a careful and trustworthy author.[1] An account given by Sir James Porter, Ambassador in Constantinople a century later, indicates but few changes, so that at the opening of the nineteenth century the organisation of the Turkish Army as described by Rycaut shows but slight change.

The progress of Turkish arms from 1380 to 1683 had been enormously aided by the formation of the great corps of Janissaries. The more closely Turkish history between those periods is examined, the more vividly is the reader impressed with the influence exerted upon the Empire by this remarkable body. Their elaborate organisation had succeeded so well that it greatly influenced and increased the fighting value of the whole of the nation in arms. They developed an *esprit de corps* almost without any analogy in history. It was they who won the great battles of the Maritza in 1371, in which the South Serbians were destroyed, and Kossovo-Pol in 1389 in which the Serbians of the north were conquered; the striking victory at Varna in 1444 wherein King Ladislaus was killed and the great Hungarian leader, John Hunyadis, suffered a crushing defeat, was gained by them; and it was they who "fresh, vigorous and invincible" completed the capture of Constantinople in 1453. At the capture of Belgrade in 1521, in the battle of Mohacz in 1526, and at Buda Pesth in 1541, they had still shown their prowess.

After 1683, though as a fighting force they continued formidable, they developed a conservatism which ultimately brought about their destruction. They had almost become lords over their masters. They repeatedly demanded and often obtained the heads

[1] The most important, "The present State of the Ottoman Empire," was translated into French, Polish, and German. Subsequently, he wrote a Continuation of Knolles' "Turkish History," bringing it down from 1623 to 1677.

of Ministers; they made and unmade Sultans. Even as late as 1807, they deposed Sultan III. and replaced him by Mustapha. When in the following year, 1808, Mahmud II. was girt with the sword of Osman the Janissaries still maintained a great reputation. But they had ceased to be generally popular. The Ulema objected to their constant interference with the succession of Sultans, and regarded them as lax Mahometans and followers of the Dervish Haji Bektash. The civilian portion of the population generally stood in awe of them. Their lawlessness even in the capital is almost incredible. The English chaplain in Constantinople describes what he saw and learned in the years between 1820 and 1830 in the streets and bazaars of Constantinople: Christians openly robbed, their houses even being taken from them; men killed for the mere lust of slaughter; a general disregard for the rights of civilians; all these abuses, largely brought about by the Janissaries, furnished an example which was imitated by other troops.

It was when they resisted the military reforms of Mahmud that the death-struggle between him and them began. A well-drilled body of gunners, trained by Frenchmen, who had seen service in the Napoleonic wars, learned European methods of fighting. Jealousy soon existed between the representatives of the new *régime* and the Janissaries. When therefore Mahmud desired to introduce European drill and especially European artillery among them, they objected and over-turned their camp kettles, their usual signal for revolt. A short struggle began on the famous Hippodrome, or as it is called in Turkish, the "At-Meidan," but the great barracks of the Janissaries being at a distance of a mile and a half in a quarter known as the Meat Market, or Et Meidan, those in revolt fled to their headquarters in that place. Thereupon the new troops of artillery, headed by a leader who hereafter became known as Kara Gehenna, or Black Hell, surrounded the barracks. The Sultan recognised that the struggle was one for life. He gave orders that the famous corps should be disbanded. Every Janissary who showed himself outside the barracks was at once shot down. A crowd of them rushed to attack the artillery under Black Hell in a dense body and in a narrow street. The renown of the famous corps was still such that many of the troops loyal to Mahmud began to flee before the rush. When the rebels faced the cannon, by which Black Hell himself stood, they halted. The cannon, however, loaded with grape, missed fire. The Janissaries rushed forward while Black Hell's own men began to give way. Discharging his pistol over the priming it went off, and, doing terrible execution amongst the massed men, checked their advance. A desperate struggle ensued. The Janissaries rushed to their death with the cry on their lips of "Haji Bektash," the name of their founder, and fought fiercely. On that day in 1826 six thousand Janissaries were slaughtered.

Their influence in the capital had been great because when retiring from active service, the Janissaries were given positions as guardians, as personal attendants, and in other capacities of trust. Indeed the word "Janissary" itself usually signified until well within the memory of living men, not a fighting soldier but a soldier guardian. Attached to each Embassy and Consulate were many whose habits of discipline made them the faithful protectors of officials, or of their wives or daughters, when they went out into the streets of the city. The destruction of the Janissaries did much to put an end to the individual insolence, tyranny and oppression of the civil population by the soldiery.

After the slaughter of the Janissaries in 1826, Mahmud introduced many changes in the Turkish Army to bring it into conformity with European armies. Down to the Crimean War, however, in spite of the adoption of European military dress and drill, the army did not strike foreigners as being an effective body. Its weak point then, and until the present time, has been its officers. This was recognised by Mahmud, as, indeed, it had been by some of his predecessors. Probably at the beginning of the last century not five per cent. of the officers could read their own language, and they knew no other. Instruction, therefore, in military matters had to be obtained from foreigners, and there was no period during the last century and a half in which some foreign officers have not held high positions in Turkey.[1] The remark applies equally to the navy and army. The navy, however, during the last three centuries has always played a very secondary part to the army. Omar Pasha, a Prussian of origin, figured largely on the Turkish side in the Crimean War, and British officers since that war have usually been attached to the Turkish Admiralty.

Besides the regular Turkish Army there existed in Turkey until the accession of Abdul Hamid, as there has done at all times in Turkish history, a large fighting rabble, ill-armed and ill-disciplined, known as Bashi-Bazuks. These were always unpaid, and had to live on the plunder of the country as they could. An attempt was made to organise this rabble at the time of the Crimean War, and regiments were formed of them which were stationed at Gallipoli and at other important parts of the Empire under British and French officers. The latest attempt to organise the Bashi-Bazuks occurred under Abdul Hamid in 1877. Those who saw regiments of them recognised a disorderly mob of savage-looking men.

It was not until well after the Crimean War that serious attempts were made to reorganise the Turkish Army on European lines. French officers remained in Turkey for such a purpose; others were invited from France and remained in the country until about 1890. The success of Germany in the Franco-German War of 1870 had turned the attention of the Sultan and his army towards Berlin, and since 1880 German officers have replaced Frenchmen as instructors and organisers of Turkish troops. In like manner Englishmen were chosen to aid in reorganising the fleet; Admiral Slade was followed by Admiral Hobart and Sir Henry Woods.

[1] The first Napoleon was desirous of taking service in Turkey. The equally distinguished German soldier, Moltke, spent two years in such service.

That they did not succeed in making the fleet efficient was not their fault.

Sultan Abdul Mejid, who died in 1861, and who had been Sultan during the Crimean War, recognised that the Turkish Army required properly-trained officers. Accordingly a military school, known as the Harbié, was established at Pancaldi, a suburb of the capital, for their training. During the last quarter of a century the chief instructors have been Germans, the most distinguished of them being General Von der Golz Pasha who died in Turkish service in 1916. It is beyond doubt that the modern Turkish military officer is superior in attainments to his predecessors.

Somewhat similar improvements were attempted in the Imperial Navy. There also the great defect was in its officers. It is true that since the great battle of Lepanto in 1571 the popular impression in Turkey was that while Allah had given power on land to believers he had left that of the sea to infidels. Nevertheless in the first half of last century the navy compared not unfavourably with that of any other country. A naval school or college was established in the time of Abdul Mejid on the Island of Halki, where there were usually two or three English instructors, some of them not undistinguished men. Just as military students had been sent to France or Germany, so also, by permission of the British Government, a few Turks were trained on our ships at Greenwich or Woolwich. Indeed, on the accession of Abdul Hamid, the Turkish Navy was probably the third in number of ships and weight of guns which was in existence.

Civil Organisation.

Military organisation always occupied the first place in accounts of Turkey. She was rightly thought of as a nation in arms. Civil organisation was indeed closely connected with military organisation. It was so even in the time of the Janissaries. Amongst the thousands of youths of Christian origin, careful selection was made, and those whose natural aptitude seemed to fit them for civil administration, for finance, or for diplomatic service, were trained, always under members of their own corps, for such services. The same connection between military and civil service still remains, and Turks in the Civil Service have nearly always been trained as military men.

When Abdul Hamid became Sultan, it was the invariable rule. There was no regular gradation which led to the office; appointments went mainly by favour. It was always well understood that such officers, while entitled to a salary from the State, were allowed opportunities of increasing their remuneration by forced contributions from the people under them. It was equally understood that they could sell the appointments to various offices in the districts over which they ruled. As their appointments were often due to the favour of ladies of the harem, or of Pashas about the reigning Sultan, they had, in order to retain the favour of those who appointed them, to send contributions to the capital. The good government of the Province, or division of the Province over which they presided, depended entirely upon the honesty and discretion of the Governor. If he kept well with the Palace, that is, in many cases, if he kept up his payments towards some of the occupants, and prevented too many complaints reaching the ears of the Sultan, his position was fairly secure for an indefinite time. The stories told by travellers in Asia Minor, Syria, and Arabia of the period between the Crimean War and the accession of Hamid, tell a curiously unanimous tale of gross forms of exaction and corruption committed by officials. The crowds of Moslem pilgrims who annually found their way to Mecca and Medina, had to pay a heavy tax to Bedouin tribes in the neighbourhood, which it was well known would be shared between the Chiefs and the local Governors. Until Abdul Hamid's accession little had been done to diminish this form of exaction and corruption. The sale of small offices under the Governor was on the same lines. The head of a Department had had to pay for his appointment, and it was natural that he would recover this payment by forced contributions from those under him.

The finances of the Empire on the accession of Abdul Hamid were in a hopeless condition. Turkey during the Crimean War had learnt that she could borrow money with facility from British and French capitalists, and she soon profited by the lesson. Even during the war she had borrowed large sums nominally for its expenses. England and France having guaranteed the payment of interest on the loan, it had become in those countries a favourite investment. She continued borrowing, the money being largely squandered, especially by Abdul Aziz, the predecessor of Abdul Hamid, in building palaces and in providing positions for the favourites of his large harem.

Shortly before the accession of Abdul Hamid a change had been made which was a distinct improvement. The Department of the Civil List was formed, meaning thereby one whose duty it was to administer the property belonging to the private domain of the Sultan and to take over the management of the sums allotted to him by the Central Government. This arrangement tended towards the regularisation of the national finance. It did not prevent Abdul Aziz or even Abdul Hamid, from demanding and obtaining sums from the public treasury, but it at least caused it to be known when great sums which ought to have been employed for the public service of the State, were abstracted for the private use of the Palace. In one respect indeed the Civil List Department, which was under the direct supervision of the Sultan, worked against the general public interest. It had become the rule that the occupants of Crown Lands, meaning thereby lands which the Sultan claimed as his own, should be free from taxation. The result in certain districts was that the keenest peasants gradually took farms on such lands and were freed not only from the illegitimate exactions of the tax collectors, but from the legitimate taxations to which other tenants were subject. The principal taxes were tithes and an *ad valorem* duty of 8 per cent. on all imports. Tithes or dimes were collected on all the produce of the country. The method of collection led to great abuses, and to discontent. The collectorship of tithes was sold, sometimes openly, but more usually by a private arrangement between the collector and the local authority. A rich Moslem in many cases paid ridiculously small sums because the assessment of his property was made on a scale which all his neighbours knew to be much below its real value. The unpopular man, and Christians generally, paid much more than the tenth permitted by law. If they objected they were liable to suffer from the ill will of the tax collector. The crops were not allowed to be gathered until he gave his permission. They might rot on the ground as in many cases they did. In a hundred ways the peasants were at his mercy. Many of them found a way of escape by bribery.

The administration of justice in Turkey continued until about 1845 to be under the direction of the Sheik-ul-Islam who was assisted by many Ulema. The Sheik-ul-Islam is the highest judicial functionary known to the Sacred Law (or Sheriat) with functions recalling those of the Lord Chancellor in pre-Reformation times. The Ulema, if Islam were a church, might be correctly described as its hierarchy. One Chief Judge presided over the Courts dealing with matters arising in Asia, and another with those in Europe. Both, however, were subordinate to the Sheik-ul-Islam. In each of these two great divisions there were a number of subordinate judges, all chosen from or connected with the Ulema. Questions regarding the ownership of land were included in the jurisdiction of all the judges mentioned. The law administered was that of the Sheri, that is, Moslem Sacred Law. Its highest source was the Koran ; other sacred or semi-sacred books furnished the Traditions and the Commentaries of the contemporary or immediate followers of the Prophet. The early Moslems had found in the Empire the wonderful collection of law contained in the Institutes of Justinian, in his Pandects, his Novels and Edicts, and while the Caliphate existed at Bagdad, great masses of these legal treatises were taken over and became Islamic law. Forgetting for awhile the prejudices which soon separated the Moslems from the Christians, and questions turning upon religious matters, the law and even its administration in these early Courts did not leave much ground for complaint. It is indeed a wonderful testimony to the lucidity of the great legal writers of the sixth century that their works should have continued to be operative down to the present day with few changes.

The Turks recognised from the first that there were inherent differences between the religions of Islam and Christ which made it desirable that Christians should have their own Courts and their own law. Christian Courts connected with the Patriarchates had jurisdiction over the members of their own community, in everything relating to matters of legitimacy, dowry, marriage, divorce, and testamentary succession, indeed in everything relating to what jurists understand by the term Personal Statute. The jurisdiction of Christian Courts came to be spoken of as "Privileges," but it may be doubted whether the Turks so regarded them during the first three centuries after the capture of Constantinople. Moslems did not wish to be troubled with quarrels among non-Moslems, who must manage these matters among themselves. Moslems were not going to extend the privileges of Islamic believers to infidels or even to Christians and Jews, the "Children of the Books." About the time of the Crimean War, however, Moslems as well as Christians came to regard the jurisdiction of the Patriarchs and other Christian authorities as privileges, and from that day to the present there has always been a tendency amongst the Turks to encroach upon them, a tendency which showed its fullest development amongst some of the Chauvinists of the Young Turk Party, who declared that as the Revolution had proclaimed the equality of all Ottoman subjects, there could be no question of privileges. Needless to say that this view was not generally adopted. On the accession of Abdul Hamid these privileges of the non-Moslem communities were in full force.

Meantime, and especially during the first half of last century, a series of questions had arisen with which the Sacred Courts were incompetent to deal. The development of commerce with its bills of exchange, laws of marine insurance, and a dozen other subjects, belonged to a condition of society widely different from that which had existed among the early Moslems or even under Justinian, and, urged by the various Embassies representing the commercial world in Europe and supported by a series of able Grand Viziers, reforms were made in Turkish Civil and Commercial Law and new Courts were established which had no connection with the Sheri or Sacred Law. The new laws were framed after the Crimean War in the form of Codes. The Commercial and Civil Codes were taken largely and often textually from the Code Napoleon and other French laws. A Commercial Court was established at Constantinople, known as the Tidjaret, with branches throughout the Empire. One of its divisions dealt exclusively with cases between Ottoman subjects and foreigners, and is known as a Mixed Court. These Codes and Courts, though certain modifications had been made, since their establishment, had come to be in full working order just about the time of the accession of Abdul Hamid.

About the same period a Criminal Code was formed after the French model, but introducing many provisions from the Turkish *Mejella*, a compilation of Moslem law from various sources.

With reference to the ownership of land, it is deserving of mention that Turkey has preserved the old Byzantine system of registration of titles. No private papers between parties prove the validity of titles to land. The true Title Deed, or *Hodjet*, is the entry in the official Register of Transfer, or a certified copy of such entry. The system, which is still in force, is simple and effectual. The buyer and seller present themselves before the Land Court which causes search to be made in the Register for the last transfer of the property in question. If it be found inscribed in the name of the person who presents himself as seller, he is asked after proving his identity whether he has sold the property in question, and if so, to whom, and for what sum. The buyer is then asked whether he has bought it and whether he has paid the price. Upon his answering and upon the seller stating that he has received payment, an entry is carefully made in the land Register, which is read over to both parties, signed by them, and their signature is witnessed by half a dozen prominent members of the Court.

There was indeed little fault to be found with Turkish law as it existed on the accession of Abdul Hamid. But even then it was in its administration that the Turk made a dismal failure. Substantially the law remains unchanged since then. There was already general complaint throughout the country of corruption in the administration of justice. Judges were then, as now, ill-paid, and their salaries were frequently months in arrears. Popular opinion constantly assumed that decisions were bought. Coupled with this statement, the observation of Bentham that it is of more importance that justice should seem to be administered impartially than that it should be so administered, and the failure of Turkish Law Courts is manifest.

Turkey was absolutely destitute of traditions of a pure administration of justice. Our fathers established an Assize system, and for centuries have surrounded the Judges who go on circuit with all the paraphernalia necessary to show that they represented the Sovereign. The ill-paid Turkish Judge had no such official dignity awarded him, and whether his decisions were just or not, he acquired no honour or dignity from his position. In these respects no improvement had been made on the accession of Abdul Hamid over the conditions which had prevailed a century earlier.

On Abdul Hamid's accession nothing worthy of the name of public education existed. It is true that attached to some of the mosques were schools in which reading and writing in Turkish were taught, but they were sparsely attended and the attempts at teaching were crude. The non-Moslems had already given much more attention to the subject. The Jews had excellent mission schools in the capital, in Smyrna, and in Salonika. Some were under the management of L'Alliance Israelite, but the most successful were under the control of the Presbyterian Church of Scotland and of the Anglican Mission to Jews. These bodies had already succeeded in raising the general status of Jewish women. No efforts, however, for the advancement of education at the time of the accession of Abdul Hamid were so remarkable as those made by the Armenians. In every Church belonging to that nationality there was a Sunday school attended by boys and men, who were instructed in reading and writing. The Greeks were not less attentive to the educational wants of their children. Stimulated by the example of Robert College, a great American institution which has rendered invaluable services, especially to Christian boys of the Empire, the Greeks established a kindred institution in the Island of Halki which in 1876 was already a flourishing establishment, and were already thinking of a scheme for the education of Greek children throughout the country. It should not be forgotten that both Greeks and Armenians have an advantage over the Turks in the greater simplicity of their written characters. It was rare to meet with a Greek, man or woman, who did not know how to read and write in his own language. It was almost unknown to find a Turk outside officialdom who could do so. An attempt had already been commenced by the Government to establish a Secondary School in which French should be the medium of instruction, but this in 1876 was languishing though undoubtedly doing useful work.

In the great towns but especially in the capital a few newspapers were in existence. There were only two in Turkish. There were probably half a dozen in Greek, and at least three in Armenian. The difficulty of writing in Turkish characters was illustrated by the fact that both Greek and Armenian newspapers existed in which the language was Turkish, but the characters employed were either Greek or Armenian.

There was no railway connection with any other State.[1] Hardly any ordinary road was in working order with the exception of one between Beyrout and Damascus, which had been formed by and belonged to a French company. The tracks which served as roads followed the course of those constructed in the time of the Greek Empire, but the bridges had been broken down and were rarely repaired. Both roads and bridges were in such a condition that they were constantly avoided by travellers. The means of transport for the peasants were miserable, with the result that while profusion existed in one district, famine prevailed in another not many miles distant.

In the towns watchmen were appointed whose particular duty was to give alarm in case of fire. Local police known as "zaptiehs" existed, but few persons had confidence in their ability or trustworthiness. A gendarmerie had not yet been thought of. Happily the great body of the inhabitants of Turkey, Christians and Moslems, were an orderly people, a fact which was probably due to some extent to the presence everywhere of men who had served in the army.

Considering the large number of non-Moslems in the country, it is remarkable how well the professors of the two faiths generally got on together. The Moslem always has a tendency to be insolent towards his Christian neighbours. He can never divest himself of the notion that he has a divine right to be dominant. The Christians accepted the fact that it was necessary for them to be subservient and, except when religious fanaticism was called into play by exceptional circumstances, there were few disturbances between them.

[1] In a subsequent chapter, railways wholly or partially constructed will be mentioned.

Fanaticism was latent and was never altogether absent. If a wealthy Moslem chose to take a fancy to a Christian woman or girl, as often happened, the parents would have to give her up, and usually found it expedient to make no trouble about it. Even in cases where an unprincipled Moslem would refuse to pay what everybody knew to be a just debt towards a Christian, he would often have the support of his co-religionists and no redress was possible in a Court of Law. These, however, were exceptional cases and a general desire for a peaceful life did much to check the outbreaks of fanaticism.

The people over whom Abdul Hamid was called upon to reign were, speaking generally, easily governed. Three-fourths of them at least were agriculturists who wished only to live in security. Their earnings and their wants were alike small. Throughout Asia Minor and to a large extent in the European Provinces peasant proprietorship was the rule. The old system of Derry Beys had ceased to exist. In the villages silver money was rarely seen and gold was almost unknown. In Bulgaria and Macedonia, Village Communities existed on similar lines to those of the Mir in Russia and the Indian Village Communities. In Macedonia, in a portion of Serbia, and in the Kurdish districts of Asia Minor, Moslem proprietors held lordship over Christian tenants, many of whom had accepted this position in order to protect themselves from other chiefs.

Industries except of a primitive character hardly existed, though nearly everywhere peasant women made woollen or cotton yarn and knitted it into socks and other garments. Bulgaria, however, was already making a species of frieze and of cloth resembling tweed with which even then the Turkish Army was beginning to be clothed. Throughout the whole length of Asia Minor carpet making found occupation for hundreds of peasants. Steam had not yet been applied in Turkey to any industry except that of grinding grain. External trade and commerce were in the hands of foreigners, but throughout the whole extent of the Empire excepting Arabia, internal trade, as represented by shop-keeping, was run by the Christian subjects of the Sultan. It was rare even in villages otherwise exclusively Moslem that the village shop was kept by a Turk. While it is true that the population generally was law-abiding, great movements had already commenced which were to receive their full development under the new Sultan. The Empire, or such of it as remained under the rule of the Ottoman Turks, was in a transition stage. The Turk, with his immobility, with the resignation which his religion and traditions had transformed into fatalism, and with his ignorance in comparison with his Christian fellow-subjects, due partly to the difficulties of Turkish script, was unwilling to make any change. The Christian, with his desire for education, already aspired to greater prosperity. It was inevitable that there should be struggles between the two opposing forces. The time required a ruler possessed of statesmanship. The great question before him was how to govern subject races. The tradition for five centuries of such rule was to put down any sign of revolt by massacre. It remained to be seen whether Abdul Hamid could depart from that tradition and could learn the lesson of treating all his subjects with justice.

CHAPTER III

REVOLUTION WHICH PLACES ABDUL HAMID ON THRONE

Revolution in Constantinople; rise of Midhat Pasha and of a party favouring reform; opposed by Sultan Abdul Aziz, who is deposed by Midhat and Hussein Avni, Minister of War; Midhat advocates religious equality between Moslems and Christians; Hussein Avni killed; Midhat's proposal accepted; Sultan Murad becomes insane and is deposed; Abdul Hamid succeeds to throne.

It was during the stirring events of the spring of 1876 that the name of Abdul Hamid first came into general notice. Sultan Abdul Aziz was then reigning and was not generally unpopular, though his extravagance alarmed his Ministers. His extravagance took the form principally of building sumptuous palaces and of keeping a large harem, but neither of these is a form of extravagance which would tend to make the ruler of an Eastern race unpopular. A more genuine cause of unpopularity among thoughtful Turks existed in his being opposed to reforms on European lines. After the Crimean War a number of able men, of whom Ali and Fuad were the most prominent, conceived the idea that Turkey's future advancement depended upon her progress on such lines.

The Rise of Midhat Pasha and a Reform Party.

In 1875-6, when the populations of Serbia, Bosnia, Herzegovina, and Bulgaria had become restive and resisted the ordinary oppression exercised by the Pashas from Constantinople, the Ministers who had ideas of better government both for the benefit of the people and the country came naturally though slowly to the front. The most prominent among them was Midhat Pasha. At a period a little earlier he had been Vali of the Danubian province, which included Bulgaria, and had succeeded fairly well in maintaining order, but without showing any indication of a desire for reform, and especially for the most necessary reform in Bulgaria, that of doing justice to the Christian population. Indeed, the stories told of him in that province show him to have had crude ideas of establishing equality between Christians and Moslems. A conversation which he had with an American, who then lived in Bulgaria, gives an indication of his insight at that period. He stated that he was informed that a Bulgarian or a Greek boy could learn to read and write in his own language in a year, and, even though he were a dullard, in two years, " whereas," said he, " one of our boys takes three or four years in order to stumble through a page of Turkish." This he considered unfair. He declared that, if he could, he would prohibit the teaching of Greek and Bulgarian in the schools and limit the teaching of language to Turkish.

When he came to Constantinople he was made President of the Council, then sent by Ali Pasha, the Grand Vizier, to Bagdad. Next, on Ali's death he was ordered to Adrianople. He refused to go until he had had an audience with the Sultan. He got his audience, and the Grand Vizier was dismissed the following day.

He was now generally regarded as the head of a party which sought to effect reforms in the Administration. All the influence of the Sultan's harem and of the corrupt officials was, however, brought against him; and the Sultan named Mahmud Pasha, of whom Midhat had complained, to be again Grand Vizier.

Finding that he could do nothing either as Grand Vizier or as President of the Council, he threw up his post—a dangerous and almost unknown procedure which greatly offended Abdul Aziz—and declared he would no longer take office as Minister. He went further and presented a report to the Palace in which he warned the Sultan that he was "drifting to the verge of an abyss." Then, like Cincinnatus, he retired to his farm.

During this time his opinions had developed. He was growing, and under his guidance the reforming party, of which he soon came to be considered the head, matured a project of reform. About November or December, 1875, the idea of a Constitution containing provisions for a deliberative Chamber seems to have been entertained for the first time in Turkey. Upwards of a year afterwards Midhat called upon Sir Henry Elliot, the British Ambassador, and explained his views on the subject, views, however, with the general tenor of which Sir Henry states that he was already acquainted.

Midhat especially wanted to control the Palace expenditure, to make Ministers responsible for it and other expenditure to a national popular assembly. To this end, for the first time, he expressed his wish to place Christians and Moslems on an equality. Hitherto his desire appeared to be to improve Turkish government by constituting an oligarchy composed of Ministers, the leading Ulema, and a Council of State presided over by the Sultan. But he recognised the difficulty of finding men untrammelled by the traditions of Turkish rule. As his ideas of political reform developed he, with his friends, desired a broader basis than the contemplated oligarchy would furnish. They sincerely desired to effect reforms which should benefit all sections of the community. They recognised that the great obstacle in their way was Abdul Aziz himself. He was the type of ruler who would tolerate anything for a quiet life except change.

Midhat by natural temperament was all in favour of activity, and when the troubles began in Serbia and Bulgaria, the remedy of reform for their restlessness came naturally to the front. The great supporters of the reform party were the Ulema and the theological students, or Softas, who were under their influence. Speaking generally, the Ulema during the last century proved themselves the most enlightened class among the Moslems. The Softas in 1876 were enthusiastic.

No doubt these young men and boys were easily moved to make political demonstration, but their youthful enthusiasm was due as much to a genuine belief in the necessity for reform as to the knowledge that most of their elders and religious teachers sympathised with them.

A significant incident occurred on May 10, 1876, when a crowd of Softas stopped Yussuf Izzedin,[1] the eldest son of the Sultan, demanding that he should return to his father and ask for the dismissal of Mahmud, the Grand Vizier, and of the Sheik-ul-Islam. Both were dismissed. Mehmed Rushdi, a responsible and popular man who insisted upon having Midhat as colleague, took Mahmud's place.

Deposition of Sultan Abdul Aziz; Murad becomes Sultan.

The feeling, however, became general amongst the ruling class in Constantinople that no reforms could be obtained from Abdul Aziz, and a movement, begun in the first instance amongst a few but soon taken up generally, commenced in order to dethrone him.

When this change was decided on, the question arose as to who was to be his successor. In accordance with Ottoman law, the heir to the throne on the death or deposition of Abdul Aziz was Murad, the eldest male of the Imperial family, and the son of Abdul Mejid. There were serious objections, however, to his appointment, for already he had shown signs of mental aberration, and his addiction to alcohol in various forms was so notorious as to shock all good Moslems. The Ulema were consulted as to whether the strict order of succession might not be set aside, and whether the brother of Murad, Abdul Hamid, could not be appointed in his place. But the judges of the Sacred Court were, as indeed they have usually been during the last half-century, conscientious men, devoted to the prescripts of their own law, and

[1] Yussuf Izzedin died in January, 1916, either by his own hand, as alleged by the Turkish Government, or, as popularly asserted, by assassination.

showed no tendency to adopt the suggestion. There was undoubtedly a party strongly in favour of the appointment of Abdul Hamid, but it was small. It was further suggested that Abdul Hamid should be named regent, but the general belief was that he had been sounded and refused to accept anything less than his appointment as Sultan. Accordingly on May 30, 1876, Abdul Aziz was deposed,[1] and Murad, his nephew, was proclaimed Sultan. A small detachment of the army and the Turkish fleet, under the guidance of Midhat and Hussein Avni, the Minister of War, accomplished the deposition. Both of them ran great risks, for failure would have cost them their heads.

The announcement of the deposition was received with general satisfaction; the press had been worked and all means taken for weeks before in order to let it be known that Prince Murad was a reformer. The news reached the British public before it reached Downing Street.[2]

England and France welcomed the change because they still clung to the idea that the independence and integrity of Turkey could be secured if only the Government would persist in introducing internal reforms. Those who have seen the entire failure of the Western Powers to induce Turkey to reform on practical lines are apt to lose sight of the honest desire and long-continued efforts of England and France to urge her to get rid of the abuses which barred her progress. The statesmen of London and Paris, as well as their ambassadors in Constantinople, desired a strong Turkey and were well aware that for two centuries she had been getting weaker. They believed that a constitutional government was essential to the progress of any race, and that Turkey could not be strong with its absolute government. Above all, they held the faith that, with a large portion of the population hostile to Moslem rule, it was necessary to grant religious equality. Few things are more pathetic than the noble and persistent efforts

[1] See note 2 at end of chapter.
[2] See note 3 at end of chapter.

of Stratford Canning, afterwards Lord Stratford de Redcliffe, to bring about religious liberty, even though religious equality were not possible. In this he was supported by his French colleagues. He considered it the triumph of his life when he succeeded in obtaining the Hatti-Humayun. With a flourish of many trumpets and self-gratulatory proclamations, the issue of the famous Hatt was hailed by the Christian population and by the reform section among the Moslems. But although religious equality was actually proclaimed, yet throughout the country it was generally disregarded.

An illustrative story may be given from Canning's Life. He heard of a Moslem who had become Christian and who was on his trial. Such an act was by the Sacred Law of the Sheriat a criminal offence. But although the Hatti-Humayun had been proclaimed, Canning knew that many had been quietly put to death for having changed their faith. In the instance in question he hastened to the Sultan with his dragoman, Mr. Pisani, to inform him that this man was either sentenced or about to be sentenced to death, and that such a violation of the famous Hatt could not be tolerated. The Sultan promised to make inquiries. Canning mistrusted the Sultan and knew that time pressed, for as soon as it was known that he had made representations to the Sultan the execution would take place forthwith. He therefore declined to leave the palace until he had the actual order for the release and surrender of the man to him in his possession. He succeeded in saving the intended victim, but many instances occurred during the reign of Abdul Aziz where Moslems who had changed their religion were quietly made away with.

While the ambassadors of the great Western Powers followed the reform party which deposed Abdul Aziz and placed Murad on the throne, Russia saw in the change a blow against her influence. Her ambassador at that time at Constantinople was General Ignatiev, a man of great determination and intelligence. It was due largely to his influence that after the Crimean War the Russian party in Constantinople recovered its influence amongst the Turks. When therefore Abdul Aziz was deposed, popular sentiment in Constantinople regarded the deposition as a triumph of Anglo-French diplomacy over that of Russia. This was supposed to be represented by a marked hostility between Sir Henry Elliot, the British Ambassador, and General Ignatiev.

Meantime every week after Murad had been proclaimed Sultan his mental aberration seems to have been more pronounced. His malady was greatly exaggerated by his addiction to champagne and cognac. Midhat, who at that time was only a Minister without portfolio, took the lead in public affairs by virtue of his persistency. Seeing the condition of the Sultan, he suggested the idea of his temporary abdication during his period of illness. Once more the chiefs of the Ulema were consulted. They objected to a regency and declared that he could not be legally deposed. Even if he were certified to be *non compos mentis*, his dethronement could only take place at the expiry of a full year. Midhat was dissatisfied with the reply and was eager to place Murad's brother, Abdul Hamid, on the throne. As the days passed the malady of Murad grew worse. The suicide of Abdul Aziz, which occurred a few days after his deposition, was a terrible shock to a man whose nerves were already shattered; and this shock was increased by a letter which his uncle, the deposed Sultan, had written to him the day after his deposition. He was too ill to be admitted to be girded with the sword of Osman, the ceremony which corresponds to coronation, and, under one pretext or another, the act of investiture was delayed.

On June 15 an event happened which still further shook his tottering reason. While the Ministers, Mehmed Rushdi, the Grand Vizier, Hairulla Effendi, the Sheik-ul-Islam, and Hussein, Minister of War, and two others, were quietly seated in a house in Stamboul, a Circassian soldier named Cherkess Hassan, a brother of one of the ladies of the harem of the deposed Sultan, rushed into the room armed with no less than six revolvers, and fired at everybody, killing the Minister of War and wounding two other Ministers. He had maddened himself with "bang," or Indian hemp. Cherkess Hassan was publicly hanged the day after his mad act. The incident increased the malady of the Sultan and to some extent augmented the strength of the old Turks who were opposed to all reforms, but all soon recognised that it was necessary to have a new Sultan.

During this period the influence of Midhat was steadily increasing; and when during the illness of Murad he produced a project of reform, it had the support not only of the Christians connected with the administration, but of the reforming section among the Moslems. He had come at length to recognise that the first reform necessary, and indeed the sum of all other needful reforms in the country, was the establishment of equality irrespective of difference of religion. His project was nominally the consummation of the principles enunciated in the Hatti-Humayun, but to put it forward in a large scheme of reform was to give it a publicity throughout the country which it had never before possessed. The objection which had been made to the principle of equality on the publication of the Hatti-Humayun was that it might conflict with certain sections of the Sacred Law. Accordingly this portion of the Sheriat Law was to be regarded as inapplicable. Christians were to be admitted to nearly all the dignities and positions in the State. A supplementary and short code was to be added to that of the Code Napoléon. The project deserves to be connected with Midhat's name because its existence and promulgation were mainly due to his foresight and persistency. After discussing it with the Ministers and the leading Ulema he submitted it to the Great Council of the Empire, which met at the Sheik-ul-Islam's palace, and in which Ministers and many notables took part. The Council finally accepted the project. It is then stated to have been submitted to the Crown Prince, Abdul Hamid, who promised to accept it in its entirety should he come to the throne. The project so accepted did not actually form the Constitution which was subsequently accepted and became law, but it contained all its essential principles. Midhat often consulted with Abdul Hamid, who at that time professed to be entirely with the reformers, and, according to Midhat's son, promised to grant more concessions in the direction of liberal reform than were contained in the project. Midhat and his fellow-reformers had, however, no intention of allowing the public to be aware of their designs. Meetings for discussion were forbidden, and the Press Bureau forbade the publication of any news regarding the proposed change.

Poor Murad got worse instead of better under the treatment of Dr. Capolini, on whom some discredit was thrown, probably unjustly, by his refusal to permit other medical men to see his patient. The Valida Sultana, the mother of Murad, sent to Vienna and obtained the services of a celebrated professor of medicine at that date, Dr. Leidesdorff. While this action was resented by Capolini, it is asserted that the Viennese specialist also disapproved of the treatment to which his colleague had submitted the Sultan. When he returned to Vienna he expressed his opinion that the illness of Murad was incurable, probably a hasty decision, which was much criticised at the time, and which was proved to be unfounded by the subsequent recovery of Murad. It was at this period, when probably all the Ministers had agreed with Midhat that it was necessary to depose the Sultan, that the proposal was made once more to Abdul Hamid to become regent. He again declined.

When all was arranged for the deposition some of the Ulema once more insisted that a full year must elapse between the declaration that the Sultan was incapable and his deposition. It is said that it was in compliance with the objection so raised that Midhat induced or compelled Abdul Hamid, the Crown Prince, to give him a declaration in writing by which he bound himself to abdicate in favour of his brother when such brother recovered. Much obscurity hangs about this matter. First of all, it is uncertain that such paper was ever given, though the belief almost universally entertained among the Turks is that there was such a document. It was believed to have been taken possession of by Midhat and to have been deposited for safe keeping in London. After the trial and condemnation of Midhat (to be subsequently mentioned) his house and all the contents were burned, and it was believed by many that amongst such contents was the declaration of Abdul Hamid. Another story was to the effect that the declaration was given to the Minister of Marine who was in power when Abdul Hamid was proclaimed and under whom the fleet took a leading part in the deposition. He remained in office until his death about 1905, and was the only Minister who had continued uninterruptedly to be in the Sultan's favour. The stories told of him point to his fearlessness of anything that Abdul Hamid could do. It is said that the Sultan on one occasion sent to say that he had learned that the Minister had received £200,000 as bakshish. The reply of the Minister was that he had received £300,000, and nothing more was heard of the matter. He was a bluff old sailor and undoubtedly made a large fortune out of his position as Minister of Marine. But the reason most commonly assigned for his being the only one whom Abdul Hamid had not dismissed was that he either had the document in question or knew where it was deposited with orders for its publication in case of his death by violence, and therefore it did not suit Abdul Hamid to get rid of him.

Murad deposed; Abdul Hamid becomes Sultan.

Meantime everything had been arranged for the deposition of Murad; the necessary *fetva*[1] had at length been obtained from the Court of the Sheik-ul-Islam, and on Thursday, August 31, 1876, Abdul Hamid left the house of Peresta Hanum, the lady who had adopted him, and, accompanied by the Minister of War and a hundred and fifty soldiers on horseback, at half-

[1] See note at end of chapter.

past eight in the morning arrived at the Imperial Palace at Stamboul, where the Ministers and high dignitaries were already assembled. At ten o'clock the boom of a hundred guns announced the deposition of Sultan Murad and the appointment of his brother Abdul Hamid. The new Sultan was then hailed as Padisha and embarked at Seraglio Point, followed by a great number of caiques belonging to the Court, and was conducted to the palace of Dolma Bagshe, which had been quitted a few hours earlier by Sultan Murad and his family. Abdul Hamid had obtained his wish and was now undisputed Sultan of Turkey.

Note No. 1.—The word *fetva*, which will occasionally occur in this volume, requires explanation. *Fetvas* correspond to what are known in Roman law as *responsa prudentum*, the "answers of the learned in the law." They are opinions given by a court which exists as part of the Supreme Court for the administration of sacred law. The *Fetva Khan* still survives. If a person desires an answer to a question involving Turkish law he may obtain it without much difficulty. The questions are usually in an impersonal form. "Hassan dies leaving one widow, two sons, a daughter, and three grandchildren, being a son and two daughters, the children of Mehmet, a third son of Hassan, but now deceased." What is the share in the inheritance of Hassan which the children of Mehmet will be entitled to receive ? A small fee has to be paid to the court, which then gives a decision in writing, known as a *fetva*.

Note No. 2.—On the deposition of Abdul Aziz, mentioned on p 37, Sir Henry Elliot, writing in the *Nineteenth Century* for February, 1888, gives the following interesting details :—

"The only persons who took an active part in it were Midhat Pasha and Hussein Avni, the Seraskier, or Minister of War, and I never could ascertain for certain whether the Grand Vizier had previous knowledge of their enterprise or not ; but I understood that, though three days before he had been persuaded to consent to it as indispensable for the salvation of the Empire, the two other Ministers alone matured the plan, without any but themselves being dangerously compromised. The risk that they had to run was very great, for their heads were at stake ; but they combined their project with skill, and executed it with courage and resolution. They passed the early part of the night of May 29 at Hussein Avni's konak at Beyler Bay, on the Asiatic shore of the Bosphorus, and from there an hour or two after midnight, when it was very dark and raining hard, they passed over to Constantinople in a small caique, attended by a single servant, and were landed at a spot where they expected to find carriages waiting for them, which, however, had not arrived. They were left standing in a drenching rain, exposed every moment to a discovery which would have been fatal to their enterprise and no doubt to themselves, till at last their servant found and brought the carriages, which had gone to a wrong place.

"Then, as had been arranged, Midhat Pasha proceeded to the Seraskerat, while Hussein Avni went to the barracks near Dolma Baghtche, where, as Minister of War, he had no difficulty in bringing a regiment quartered in them to the palace, which he surrounded without any alarm being taken. He then knocked at the gates, and desired the Kislar Agha, the chief official of the household, to inform the Sultan that he was a prisoner, and to urge him to put himself into the hands of the Seraskier, who answered for his safety. The Sultan's first and natural impulse was to resist, and it was not till Hussein Avni appeared before him and convinced him that resistance was impossible that he could be persuaded to submit to his kismet. A guard was placed over him without a blow being struck, and, as had been agreed upon, a gun was fired to announce to Midhat Pasha at the Seraskerat that the arrest of the Sultan had been successfully carried out.

"In the meantime Midhat's position had been intensely critical. He had no authority over the troops, no right to give them orders, and he had to rely solely on the personal influence that he might be able to exercise. He had arrived at the Ministry of War under the most suspicious appearances, in the dark, unattended, and drenched to the skin; and it was with the utmost difficulty that, by representing himself as authorised by the Seraskier, he at last succeeded in inducing the commanding officer to call out his men and draw them up in the square. He had a long and anxious time to pass, during which at any moment, if sinister rumours arrived from the palace, the troops might assume a hostile attitude, for it was not till close upon daybreak that the signal gun put an end to the suspense, and announced the successful accomplishment of the enterprise.

"Midhat then came out into the square to harangue the troops, and not a murmur of discontent was heard when he informed them of the step that had been taken, and explained the necessity for it. He was cheerfully obeyed when he ordered a guard of honour and an escort to proceed to the palace of Prince Murad to announce to him his accession to the throne, and to conduct him to the Seraskerat, where he was at once proclaimed and saluted as Sultan by troops drawn up there, and by the people, who by that time had begun to assemble."

Note No. 3.—With reference to the statement that the news of the deposition first reached the British public on p. 38, Sir Henry Elliot says: "One newspaper correspondent alone had contrived to send the news to his employers. He was at the head of the Turkish Post Office, and, with a view to some possible emergency, he had arranged a private code by which he could communicate political intelligence, while appearing to deal with purely private concerns, and he obtained permission to forward a message 'of an urgent private nature,' which ran as follows: 'The doctors have found it necessary to bleed' (depose) 'poor Jane' (Abdul Aziz). 'Grandmamma' (the Validé) 'is with her. Cousin John' (Murad) 'has taken charge of the business.' This ingenious telegram conveyed, I believe, the first intelligence of what had occurred that reached any European capital."

CHAPTER IV

ABDUL HAMID ENDEAVOURS TO STRENGTHEN HIS OWN POSITION; STORY OF MIDHAT

Two attempts in favour of Murad; Midhat Pasha dismissed from post of Grand Vizier February 7, 1877; the Chamber of Representatives under his Constitution meets March 19, 1877; clauses of Constitution *re* representative government suspended; charge of murder against Midhat; story of suicide of Abdul Aziz; of post-mortem; testimony of nineteen medical men and of Sultana Valida; sentenced to death June 30, 1881; murdered July, 1883; Sir Henry Elliot's remarks in February, 1888.

ONCE seated on the throne, Abdul Hamid found himself in presence of many difficult problems. The most pressing in his own opinion related to the strengthening of his position, the second to putting an end to the serious difficulties which had arisen in his Danubian provinces.

The Sultan probably considered his position to be in more serious danger than did observers in his capital. His right was not contested by any class of his subjects. Murad had been deposed after a formal judgment of the highest religious court. Moslem public opinion sanctioned it. The rest of the population either approved of the deposition of a ruler who was insane or a drunkard, or were indifferent. It is true that there were a few among the Mollahs or Ulema who held to the belief that a year ought to elapse before the deposition took place, and they were joined by some who were opposed to any proposals which appeared to favour the Christians. They made a demonstration almost immediately after the accession. But it was easily suppressed in the last week of October, 1877. A few arrests were made, and the opposition seemed to die a natural death. It broke out again, however, in a more serious form eighteen months later (May 20, 1878) under a half-crazy Mollah named Ali Suavi. He was supported by a few men who were dissatisfied on various grounds with the conduct of Abdul Hamid, and who avowed themselves in favour of Murad. Their plot was hardly concealed, and when they made an attack upon the palace, the leader and all the assailants were killed. The incident was the last attempt in favour of Murad.

Abdul Hamid was much more concerned with strengthening his position against Midhat Pasha and the group of reformers. From his accession to his death, like probably most Sovereigns, he was extremely jealous of any encroachment on his sovereign power. He was believed to have promised the reformers that he would grant even greater reforms than they asked for, but such promises were made when he was asked to become regent. When he became Sultan, his Ministers and many others soon recognised that he hated the notion of any change in the form of government.

The events in Bulgaria, however, forced his hand. When a Conference of the European Powers was decided to be held in the capital in December, two months after his accession, to submit a scheme of reform to him, he found himself in a difficulty. To accept what foreign Powers desired—for no secret was made of the general lines on which the Powers would act—would humiliate him in the eyes of his subjects; to reject it would be to risk war with all Europe. Then Midhat saw his chance. He suggested to Abdul Hamid a step which appealed to his vanity and gave him hope of a triumph. Abdul had promised to accept Midhat's scheme of reforms. Let the Sultan outbid the European delegates; let him proclaim a scheme which should apply not to the disaffected European provinces only, but to the whole Empire. If his Majesty would proclaim a Constitution the wind could be taken out of the sails of the Conference. The representatives would go home defeated men, and his Majesty's reputation would be enhanced. Abdul Hamid accepted the proposal. On the day fixed for the meeting of the Conference, December 23, 1876, a salute of a hundred guns from the Turkish fleet (anchored near the Admiralty buildings on the Golden Horn, where the delegates were sitting) should announce to them that the Sultan had granted reforms greater than they proposed. We shall see in the following chapter how this arrangement was carried out. For the present it is sufficient to say that it signally failed.

On January 20, 1877, the Conference ended, all admitting that they had not succeeded in obtaining the objects for which they had met. The Sultan's proposals had not taken the place of those of the delegates. Thereupon Abdul Hamid's resentment turned upon his Grand Vizier. Midhat and other members in favour of the Constitution were ignominiously dismissed on February 5, 1877.

But the Constitution had been not only proclaimed, but that part of it especially which established a Parliament was so welcomed by the populace of the capital that it would have been dangerous to set it aside at once. Accordingly a Turkish representative Chamber was convoked. The experiment was a new one for Turkey, and its results were in many respects noteworthy. The Chamber met on March 19, 1877. It showed that representative Chambers are not institutions to be trifled with, and that, if freedom of speech be permitted, they will be an effectual means of bringing about reforms, since they will create a public opinion which no ruler can long defy. The convocation of the Chamber was probably largely influenced in popular opinion by manipulation from the capital. Few, however, objected because the voters were entirely inexperienced. The result obtained was an assembly of a number of real representatives who had the desire to secure better government, and some of whom were determined to substitute a constitutional form of government for absolutism. It was the first time that representatives from such distant places as Bagdad, Albania, Armenia, and Syria met together. Their discussions were singularly full of interest and even surprises. Though most of the members spoke of serious grievances which required redress in their own districts, they were surprised to learn that their own constituencies were not alone as spheres of misgovernment. When the members for Jerusalem, Bagdad, Erzerum, and Salonika met together, they found that the administration throughout all the country was corrupt, and they set themselves honestly to discuss their grievances and the changes in the system which were necessary to secure a remedy. Amongst the deputies were several able and thoughtful men. They had no traditions of parliamentary government, and some of the speeches were banal, speeches which would have been brought to an end by authority had they been delivered in the Legislative Chamber either of England, America, or a British colony. They often had a tendency to personalities unconnected with public affairs, but more usually they attacked this pasha or that for abuses, for receiving bribes and refusing to do what was right unless he were paid for it. Had the Sultan been as wise as his sycophants represented him to be, he would have seen the value of such statements and would have allowed the deliberations of the Chamber to continue. There were at first absolutely no attacks whatever upon him, though many of his Ministers were personally charged with specific irregularities and misconduct. The discussions were a revelation to Turkish subjects. They showed that the government from one end of the country to the other required radical reform. The Chamber had at its head a President, Ahmed Vefyk, who had been Ambassador of Turkey at the Court of Napoleon III., was an excellent French scholar, and in education was no doubt the superior of nearly all the deputies. But in public and private life he had become despotic, and his superior, schoolmasterly manner as Chairman of the House was arrogant and sometimes amusing. He frequently stopped deputies in the midst of speeches, telling them that they knew nothing about the subject and were talking nonsense. Dr. Washburn, the President of Robert College, was present when a white-turbaned deputy,[1] who was making a long and prosy statement, was suddenly pulled up by a stentorian shout from the President of "Shut up, you donkey!" (*Sus eshek*). The orator sat down as if he were shot.

Meantime the accusations brought by members against the corruption of individual Ministers became more serious and definite in form. The claim that certain of the Ministers should be brought before the Chamber in order to answer charges against them was naturally opposed by the accused Ministers, and was distasteful to Abdul Hamid. The hostility between the Chamber and the pashas became serious, and various correspondents predicted that within a short time the Chamber would upset the rule of the pashas, or the pashas would get rid of the Chamber. Abdul Hamid never lost sight of the fact that the calling of the Chamber and the proclamation of the Constitution had been imposed upon him by Midhat. Accordingly, when the charges against three of the Ministers became definite, and a resolution was adopted that the accused should answer them before the Chamber, Abdul Hamid took the resolution to dissolve the Chamber and to expel the members from Constantinople. The capital learned that the night after the Chamber had made the request above mentioned all the deputies had been packed off to the places which they represented. No more was heard of attempts to govern Turkey constitutionally until the revolution of 1908. The dismissal of the Chamber was followed by an Imperial edict declaring that the whole of that part of Midhat's Constitution which related to the Chamber of Representatives was suspended. The Chamber, opened on March 19, 1877, sat for barely two months.

Though Abdul Hamid had got rid of the Chamber and was now free to exercise arbitrary control, though he never forgave Midhat or others who had urged him to try the experiment, though its labours had not

[1] The Ulema class wear white turbans and are spoken of as Seraclis or Mollahs.

placed upon the Statute Book any measure of importance, its sittings were nevertheless not valueless. They gave the thoughtful portion of the community an insight into a means of checking arbitrary authority. They helped to furnish to it an ideal of better government. Though that portion of the Constitution which provided for representative government was in abeyance between 1877 and 1908, it was never forgotten, and in the interval, which was crowded with instances of misgovernment due to the vindictiveness, the short-sightedness, the ignorance, and the incapacity of Abdul Hamid, men recalled the attempt of Midhat and the reformers, forgot the blunders of the representatives of the people, remembered their honest attempts, and came to think of government by an elected Chamber as the best means of putting an end to arbitrary government.

The story of the subsequent dealings of Abdul Hamid with Midhat Pasha is a tragedy, and shows the worst side of the Sultan's character. He never forgave Midhat for his attempt to establish constitutional government. The members of the Conference of Constantinople having failed to be cajoled or deluded by the salute which was intended to make them believe that the Sultan of his own free will had inaugurated a wide scheme of reforms for the whole Empire, Midhat, then Grand Vizier, was sent for to the palace to be ignominiously dismissed. He was met before entering it by an aide-de-camp, who ordered him in the name of his Majesty to surrender to him the seals of office and then conducted him on board a steamer leaving at once for Brindisi. Thither he went, but soon afterwards at his own request was permitted to return to Turkey.

The dismissal on February 3, 1877, was before the meeting of the representative Chamber which was in truth Midhat's creation. The Sultan had concluded not only that he must no longer be a Minister, but that it was dangerous to allow the man who was notoriously the principal author of the Constitution, and who was not unpopular with the inhabitants of the capital, to remain in it. After his dismissal until his death Midhat was treated with remarkable vindictiveness. Upon his return to Turkey, though he was not permitted to reside in the capital, he was not molested. Abdul Hamid was waiting his time.

A charge was being formulated against Midhat of an extremely grave character. In order to understand it the deposition of Sultan Abdul Aziz must be recalled. After that event the deposed Sultan was kept in an honourable confinement for a day or two in his palace and was then sent for two or three days to Seraglio Point to a beautiful little kiosk which is one of the most conspicuous objects to travellers descending the Bosporus. Then he was taken back to the Cheragan Palace, which adjoins that of Dolma Bagshé. On the fifth day after his deposition, namely on June 4, 1876, it was announced that he had been found dead in his chair in one of its rooms. The story given of the circumstances in which he was found was plausible, but in Constantinople accounts of the sudden death of distinguished Turks are always, and justly, looked upon with suspicion. The circumstantiality of the then uncontested evidence convinced most people that in this particular instance death was the result of suicide, and not of assassination. The late Sultan was found dead in an arm-chair with his head on one side. Great spurts of blood which had come from his left arm were on the floor, while smaller spurts had come from the right. By his left side was found a pair of long pointed scissors such as the Turks commonly employ for personal use. The room where he died, and which he occupied, adjoined the harem, and its ladies could look into the part of it where the Sultan's chair stood from a projecting gallery whence they could see only the back of his head as he sat in it. Some of them saw the Sultan's head fall forward. Alarm was immediately given, and the Sultana Valida had the door forced open. On entering Abdul Aziz was found to be dead with the scissors lying as if they had fallen from his hand. The Sultana at once declared that her son had asked for the scissors in order to trim his beard, and that she, after some hesitation, had complied with his request. The hesitation, she subsequently explained, was caused by the fact that she believed that Abdul Aziz had a predisposition to insanity. His brother, Abdul Mejid, whom he succeeded, had indeed at one period of his life suffered from the same malady.

The Ministers recognised that for their justification before the country and the Powers an immediate examination was necessary. Every embassy and legation in Constantinople was requested to send its medical officer in order to take part in a post-mortem. Nineteen medical men, including the most eminent foreign and native physicians, attended and signed a report declaring that after careful examination they found that death was due to suicide under the circumstances already mentioned. Sir Henry Elliot, our ambassador at the time, immediately summoned Dr. Dickson, already an old and well-trusted British medical officer, to attend with the rest. By an accident in the transmission of the message Dr. Dickson arrived at the palace a few minutes after the others had concluded their investigation. He was accompanied by Dr. van Millingen, who had been with Lord Byron at Missolonghi when he died. Dr. Dickson in after-days repeatedly stated that he went to the palace with the firm conviction that Abdul Aziz had been murdered, and that the story put forward by the Ministers was an ingenious invention, which he was determined to expose. He and Dr. van Millingen examined the body carefully and found no traces whatever of injury except the piercing of the arms. The Sultan was known to be an exceptionally powerful man, and there was no trace of a struggle. The fewer spurts of blood from the right arm as compared with those from the left impressed them as being what would naturally happen from the fact that most men are less skilful with the left arm than the right. Having completed the examination of the body, they reported that it was healthy and bore no traces of violence or injury from the crown of his head to the soles of his feet except on the arms. There was not a scratch, mark, or bruise on any part of it. They examined the body also for traces of poisoning, giving details which need not be printed. Thereupon Dr. Dickson addressed a report to Sir Henry Elliot confirming in all particulars that which had been drawn up by his colleagues. His preconceived idea of murder had to be abandoned. He found a clear case of suicide. He confirmed these statements shortly afterwards in a careful letter to the London *Lancet*.

After these examinations and reports Constantinople settled down to the belief that the death of Abdul Aziz was due solely to his own hands. The attitude taken by the Sultana Valida confirmed the public judgment. Everybody recognised that if she had any suspicion of assassination she would have given utterance to it. But her declaration that she had given the scissors, and that the wounds had evidently been inflicted by them, was strong corroborative evidence of the truth of the suicide story. She was satisfied as to the cause of death. The poor woman was distracted; and when Dr. Millingen saw her, she bemoaned her fate and declared she was the author of his death by lending him the scissors.

The outside world had almost forgotten the incident of the suicide of Abdul Aziz when it was startled by news that Midhat with Hairulla Effendi, the ex-Sheik-ul-Islam, Mahmud Damat, together with a wrestler and a gardener attached to the Palace, had been suddenly arrested and were to be put on trial for the murder of their Sovereign. Common report had long attributed to the Sultan strong personal animosity against Midhat, but anticipated with confidence that legal proceedings would show that the death was suicide. The public did not know that some of the creatures of Abdul Hamid had prepared carefully a case against the leaders of the reforming party. Indeed, the case got up on behalf of the Sultan was ingeniously put together. It alleged that no suspicion had been awakened against the report of the medical men until an accidental examination of the books of the Civil List in reference to the expenditure of Yildiz Palace disclosed the fact that there were two men kept on, nominally as gardeners or in some other subordinate capacity, to whom no specific work had been assigned. Upon inquiry it was found that they received their salaries because they had assisted in killing Abdul Aziz. It was alleged that under examination they admitted the charge and declared that they were acting under the orders of Midhat Pasha. One of them, a wrestler, held the Sultan's arms pinioned while the other carefully thrust a stiletto from the shoulder to the heart. They claimed that the deed had been done so skilfully that no external signs could be detected by any of the medical men who took part in the examination.

The judgment of the Turkish Court was delivered on June 30, 1881. All the judges, with the exception of one Ulema who ever afterwards was the subject of Abdul Hamid's enmity, concurred in pronouncing a verdict of "Guilty" against all the persons accused. All were sentenced to death.

Those who knew the Turkish Courts and Turkey found no difficulty in believing that the witnesses were suborned and that the whole trial was a monstrous mockery of justice. It is true that a few intelligent foreigners were inclined to believe the story told by the prosecution, but their belief was due to ignorance of the facilities by which false evidence could be obtained. The witnesses had been carefully coached before they told their tale in Court. In defiance even of Turkish law, no cross-examination was allowed. Midhat himself throughout the trial was specially aimed at, although all the other accused were also sentenced. It is doubtful whether more than three of them were intended for punishment.

Abdul Hamid had succeeded in a foul conspiracy which Sir Henry Elliot justly characterised as "an indelible blot upon his reign."[1]

[1] *Nineteenth Century* for 1888, p. 288. The article of Sir Henry is entitled "The Death of Abdul Aziz and of Turkish Reform." (See note at end of chapter.)

Every Power in Europe, acting upon the reports of their own embassies, recognised that the verdict was at least a doubtful one, and that to execute the sentence of death on Midhat would be a disgrace to them as well as to Abdul Hamid. The matter was brought before both Houses of Parliament in England. Both political parties used their influence upon the Government to save Midhat's life. All that they could accomplish was to reduce the sentence from death to banishment for life to Arabia. Probably no act by the Powers was so resented by Abdul Hamid as their interference between him and his intended victim.

Abdul Hamid's vindictiveness was baffled for the time, but his determination to get rid of Midhat continued. He and Hairulla were sent to Taif, in Arabia. The Sultan had succeeded in getting rid of the principal man whose presence would make it difficult for him to recall the shadowy reforms which he had granted in that part of the Constitution which he had not suspended. In Constantinople, however, it was generally believed that the author of the Constitution had been sent to Taif simply to get rid of his influence; but the popular judgment had not yet taken the measure of Abdul Hamid's enmity. According to Midhat's fellow-exile, Hairulla Effendi, the reformer was strangled by order of the Sultan on July 26, 1883. Hairulla records the details of the manner of his death. Midhat's son, Ali Haydar Midhat Bey, gives interesting particulars.[1] Midhat was sixty-one years old at the time of his death.

It is interesting to recall that the British Government took the most active part in the intervention which saved him from being hanged in Stamboul. The report of the debate in the House of Commons on July 1, 1881, upon the trial of Midhat shows the great interest taken in England both during his trial and after his condemnation. Lord Granville, then Foreign Secretary, was in communication with Lord Dufferin, who was then Ambassador to the Porte and had received instructions to

[1] See note at end of chapter.

use all his influence together with that of the other Ambassadors to save Midhat's life. In reply to the questions of Mr. McCoan, an Irish M.P. who had lived many years in Constantinople, practising at the Bar of the Supreme Consular Court, Sir Charles Dilke suggested that it was better not to press him further with questions, or the members might be defeating the object they had in view.

Midhat, a man not without serious faults, had sown the seed which was destined after long years to be productive of a useful harvest. The quarter of the century which followed his death showed Turkish subjects of all ranks and creeds what were the evils of despotism. The faults of Midhat were forgotten, but it will ever be remembered that he struggled hard to substitute a constitutional government for absolutism and lost his life in consequence. His trial and death will ever remain as one of the most conspicuous blots upon the career of Abdul Hamid.

Note, p. 57.—See "Life of Midhat, with a Preface by J. L. de Lanessan, formerly Minister of Marine in France." The author repeats the story elsewhere alluded to that Midhat's body was dug up and the head cut off and sent to Abdul Hamid at Yildiz in a box labelled "Ivoires Japonnaises, objets d'art. Pour S.M. le Sultan."

Note on Midhat's trial by Sir Henry Elliot.—In February, 1888, writing in the *Nineteenth Century*, on p. 288, Sir Henry Elliot says: "If at the time there was no ground for a suspicion of assassination, there was certainly no evidence deserving of the slightest attention brought forward at the iniquitous mock trial instituted three years later, when the ruin of certain important personages had been resolved upon. The fact that the charges against them could only be supported by evidence which could not by any possibility be true, and the falseness of which could easily have been exposed if, in flagrant defiance of the law, the accused had not been denied their right of cross-examining the witnesses, affords sufficient proof that no real evidence against them existed. As the disgraceful mockery of the whole proceedings was admitted universally even by those who entertained no friendly feelings towards the accused, it is unnecessary to enter into an examination of them. The object, however, was attained, and eminent persons who were considered dangerous, and who might stand in the way of the resumption of the absolute power of the Palace, were effectually got rid of; while the men on whose perjured and suborned evidence the convictions were obtained, although they declared themselves to have murdered the Sultan with their own hands at the instigation of the pashas, were not only not executed, but are believed to have continued in the enjoyment of comfortable pensions ever since.

"There is no way of explaining why, after the lapse of three years, a wrestler and a gardener should come forward and declare that they had assassinated the Sultan except by the assumption that they had been promised not only immunity, but reward, if, while making their confession, they procured the conviction of Midhat and the other pashas as the instigators of their crime. They duly earned the promised recompense, and the Sultan secured an iniquitous conviction that enabled him to rid himself of the men whom he dreaded; but it was at the cost of an indelible blot upon his reign."

CHAPTER V

THE PACIFICATION OF BULGARIA AS SETTLED AT SAN STEFANO AND BERLIN

Abdul Hamid resists reforms; condition of Balkan provinces on his accession; oppression of Bulgarians; attitude of Orthodox Church; massacre of Bulgarians; reports by Mr. Schuyler and Mr. Baring; agitation aroused in England; Mr. Gladstone publishes "Bulgarian Horrors and Questions of the East"; Conference of Powers at Constantinople; proclamation of Constitution; declaration of war by Russia; siege and fall of Plevna; Gourko and Skobeleff advance; Abdul's attempt to delay it fails; establishment of principality of Bulgaria; Bismarck intervenes with Austria to throw odium of saving Turkey on England; Treaty of San Stefano; Congress and Treaty of Berlin; the Cyprus Convention.

WHILE giving attention to the strengthening of his own position, Abdul Hamid had to concern himself with the condition of Bulgaria, Serbia, Bosnia, and Herzegovina. Insurrection had broken out in the latter province in the summer of 1875. It spread rapidly into Serbia and neighbouring provinces. In July, 1876, war was declared against Serbia and Montenegro. In April, May, and June massacres occurred in Bulgaria. Abdul Hamid had of course no responsibility for these atrocities, since they took place before he ascended the throne. Nor can he reasonably be held responsible for what took place immediately after September 1, for the savage cruelties, including the hanging of many suspected persons in order, as was alleged, to punish those who had stirred up the disaffection which led to the massacres.

In view, however, of what happened after Abdul Hamid's accession and his many dealings with that province, it is expedient to notice briefly what was the condition of Bulgaria, and especially what were the events of 1876.

The Bulgarians had hardly attracted any notice in Europe for centuries. They belonged to the Orthodox Church. Matters ecclesiastical were under the Patriarch of Constantinople. The bishops sent into Bulgaria were Greeks, who usually spoke no language but their mother-tongue. If they possessed a second it would in most cases be Turkish. Travellers who in the eighteenth and first half of the nineteenth century passed through Bulgaria to the capital (the chief road always being from Belgrade to Sofia and thence to Philippopolis) often seemed to have believed that all the Christians whom they met were Greeks. Lady Mary Montague in the eighteenth and Kinglake, the author of "Eothen," in the nineteenth, saw churches and usually took them and their congregations to be Greek. A British statesman now living has stated that when he travelled over the same ground as Kinglake in the early fifties he fell into the same error.

The Bulgarians had ceased to regard their Church as a protector. Its liturgy was Greek. The Bulgarians suffered much from the exactions not only of the Turkish governors, but of their ecclesiastical authorities. Many of the younger members of well-to-do families were sent into Russia for their education, usually to Odessa. The first service these young men rendered to their country was to give voice to a public opinion in favour of the use of Bulgarian instead of Greek in their churches. Like all the Christians of the Balkan States, they looked to Russia for sympathy and aid. Their language, like that of Serbia and Russia, is Slavic. Even before the Crimean War a committee had been formed at Odessa which became the centre of Bulgarian national activity and aspirations. The Crimean War caused it to suspend some of its operations, but the struggle for the use of Slavic in their churches continued even during the war, and had the effect of causing the Russian nation to sympathise with the Bulgarian people. Russia, however, hesitated for a considerable time even after the war to interfere. She was not going to renew a great struggle for the sake of an oppressed province in Turkey. She, however, and other European Powers changed their attitude when an influential deputation of Bulgarians went to Italy in order to negotiate a union of their Church with that of Rome. The Greeks of Constantinople naturally opposed this movement. Under the threat that if the concession to substitute a Slavic for the Greek liturgy were not granted a formal demand would be made for the union with Rome, the substitution was granted. The menace of such union brought about the active intervention of Russia. England and France recognised that the only equitable solution of the difficulty was to allow the Bulgarians to have their own Church. When Napoleon III. advised union with Rome, Russia pressed her demands on Constantinople for the establishment of an autonomous Church. The Porte was always ready to adopt any suggestion which divided the Christians; and once the project was supported by Russia and the two Western Powers, Abdul Aziz disregarded the opposition of the Greeks and in February, 1870, granted a Firman recognising the Bulgarian Church. Its authority was to extend over all Bulgarian-speaking communities in the Empire. In order to lessen any conflict with the Patriarch, with whom Russia had always desired to be on good terms, the head of the Bulgarian Church was called the Exarch.

The Orthodox Church, partly from its desire to force the Bulgarians to preserve unity and partly from its wish to guard its right of appointing bishops, declared the Bulgarian Church to be schismatic, and still refuses to admit its members into communion with her. Unfortunately the separation of the Churches emphasised the century-long hostility between Slavs and Greeks in the Balkan peninsula. When the struggle commenced by the Bulgarians for their independence in the spring of 1876 the Greeks constantly and persistently opposed them.

During the revolt of the Serbians against Turkey in 1875 and 1876 an agitation of apparently slight importance had commenced in Bulgaria. The Turks in the latter province were engaged in trying to find out and punish all who were disaffected towards their Government. They were particularly severe against schoolmasters, priests, and persons of education. Many were imprisoned, others tortured or exiled unless they were able to escape from the country. The exiles who had reached Bucharest formed a committee whose object was to obtain reforms in Bulgaria. Thereupon the Turk, who has never known any means of governing a disaffected section of his community other than by massacre, tried his usual method. He would strike terror into Christians from one end of the province to the other. Orders were issued in April, 1876, by the Ministers of Abdul Aziz to attack the Bulgarian malcontents. Then there commenced a series of atrocities which recalled to old men the loathsome brutalities of Chios in 1822. All the cruelties which had attended the devastation of that beautiful island were reproduced. The reports of them in the London press in June and July, 1876, attracted great attention in England.[1] The statements were denied by Mr. Disraeli, but his denials contributed to bring about the greatest political agitation which had ever arisen in England in reference to the affairs of Turkey. The popular sentiment in favour of Turkey which had existed during the Crimean War still remained. Many doubted the truth of the allegations

[1] According to the testimony of Mr Gladstone, I was the first person who "sounded the alarm in Europe." This was done by a letter to the *Daily News*, under the head of "Moslem Atrocities in Bulgaria," which was dated from Constantinople, June 16. In this and a subsequent one, written on June 30, I gave the names of sixty villages which had been destroyed and whose inhabitants had either been tortured or killed. These letters were followed by others in the *Times*, written by Mr. Gallenga, and attracted much attention in Parliament. Mr. Disraeli, then Prime Minister, made light of the matter. He professed a doubt whether torture was practised on a large scale among the people, who "generally terminated their connection with culprits in a more expeditious manner" He spoke of the Circassians who had been mentioned as sharing in the cruelties and plunder as "settlers with a great stake in the country." His statements were untrue, for torture was constantly practised throughout the Turkish Empire until the revolution of 1908, and the Circassians were not settlers, but consisted of a few bands of robbers, who looted all property which they could seize. The statement had been made that they had seized and sold girls, and that the latter could be bought for two or three pounds each.

in the *Daily News* and *The Times*, but the denials called forth fresh confirmatory evidence, and the earnestness and zeal of two men especially, the Duke of Argyll in the House of Lords and Mr. W. E. Forster in the House of Commons, supported as each was on account of the moderation and precision of their statements, had their effect. A general demand was made in both Houses of Parliament that an authorised representative should be sent to examine and report on the charges which had been made. After considerable discussion Mr. Disraeli acquiesced in the general demand, and Mr. Walter Baring was named Commissioner. In the meantime, however, Mr. Eugene Schuyler, the American Consul-General, went into the disturbed province to learn the truth by personal observation. He was accompanied by Mr. MacGahan, acting as special Commissioner for the *Daily News*. Thus the reports of two independent commissioners were obtained. Mr. Baring found the number of villages destroyed to be fifty-nine and the number of killed to be 12,000. Mr. Schuyler's report made the number of villages destroyed to be sixty and the persons killed 15,000. It was when these reports were published in England that Mr. Gladstone, who had remained silent during the discussion in the House of Commons, published his pamphlet "Bulgarian Horrors and the Question of the East." The publication of these reports and the agitation which ensued did more than anything else to dispel the illusions in the Western mind which had grown up during the Crimean War. The attitude of Europe towards Turkey changed at this period, which exactly coincides with the accession of Abdul Hamid.

In justice to him, it should be noted that, while he had nothing to do with the outrages in Bulgaria, the massacres, the torturing, and the many methods of cruelty which were practised during the autumn of 1876 in Bulgaria, were all in accordance with the traditional methods of government in Turkey.

The most burning question with which Abdul Hamid had to deal was the pacification of the disturbed Balkan provinces, a pacification which implied the establishment of a government in the Balkan Peninsula which would prevent a recurrence of the recent horrors.

In England and in Russia popular sentiment was loudly expressed. With the object of finding a remedy, the proposal made by England to hold a Conference in Constantinople to draft reforms was accepted without much difficulty. The Conference met on December 21, 1876. Lord Salisbury was the Envoy Extraordinary and Minister Plenipotentiary of England, but was associated with Sir Henry Elliot, who was at this time the Ambassador to the Sublime Porte. Sir Henry was a favourite with the Turks, and during this portion of his career owed much of this repute to a curious incident. Mr. Disraeli in the House of Commons had not only defended the Turks and spoken slightingly of their misconduct, but produced a telegram, which, according to him, purported to come from Sir Henry Elliot, denying some of the statements in the leading British journals regarding Bulgarian horrors and declared others to be greatly exaggerated. The telegram itself brought great inconvenience and odium on Sir Henry, who, it appears, never sent any telegram of the sort. But the statement increased his popularity with the fanatical party in Turkey, for whose opinion under ordinary circumstances he felt and expressed contempt.

Lord Salisbury, on his arrival in Constantinople, expressed his opinion quite freely as to the necessity of reform, and the notion soon grew that he and Sir Henry Elliot were at loggerheads. This opinion was probably increased by the fact that Lord Salisbury and General Ignatiev, the representative of Russia, got on extremely well together. They two, beyond doubt, were regarded as, and in fact were, the most important men in the Conference. The Turkish delegates were Savfet Pasha and Edhem Pasha.

The scheme of reform which was submitted by the Conference alarmed Abdul Hamid. He declared that all the proposals were in derogation of his sovereign authority, and that he would not consent to anything which left him less powerful than any of his predecessors.

The Turkish newspapers, all subsidised, which the Sultan had already learnt to cultivate, strongly supported his Majesty's views, and, acting on the principle which Abdul Hamid not infrequently avowed of *divide et impera*, they were instructed to declare that Lord Salisbury did not represent the views of Mr. Disraeli, the British Prime Minister. Many articles in this strain, evidently inspired, appeared in the local journals. One headed "Bravo Sir Elliot" was shown in the House of Commons by Mr. Forster.

Abdul Hamid was perplexed. Even before the formal meeting of the Conference on December 23, he was informed what it would propose, and that its scheme of reform was accepted by the representatives of all the different Powers. Turkey's representatives dared not accept anything without Abdul Hamid's permission. Meantime even the Sultan recognised that something must be done to satisfy the demands of all Europe. He had accepted Midhat's proposal and it was now to be carried out. The Constitution would be proclaimed. Apparently Sir Henry Elliot knew of what had been arranged, for when a salute of a hundred guns disturbed the first sitting of the Conference, he rose and declared that the salute announced that their work was at an end. They had been gathered together to draft a scheme of reform for Bulgaria, Serbia, Bosnia, and Herzegovina. The salute announced that his Majesty had granted a Constitution which accorded wider reforms to the whole of the Empire.[1]

For the moment the members of the Conference were dumb. Then Ignatiev expressed his opinion that each of the delegates was charged by his Government with a special mission and that officially they knew nothing of the proclamation of a Constitution. Lord Salisbury hastened to support the view of his colleague. The sittings were resumed and went on almost daily. The Turkish delegates continued for awhile to refuse any useful concessions or even modifications. Unfortunately Abdul Hamid knew that the Powers were not

[1] See note at end of chapter.

united to coerce Turkey in case they failed to persuade her. The project of reform, accepted at first by all the Powers except Turkey, was however finally whittled down so that outsiders spoke of it as useless, and the meetings of the Conference a waste of time. The unanimous desire, however, of every nation was to avoid war, and the representatives would have been content with the simulacrum of reforms. But the Turkish delegates were obdurate. The representatives lost hope, and when on January 18, 1877, the Conference broke up, it had accomplished nothing.

It is an interesting subject for speculation whether at the time of the proclamation of Midhat's Constitution a better course might not have been taken than merely to reject the Sultan's proposal. If the delegates had asked for an official copy of it, and having found, as they probably would have done, that it contained useful provisions for the establishment of representative government and others against arbitrary arrest and imprisonment, had accepted it on condition that guarantees were given by Abdul Hamid for its execution, possibly the course of Turkish history might have been changed for the better. One can well understand that experienced statesmen, as the delegates of the Powers were, did not believe in the sincerity of a Constitution which appeared to have been promulgated simply to overcome what the Turks regarded as a temporary difficulty.

What is certain is, that the delegates went to the extreme limit of their powers in order to obtain better government for all elements of the population, but especially for the oppressed Christians. It is equally certain that the two nations most concerned after Turkey, namely England and Russia, earnestly sought to avoid war. It is hardly necessary to point out why Great Britain so desired. The integrity and independence of the Ottoman Empire was accepted by both parties as an article of political faith, and a war in defence of Turkey occasioned by the events in Bulgaria and the refusal of Turkey to accept reforms was unthinkable.

As to Russia, the general belief existed that she was not prepared for war. Probably it was well founded. An intelligent correspondent, who had come overland from Petersburg to Constantinople, declared that everywhere the Russians were unprepared and would not and could not fight. He was received by Abdul Hamid with every mark of favour, was decorated, and became the recipient of many presents, his statements on the subject being regarded as conclusive. As a fact, however, Russia was not well prepared for war, and she joined with England in the few weeks following the break up of the Conference in making strong representations to Abdul Hamid in order to obtain a show of reform and thus avoid war. Abdul Hamid was proud of his success and would not give way. His delegates, Savfet and Edhem, were both reasonable men and endeavoured to induce him to reconsider his decision. The only effect of their efforts was to cause both of them to be regarded henceforward with disfavour by their master.

On April 24, all efforts having failed, the Czar of Russia issued a manifesto, dignified in tone and reasonable in its statements, in which he declared that, having exhausted all pacific measures, Russia was brought " by the haughtiness and obduracy of the Porte to proceed to less pacific acts." On the same day he declared war.

Both the delegates of Abdul Hamid up to the declaration of war had urged him to grant concessions which would have avoided it. Their persistent arguments were in vain. Abdul Hamid therefore must be held responsible primarily for the war between his country and Russia, a war which contributed largely to the disintegration of Turkey.

It is no part of my task to write the history of the Turco-Russian War; but readers may usefully recall its chief incidents. Turkey has never been without soldiers of ability. In the war which ensued there were many vicissitudes and surprises. Muktar Pasha proved an able general. He commanded the Turkish divisions in Asia Minor. The Russians advanced against Turkey both there and in Europe. For some weeks in Asia

Minor they carried everything before them, but Muktar by his generalship checked their progress towards the capital and threatened them for a time with complete defeat. The great body of the Turkish Army in Europe was sent to oppose the Russians on the south shores of the Danube and opposite the provinces now known as Rumania. Another division under the command of Mehmet Ali went to put down a rising in Bosnia and Herzegovina. Mehmet Ali was a Prussian renegade who had come to Turkey as a youth, embraced Mahometanism, and rose to high command. He was murdered on the campaign in the autumn of 1877. The Russians, aided by the Rumanians, who had been hitherto regarded as an unwarlike people, successfully crossed the Danube, and made their way, almost without opposition, across the Balkans. They were of course welcomed by the Christian population, but on the approach of a large body of Turks, one division of which was under Suliman, they retreated across the Balkans. Thereupon a series of retaliatory outrages commenced by the Turkish soldiers upon the Christian population. The Russians, however, successfully and skilfully aided by the Rumanians, steadily advanced until a large Turkish Army was surrounded at Plevna. Osman Pasha, in command at that place, intrenched himself and successfully stood a siege which showed the Turks at their best. Plevna was captured, however, on December 10, mainly through the efforts of Skobeleff. The Russian general in actual command was Gourko, though he was nominally under a Grand Duke. Gourko, the real hero of Sebastopol, and Skobeleff arranged the subsequent plan of campaign; Gourko marched with a large division of the army to the miserable little village of Sofia, now the capital of Bulgaria. His intention, easily accomplished, was to capture it, and by pushing on over the great plain through the Iktiman Pass, of which the famous Trajan Gates formed part, to occupy Philippopolis. Skobeleff arranged and executed a project entirely in accord with his daring spirit. The one great road over the Balkans debouched at Shipka.

It was one of the few military roads made by the Turks, and was commanded by the strong Forts of St. George. The time was winter and exceptionally cold; but he learned from Bulgarian peasants that some five or six miles to the east of the great road there existed a sheep track, and about the same distance to the west of it another. He sent a body of men to endeavour to capture the Forts of St. George, a task which he recognised to be impossible of accomplishment within the time for the execution of his design. Another body he placed under Prince Mirska, to cross the range by the pass to the east of the road. He himself took charge of the remainder and set out to cross by the pass to the west. It was arranged that the men under Mirska and Skobeleff respectively should take up defensive positions immediately they had left the mountains and then act together. The pass was long and narrow. The men travelled in Indian file, and the first man had reached the southern extremity before the last man had started. They, however, successfully accomplished their design, for, although seen by the Turks in command at St. George, no efforts could be made to interrupt either of the long thin lines. The division under Mirska arrived first and was apparently impatient to get to the enemy. A large Turkish army under Vessel Pasha was encamped at Shenova, which commanded the pass. Mirska failed in his attempt against Vessel's army of 100,000 men. On the following day his force united with that of Skobeleff, and the most important battle of the campaign took place at Shenova. Skobeleff claimed that in it there was a hand-to-hand bayonet fight which lasted seven minutes. Then Vessel asked for the terms of surrender. Skobeleff replied that the whole of the army must lay down their arms and become prisoners and that orders must be sent to the Forts of St. George for their surrender. These terms were accepted, and before night fell a large host of Turkish soldiers, variously estimated at from 50,000 to 80,000 men, was on its march across the Shipka Pass to Russia as prisoners. The whole movement ending at Shenova was the most brilliant feat of the war.

Gourko's army was opposed by Suliman, a man of little ability, and who so conducted himself that Baker Pasha (Valentine Baker, formerly Colonel of the 10th Hussars), who had accepted service with the Turks, was persuaded that he was a traitor to Abdul Hamid. The two armies of Gourko and Skobeleff joined forces and continued their march to Philippopolis. Then Abdul Hamid, who from the first had taken upon himself the direction of military movements, recognised that the Turkish Army was beaten, and proposed to make terms. He sent Commissioners to treat for peace, but, with a trickiness which characterised him throughout his reign, gave them no instructions and no power to sign on his behalf. These Commissioners asked that the advance of the army should be stayed pending negotiations. Naturally the Russians refused.

It is probable that Abdul Hamid was aware of an agreement, then regarded as secret, between Austria and Russia, by which Austria consented to the entry of the Russian troops into Turkey, and to the establishment of a principality north of the Balkans, in return for Austria having the right of administration over Bosnia and Herzegovina. Once, therefore, the Russian Army had reached Philippopolis, they had come within the operation of a clause in the agreement which only allowed them to pass south of the Balkans in case of military necessity. Meantime messengers had been sent in hot haste to inform Abdul Hamid that the Russians were advancing and that they refused to treat with Commissioners not furnished with powers. There was no railway at the time and the roads, when not covered with snow, were heavy with rain. Delay in negotiations took place entirely owing to the inaction of Abdul Hamid. No powers authorising the delegates to treat having arrived until the Turks had fallen back beyond Adrianople, the Russians pushed on towards San Stefano, about twelve miles from Constantinople. An armistice and preliminaries of peace were signed on the last day of January, 1878, but the Russians continued to advance until these were completed and signed.

When negotiations commenced the Russians had an army of 150,000 men in the neighbourhood of Constantinople. Having free access by sea through the Bosporus to Odessa and the Crimea, and having no fear of the Turkish fleet, their position was fairly safe. Peace was signed on March 3, 1878, at San Stefano. Events during the end of the war had followed each other rapidly. Plevna fell on December 10, 1877; Gourko's army was at Sofia on January 5, 1878; a week later it had joined with Skobeleff, who crossed the Balkans on January 9, and was on its way towards Constantinople.

The most important event of the war was to establish the principality of Bulgaria.

Even before the fall of Plevna Abdul Hamid built great hopes on the interference of England. Mr. Disraeli had brought Indian troops to Malta which were regarded as an earnest of a great Indian army which was preparing to be despatched, and, most important of all, he had sent the British fleet into the Marmora, which it entered on February 13. Abdul Hamid was convinced that England would save him. He, however, grew greatly alarmed when he learnt of the progress of the Russian Army. The Ambassador in Constantinople at the time was Sir Henry Layard, who had replaced Sir Henry Elliot at the end of April, 1877. He learnt that preparations were being hurried on by the Sultan for leaving Constantinople. The Sultan's very kitchen utensils and all the paraphernalia of a Turkish *ménage* were already packed for Brusa. Speaking generally, Sir Henry Layard got on well with the Sultan, because he was regarded as owing his appointment by Mr. Disraeli to his friendly relations with the Turks. But on this occasion he spoke very strongly to Abdul Hamid, and warned him that if he quitted Constantinople he would be abandoned by Great Britain and never be allowed to return. At the same time the Sultan was assured that the presence of the English fleet would be a safeguard to him and to Turkey.

It is not out of place here to mention that while Great Britain incurred the credit or the odium of opposing the entry of the Russians in 1878 into Constantinople by sending a fleet under Admiral Hornby into the Marmora, other causes had at least contributed to such a result. On the authority of the late Sir William White, the Ambassador at Constantinople, what hindered the occupation of the capital by the Russians was not primarily the British fleet, but a secret agreement between Russia and Austria. According to this agreement, as already mentioned, the Russians were not to advance beyond the Balkans except in case of military necessity. When Austria learnt that they were advancing to San Stefano she began quietly to mobilise her army. Bismarck, who according to Sir William White was the only statesman in Europe besides the immediate parties who knew of the secret treaty, immediately communicated with the Emperor of Austria and informed him that he had trustworthy information that Great Britain was sending a fleet and Indian troops and that the wiser course was to remain quiet and allow our country to take action.

The British fleet in entering the Marmora had not formally obtained the permission of Abdul Hamid as required by the Treaty of Paris. One or more of our ships actually grounded in the Dardanelles under the Turkish guns, and anxiety prevailed in the capital lest they should be fired upon. But Abdul Hamid made no objections and probably gave his consent to Sir Henry Layard. The fleet proceeded to Ismidt, the ancient Nicomedia, but the position being unhealthy, and moreover being forty miles distant from Constantinople, our Ambassador yielded to the request of the Sultan and the fleet took up its anchorage on the northern side of the island of Prinkipo. Admiral Hornby was in command, his flagship being the *Alexandra*. In the fleet under him were the *Temeraire*, the *Devastation*, the *Achilles*, and seven smaller vessels. Their distance from the south end of the Bosporus was about ten miles. A large detachment of the Russian Army took up its position at San Stefano, about twelve miles distant from Constantinople and on the northern shore of the Marmora and fourteen miles from Prinkipo.

In the negotiations concluded at San Stefano on March 3, Abdul Hamid found himself compelled to recognise the independence of Rumania, Serbia, and Montenegro and to cede Bessarabia and the Dobruja to Rumania, to consent to the razing of all forts on the Danube, and to recognise the right of passage to merchant ships of all nations through the Dardanelles and the Bosporus.

The most important concession, however, was the establishment of Bulgaria, which by the San Stefano Treaty not merely included the whole district north of the Balkans, but Southern Bulgaria, as Eastern Rumelia was popularly called, and a large district including the Rhodope Mountains and the sea-ports on the northern shores of the Ægean. This "Big Bulgaria," as it was commonly called, was constituted mainly on the lines of nationality. It was open to some objections, of which the greatest was that many Greeks were comprised in it. All along the northern coast of the Ægean, the Marmora, and even on the coast of the Black Sea, there have been for many centuries Greek settlements. It may be said, indeed, that the Bulgarian sea coast was largely, and in some places almost exclusively, Greek, while the back country was Slav. In the course of centuries in all the coast districts, and very largely in Southern Macedonia, the population became mixed. Villages exclusively Greek existed; others were exclusively Slav. A story illustrative of this admixture of the population was told of General Ignatiev. When the proposal was made to mark out the confines of Bulgaria, he is reported to have said to the Turkish delegates, "I will take the boundary you yourselves have drawn." The delegates expressed their astonishment and declared they did not know of any. Ignatiev's answer was to point, on the large map which had been prepared, to villages which had been burned by the Turks because they were Bulgarian. One of these, that of Dervent, was barely thirty miles from Constantinople. The proposal was of course not acceptable and probably never seriously made, but it illustrates the difficulty in marking out a boundary which would be in accordance with the ethnography of the inhabitants. The Turks were singularly ignorant of the geography of their own country, and naturally the Russians knew even less. It is a remarkable fact that the man who had studied the ethnological conditions of the country, and whose advice was most followed by the Russian Commissioners because he knew most about it, was Mr. Schuyler, the American Consul-General, and it was with this aid that the outlines of Big Bulgaria were traced.

Great Britain was of opinion that the provisions of the Treaty of San Stefano should undergo revision. The principle of which Mr. Gladstone was a great advocate, that in all matters relating to Turkey a concert of the European Powers should be sought and ultimately decide, was acted upon by the Conservative Government, and after negotiations with the Powers, and especially with Bismarck, a Congress was called at Berlin to revise the San Stefano Treaty. Russia hesitated. Her army was still in the Balkan Peninsula; probably at least 180,000 men were within twenty miles of Constantinople. An Austrian army would have been able to drive a wedge in between Russia and the Balkan Peninsula and to cut off the retreat of the Russians. It was well known that Skobeleff and probably the Grand Duke, who was now with the army in San Stefano, would have liked to occupy Constantinople, but the military situation would have been extremely dangerous if Austria, probably with Germany behind her, had declared war. Accordingly Russia accepted the proposal for a Congress in Berlin. It met on June 13, 1878, and continued its sittings for a month. The main outlines of a revised Treaty were settled beforehand by an arrangement between Lord Salisbury and Count Schouvaloff, the chief delegate of Russia. On July 13 the Treaty of Berlin was signed. It cut down the San Stefano Treaty. It sanctioned the establishment of the principality of

Bulgaria to consist of the territory north of the Balkans and bounded on the north by the Danube. It created a new province under the name of Eastern Rumelia, which was to be under a Governor named by the Sultan, but with the consent of the Powers. The Prince who should be chosen for Bulgaria, with his territory north of the Balkans, should recognise the suzerainty of Abdul Hamid. The Sultan was to have no right of interference with the principality, but in Eastern Rumelia it was expressly stipulated that in case of disturbance his troops should have the right to enter in order to restore order. The Treaty further stipulated for the payment of a large war indemnity.

An article in the San Stefano Treaty which occasioned great irritation in Rumania stipulated that Turkey should cede Bessarabia to Russia. This was modified at Berlin so that Rumania appeared to make the cession to Russia. In return a large portion of the Dobruja was handed over to Rumania. People wondered much at Russia's persistency in pressing and in obtaining Bessarabia. It was felt as an uncalled-for injury inflicted on Rumania. The only explanation put forward was that the Czar wished to obliterate all traces of concessions forced upon him by the Crimean War, of which the surrender of Bessarabia was one. As the Rumanians had lent valuable aid to Russia during the war, an aid which, though not perhaps so important as the Rumanians believed it to be, was really great, the act on Russia's part appeared to be extremely ungracious.

Rumania, Serbia, and Montenegro were recognised as independent kingdoms.

Many stipulations of less importance appear in the Berlin Treaty. There were provisions for the better government of Crete, contained in what was known as the "Organic Law," which remained to be drafted. Greece and Montenegro each received a cession of territory; but in regard to both these States it may be here observed that, though the representatives of Turkey in Berlin had signed it, Abdul Hamid refused to carry out the stipulations in regard thereto and continued to do so for three years until convinced by naval demonstration by Great Britain that he must no longer resist. Another article made provision which, if carried out, would have been useful for reforms in Armenia.

The general lines of the changes to be made in the San Stefano Treaty, previously agreed upon between the representatives of the British and Russian Governments, were not seriously modified except as regards Armenia, where, as we shall see, the useful article 16 of San Stefano was abandoned for one of less value. *Punch* fairly reflected the situation in Berlin in a cartoon, which represented Mr. Disraeli as asking his colleague for the French word for "compromise," because the arrangements were a compromise or "transaction" between the claims of Russia and the provisions which Mr. Disraeli desired to insert for preserving so far as possible the integrity and independence of the Ottoman Empire.

Lord Salisbury had accompanied Mr. Disraeli to Berlin, and when the two statesmen returned to London it was Mr. Disraeli who, on the platform of the station at which they arrived, declared in his best theatrical manner to the crowd who had gathered to welcome them, "We bring you peace with honour."

During the negotiations at the San Stefano Congress, and for many weeks after that of Berlin had been concluded, the British fleet remained in the Marmora. It left Turkish waters in the beginning of October, 1878.

On June 4 Sir Henry Layard concluded with Abdul Hamid what is known as the "Cyprus Convention." It astonished Europe when it became known, but was intentionally kept secret until after the Berlin Congress. The late Sir Campbell Clarke, who acted as the representative of the *Daily Telegraph* at Berlin and had the instincts of an able detective, realised from many indications that such a Convention had been made, and in Berlin mentioned his conclusions to Lord Salisbury, who, while admitting that he was right, urged him not to make them publicly known. No one has yet arrived at a satisfactory conclusion as to the reason why it was made. The suggestion that it would serve as a naval base for our fleet in the Levant is futile. It has not and never can have any value for such purpose. The further suggestion that it should be used as a base of operations against either the Northern Syrian coast or that of Cilicia is not only improbable, but open to the remark that it is hardly likely that Abdul Hamid would have consented to the cession of a portion of territory which might be used as a basis of attack against Turkey. The only plausible explanation advanced is that Disraeli had suggested in one of his earlier novels that England would take possession of it. The island has been of no use to us, but has been a burden. The whole negotiations were done secretly, and in a great hurry Sir Henry Layard consented to pay over to Turkish account a revenue amounting to £87,800 per annum. This has been employed to pay the interest on a loan contracted during the Crimean War and guaranteed by the British and French Governments. The bargain was a bad one, but Great Britain has kept her word, with the result that the revenues of the island, when the aforesaid interest has been paid, have been insufficient to meet the costs of government, let alone of improvement.[1] The Treaty bears evident signs of great haste. Abdul Hamid on all occasions showed the utmost reluctance to surrender any portion of territory, and the only article in the Convention which probably appealed to him was one which provided that in return for the cession and for the acceptation of reforms to be made in Armenia, which Abdul would never even consider, Great Britain took the obligation to defend Turkish territory against any attacks by Russia.

In one respect the Cyprus Convention has been of use as showing that British administration can mete out even-handed justice to Christians and Turks alike. The Turkish population of the island have been content, as they well may be, with their just government and with the permission granted them to retain all their revenues

[1] Whitaker's Almanack for 1916 speaks of the amount to be paid "as a heavy burden," but adds "Taxation is at least better apportioned than formerly."

from pious foundations. The Greeks, who form by far the largest element in the population, have chafed under the burden of taxation which remains practically the same as under Turkish rule. It may be safe to predict that ultimately Cyprus, with the consent of Great Britain, will be handed over to the kingdom of Greece.

In November, 1914, Cyprus was formally annexed to the British Empire.

Note.—Edhem (p. 65) was a man of great ability, whose history is noteworthy Captured at the age of three or four in the massacre of Chios, he was taken to a harem, brought up as a Moslem, and, as has happened to Christian children in many cases in Turkish history, rose by his singular talents to become Grand Vizier. His eldest son was Hamdi Bey, who became the real founder of the great Museum in Stamboul. Though professing the religion of Islam, he became a painter and exhibited at the Salon in Paris and at our Royal Academy. Some of his works have found a permanent resting place in British galleries. The conferring upon him the degree of D.C.L. by Oxford in 1909 was regarded by him as the crowning of his career. Unfortunately he died the following year.

Note.—It is right that something should be said in justice to Sir Henry Elliot. He incurred much undeserved obloquy, largely due to the unfortunate misrepresentation which led the public to believe that he sympathised with the Turks in their treatment of the Christians. He was an honest and intelligent British Ambassador, who, like most Englishmen, was a firm believer in the advantages of Constitutional Government. He was cognisant from the first of the doings of Midhat and the reformers; trusted them; believed in their honesty and that they were on the right track to put an end to the corruption and misgovernment of the country. When he interrupted the proceedings of the Conference by stating that the salute implied a more radical change in the government of the country than that likely to be granted to the European delegates he honestly believed in what he said. He knew more about the provisions of Midhat's proposal than any of his colleagues and regarded the experiment which was to be tried as hopeful. It was unfortunate that when Lord Salisbury came to the country the two men did not get on well together. Probably at that time Sir Henry did not recognise that the new Sultan would be the great enemy of all reform, but he steadfastly worked on the lines of the great Canning for the amelioration of all sections of the population in Turkey.

CHAPTER VI

QUESTIONS ARISING FROM BERLIN CONGRESS

Abdul Hamid's treatment of questions remaining unsettled at the Berlin Congress; Article 61 regarding reforms in Armenia; negotiations; Sir Henry Layard's struggles, failure, and recall. Incident of letter in Greek written by Mr. Gladstone. Sir Henry leaves Constantinople; is replaced by Mr. Goschen. An ultimatum delivered: Abdul Hamid yields regarding Montenegro; questions regarding Greece; Eastern Rumelia; Commission appointed for its organisation; Russian troops leave Bulgaria; Lord Edmond Fitzmaurice's Commission for Macedonia; appointment of Gavril as Governor of Eastern Rumelia; bloodless revolution in Philippopolis. Abdul Hamid's conduct regarding Bulgaria; Gavril replaced by Prince Alexander, who is kidnapped; subsequently abdicates September 7, 1887; interregnum; Ferdinand of Coburg elected; persistent opposition of Russia; war with Serbia; Battle of Slivnitza; Russia proposes intervention with Turkey; Sultan refuses; Stambuloff becomes practical Dictator; is murdered; all Powers recognise Ferdinand.

THREE principal questions were left by the Berlin Congress for further action by the signatories of the Treaty. They concerned:—The introduction of reforms for Armenia; an increase of territory to Montenegro, and another increase of territory to Greece; arrangements for the government of Eastern Rumelia, including the appointment of a Governor.

In reference to reforms in Armenia, Article 61 of the Berlin Treaty provides:—

"The Sublime Porte undertakes to carry out, without further delay, the improvements and reforms demanded by local requirements in the provinces inhabited by Armenians, and to guarantee their security against the Circassians and Kurds. It will periodically make known the steps taken to this effect to the Powers, who will superintend their application."

NEGOTIATIONS FOR REFORMS IN ARMENIA.

The Ambassador charged with the presentation of a scheme of reforms for Armenia to the Sultan, in accordance with the article just quoted, was Sir Henry Layard. He had come to Turkey from being her Majesty's Ambassador at Madrid, and arrived in Constantinople on March 31, 1877. Though a Liberal in politics while in the House of Commons, Sir Henry was appointed by Mr. Disraeli's Government because of his well-known friendship for the Turks. His great reputation had been made in his early manhood by his discovery and exploration of Nineveh.[1] His volume on the subject marked a great advance in the archæology of Assyria. Though in his narrative he recognised the corruption of Turkish officials, he liked the Turks personally, as did perhaps most Englishmen, and on his return to England fell under the influence of Mr. David Urquhart, a typical and able philo-Turk, whose singular energy both on his travels, in voluminous writings and in Parliament, but especially in his "Spirit of the East," struck a popular note and made many converts to his views. His followers were probably more philo-Turk than himself, and were animated by philo-Turkism and by the utmost distrust of Russia. Small societies known as Foreign Affairs Committees were formed in many British towns for the advocacy of his views, especially in the northern counties; probably he found his strongest supporters in Newcastle-on-Tyne, where his influence remained for many years after the Crimean War. Sir Henry Layard was a fair representative at one time of the general spirit of hostility towards Russia and of friendship towards Turkey prevailing in the Urquhart group. When therefore Sir Henry Elliot was made Ambassador

[1] See note at end of chapter.

in Vienna it was a reasonable suggestion on the part of the Disraeli Government that a man, known by his admiration for the Turks, should be appointed as his successor. He took up his task with reference to Armenia with great confidence. He was convinced that the reforms which he submitted to the Porte were for the benefit of Moslems and Christians alike, and that when explained by him to his Majesty they would be carefully considered. He was received by Abdul Hamid as a welcome successor to Sir Henry Elliot, and anticipated little difficulty in procuring their acceptance. This hope would probably have been justified had the rule of the country been in the hands of any of the three or four able Grand Viziers in office during the time of Abdul Hamid's immediate predecessors. But government by Ministers was almost at an end. Amongst the successors of such men, Midhat, the only open advocate of reform, had already been dismissed (February 5, 1877). When the *coup de théâtre* of proclaiming the Constitution failed, Abdul's hostility towards reform became more virulent than before. He hated the very word "constitution" and everyone who approved of it.

Sir Henry Layard presented his scheme of reforms. They were discussed seriously with the other Ambassadors and with the representatives of Abdul Hamid. It soon however appeared that the Turkish Ministers were powerless, and that their master would not permit them to exercise their judgment. Layard found out subsequently that the Minister for Foreign Affairs who took the leading part on the Turkish side had been ordered to make opposition to all projects of change. Article by article of the projected scheme was discussed and rejected. For the sake of appearances a new draft of projected reforms was submitted on the part of Abdul Hamid. Gradually Sir Henry Layard and all the Ambassadors learned the disagreeable truth, that the Sultan, in spite of his professions of friendship to Sir Henry personally and to the country which he represented, was determined not to make any concession.

Sir Henry was in a difficult position. He had to maintain his reputation in England as a friend of the Turks. Yet he had to obtain Abdul Hamid's consent to changes which he soon saw were distasteful. Perhaps it may fairly be said that he had been too violent a partisan to have been sent as a representative to Turkey, for the extreme philo-Turk party in England expected too much of him. He worked steadily and persistently in endeavouring to obtain from the Porte, that is, from the Sultan, some definite promise of reforms for Armenia. But as months passed away while all his proposals were rejected, and those of the Porte were manifestly futile, he gradually realised that it was hopeless to obtain from Abdul Hamid any amelioration whatever of the lot of the Armenian population.

After long negotiations he succeeded in obtaining as a great and almost as the sole concession a declaration that in the Armenian Provinces the sub-Governor in each of such provinces should be a Christian. It is impossible to say that the provision was valueless, because a sub-Governor who chose to risk his place might take up a strong position with his Chief in favour of a particular line of action, and, if a sensible man, could use his personal influence to induce him to make the provisions of existing law as little harsh as possible for his co-religionists; but as he was appointed by Abdul Hamid he knew perfectly well that if he opposed the wishes of his Chief he could be easily dismissed. To anticipate the result of this reform for which Sir Henry Layard, at the time, claimed a good deal of credit, it proved utterly illusory. The sub-Governor, so appointed, gradually came to be known as "Evet Effendi" or "Yes, Sir," because in popular belief he invariably agreed with his Chief. Sir Henry Layard undoubtedly did his utmost to obtain reforms. His reputation and interest coincided with the interest of the Turks, whom he liked, and stimulated him to great activity: but he entirely failed. In his diplomatic correspondence, so far as it has been published, he gave no indications that he had been unsuccessful during his negotiations. When at length the concession was granted of which I have spoken, the project accepted was a mere simulacrum of what had been originally proposed. Sir Henry expressed his disappointment in very strong terms at the stubbornness of the Porte, but remarked that the sub-Governor clause would always be something gained.

A General Election took place in England in April, 1880. The Liberal Party came into power and an outcry was raised for the recall of Sir Henry Layard. At the crisis of the election the first despatch from him indicated his failure and especially pointed out that though the reforms would be of as much benefit to the Moslems as to the Christians, the Sultan would have none of them. The despatch was taken by British public opinion as a *volte face* and a bid for popular favour.

The Liberal Government would possibly have continued Sir Henry in office but for an unfortunate circumstance which justly offended its members, and for which Sir Henry's too great party zeal must be held responsible. A letter had been written to Mr. Gladstone from Constantinople of no special importance by a Greek gentleman. Mr. Gladstone replied in Greek but did not keep a copy of what he had written. The Greek who had received it showed it to Sir Henry Layard and gave him what he chose to call a translation. Sir Henry Layard, without having the translation verified by one of the able Greek scholars at the Embassy, accepted the translation as correct, and informed the correspondent of a London newspaper, which was at that time strongly pro-Turkish, of its contents. The correspondent in good faith communicated to his journal that Mr. Gladstone had made statements which, if true, it was at least inexpedient for him to have made. The pro-Turkish party in England made a great outcry. Mr. Gladstone asked that a copy should be furnished to him. Sir Henry persisted that he had read the offensive statements in Mr. Gladstone's own handwriting, in other words he "gave the lie" to the Liberal leader. When the copy was obtained it was found that

Mr. Gladstone had not said what he was reported to have said, and the odium of the incident fell upon the Ambassador. The result was that one of the first decisions arrived at by the Liberal Government was that Sir Henry must leave Constantinople.[1] On his departure the Armenian question was allowed to sleep for some months. Abdul Hamid considered that he had inflicted a defeat on Great Britain through her Ambassador.

Sir Henry Layard was replaced by the Right Hon. George J. Goschen, who was then Member of Parliament. The special object of his mission was to induce the Sultan to carry out certain other provisions of the Treaty of Berlin, which he had hitherto declined to do.

Negotiations regarding Montenegro.

The first of these related to Montenegro. The Mountain State had had its independence acknowledged for the first time by European Treaty. The Berlin Congress decided that the port of Antivari on the Adriatic should be given to it. Abdul Hamid from the first made the strongest opposition and declared that he would never consent to it or to any other sacrifice of territory. In connection with such sacrifice let it be said generally that a curious superstition has existed for centuries in Turkey. On many previous occasions before the Berlin Congress it had been the habit of the Porte to appoint a Christian delegate in order that he might take the odium and responsibility of ceding Moslem territory to the Unbeliever. It had happened on various occasions that the Sultan had sacrificed his Christian delegate to popular clamour, though it was by his express or implied instructions he had consented to yield territory. Even at the Congress of Berlin the practice had been followed, and Alexander Pasha Caratheodori, who was perhaps the ablest statesman in Turkey, was appointed Minister of Foreign Affairs and the especial Turkish representative at Berlin because

[1] See note at end of chapter.

he was a Christian. In justice to him it should be said that he fought a hard battle against Bismarck and Lord Salisbury, the first being personally rude to him, telling him bluntly on one occasion that he and his colleague had nothing to do with the decisions of the Congress but to accept them.

Abdul Hamid in opposing any cession of territory to Montenegro was acting in accordance with the traditional practice. Nevertheless the Turkish delegates had accepted the decision which Berlin had taken and Abdul must abide by it. He had defeated England in his first encounter regarding Armenia and entered upon the second with confidence. Upon his emphatic refusal to surrender Antivari, the British Cabinet invited the States who had signed the Berlin Treaty to join in making a naval demonstration before that town. Men-of-war of various nations assembled in the Adriatic. It was believed that their appearance would induce Abdul Hamid to give way. When, after some weeks, the Sultan showed no signs of yielding, and the ships of the other nations which had taken part in the demonstration withdrew one after the other, Abdul Hamid considered himself justified in his belief that his firm will would prevail, and that he would gain the credit from his subjects of once more successfully defying Europe. He, however, was not aware that in defying Mr. Gladstone and Mr. Goschen he was matching himself against two strong men. The British Government supported Mr. Goschen's recommendation that the British fleet alone should execute the mandate of the Powers, and prepared to take severe measures. Mr. Goschen went to see Abdul Hamid and delivered an ultimatum. The event was a trying one for the Ambassador, because he knew that the Sultan had proclaimed his determination not to make the cession and believed that the withdrawal of the ships of other nations indicated that England stood alone. Indeed the belief in Turkey was general that Great Britain was undertaking more than she could accomplish. Some of the Powers would probably have liked to have seen a rebuff inflicted by Turkey on Great Britain. Mr. Goschen informed Abdul Hamid that if he did not give way, British ships would occupy and hold an important, but unnamed, port in his dominions until he had given in. Abdul Hamid once more refused. The Concert of Europe had failed, and Turkey had now only England to deal with. If Mr. Goschen at the interview was nervous, Abdul Hamid was probably still more affected, for the story was current in Constantinople the next day that during the evening he had broken out into a paroxysm of anger and professed that he would be happy if he could see London destroyed. Mr. Goschen probably kept his own counsel. There was intense interest and some jealousy on the part of some of the other Ambassadors who watched with eagerness to see whether England would act alone. Meantime the British Government and Mr. Goschen had decided upon their measures. The Admiral in command of the British fleet had secret instructions and the ships under him were ready to heave anchor under sealed orders when word came from Constantinople. Everything indeed was ready for their departure and the signals were actually "bent on" when it was reported that a local boat was coming in haste from the shore and that some-one in it was frantically waving a paper. The messenger arrived bringing the announcement that the Sultan had given way. It was not until three months afterwards that the British public learnt that the sealed orders were for the occupation of Smyrna. A legend had grown up in England which was widely current at the time that the Liberal Party was incapable of what was called "a spirited foreign policy." The concealment of what had been done at Antivari until Parliament had risen was an act which suggested that the Government were still a little afraid of what their supporters would say about their spirited policy.

Questions regarding Greece.

Some of the questions in reference to Greece were asily settled. The popular belief, probably not unfounded, was that, on condition of her abstaining from taking part in the Russo-Turkish War, she was to receive compensation. In June, 1880, a Conference met in Berlin to bring about a friendly arrangement between Turkey and Greece. Meantime the Greek Army was mobilised. After months of negotiations, in July, 1881, Thessaly was ceded to her. Other questions were settled without much difficulty. The most important, however, had to stand over until a later development occurred, and was concerned with the better government of the Island of Crete. As this question did not take an important shape until at least ten years later, it need not be yet considered.

Questions regarding Bulgaria.

As already mentioned, the provisions of the San Stefano Treaty had created a Great Bulgaria, which extended as far south as the Ægean. By the Berlin Treaty the country north of the Balkans was formed into a Principality, and little difficulty occurred in the appointment of Alexander of Battenberg as its first Prince. A large strip of country which was included in the Great Bulgaria of the San Stefano Treaty was returned to Turkey; and the remainder, officially known as Eastern Rumelia, was constituted into a tributary province to be under the Sultan's suzerainty, presided over by a Christian Governor, named by the Sultan with the approval of the Powers.

Before, however, a Governor was named much preliminary work required to be done. A Commission was appointed for the organisation of Eastern Rumelia in 1878. Sir Henry Drummond Wolff was named by Great Britain in August. A scheme for the better government of the province was drawn up and approved by the Commissioners of the Powers and by the Sultan in the following November.

The precaution had been permitted of allowing Russian troops to remain in occupation of Southern Bulgaria until these arrangements were completed. When the Commissioners had created and put the machinery of government in motion in accordance with the provisions of their scheme, the Russian troops left in May, 1879.

Macedonia having been detached from the Great Bulgaria, a Commission was appointed to draw up an "Organic Law" for its government. It was presided over by Lord Edmond, now Lord Fitzmaurice. It did its work excellently and was approved by the Powers. Had its provisions been loyally executed by Abdul Hamid, the history of Europe might have been changed, and a semi-autonomous province created which would have probably worked harmoniously. No reasonable doubt can be entertained that the province could have been made as great a success for some years at least, as the district of the Lebanon had become after the arrangement made consequent upon the troubles between the Druses and the Maronites in 1860. We shall see that from the first Abdul Hamid, with the short-sightedness which characterised all his dealings both with the Powers and with his own subjects, placed every obstacle in the way of reforms in Macedonia and thus led to the twenty-five years of anarchy which prevailed in that country, and which resulted directly in the formation of a Balkan League, the series of events which precipitated the disturbances in the Balkan States, and contributed to add a dangerous and disquieting element to the present European War.

To return, however, to the question of Southern Bulgaria. It was not thought advisable that a Governor should be appointed until the scheme of organisation already mentioned was ready to be put in operation. Then, after negotiations with the Powers, the Sultan named a certain Christovitch, known by the Turks as "Gavril Pasha," to be Governor in 1884. In Constantinople he was often spoken of as a "schoolmaster President" in allusion to his conduct as President of the Turkish Mixed Court. He was not a man of great knowledge or of good judgment. Nevertheless, he had effected improvements in his office in the capital, and as there was absolutely nothing against his personal character, he was accepted by the Powers when named by Abdul Hamid. When he went to take up his position at Philippopolis, the capital of Eastern Rumelia, it was expected by the Sultan that he would wear the red fez, as a mark of subjection to Turkish authority, which everyone indeed in the Sultan's employ had to wear. The story went that as soon as he crossed from Turkey into Rumelia he put the fez in his pocket and produced a Bulgarian headdress known as a kalpak. He was a good-natured man and had no special difficulty with the Bulgarians, but the population resented their separation from their brethren and neighbours of Northern Bulgaria, and looked with suspicion on every measure introduced by Gavril, fearing that it might have been dictated from Constantinople. Nevertheless they tolerated the representative of the Sultan because all knew that in the Treaty of Berlin express authority was given to Abdul Hamid to send his troops into Rumelia in case such a measure was necessary to preserve his authority.

We can all now recognise that the provision in the Balkan Treaty which separated the Bulgarian people was a foolish one, for the inhabitants were of the same race, religion, and language as those in the Principality, and would only consent to be separated from their brethren so long as they were prevented by actual or anticipated force. Indeed it was this consideration which furnished the reason for the provision allowing Turkish troops to be sent by the Sultan to Philippopolis and other portions of the province in case of disorder. Hence, though the inhabitants were not dissatisfied with their Governor, the feeling grew stronger every day that they must be united with the people of the Principality.

They would probably have waited longer and might even have become contented to remain Turkish subjects but for the perversity of Abdul Hamid. He insisted upon suppressing the popular clamour for union with the Principality and especially objected to the display of Bulgarian flags. Acting on orders from the Sultan,

Gavril—now become Pasha—forbade the hoisting of the Principality flag in Philippopolis. A few days after an order to this effect was published a religious feast-day occurred and nearly every house displayed it. Then on September 13, 1885, a "bloodless revolution" occurred in Philippopolis amid popular cries of "Long live the Union." Gavril felt himself powerless and at once left Eastern Rumelia and resumed the fez. He could hardly have been surprised when the revolution broke out. No one wished him any harm, and he went away without hindrance or disturbance; his occupation of the post of Vali in Philippopolis being added to his many pleasant reminiscences.

Five days after the "bloodless revolution" of September, 1885, Prince Alexander at Tirnova, the ancient capital of Bulgaria, received a deputation of the leading people of Eastern Rumelia who demanded union with the Principality. Two days later the Prince entered Philippopolis and was generally acclaimed as ruler of Eastern Rumelia.

The population of Bulgaria naturally rejoiced at the decision of their brethren south of the Balkans. At the same time, however, they at once commenced preparation to resist the Turkish troops if Abdul Hamid determined, as they expected he would, to exercise his right to send them into the country. Europe, however, had by this time come to recognise that the two Bulgarias ought not to have been divided. Upon the advice of the representatives of all the Powers except Turkey, Prince Alexander of Bulgaria did not mobilise.

The Grand Vizier at the time was Said Pasha, commonly known as "Kutchuk Said" from his short stature. He and other Ministers urged the Sultan to exercise his right of intervention. Abdul Hamid happily objected to do so. The explanation which he gave to Said and to the British Embassy was that he knew that in his army were a number of rough fellows who would treat the Bulgarians badly, and having had experience of the result of such treatment in 1876, treatment which had brought about the war with Russia, he was not going to risk the experiment. On the whole it was a satisfactory decision both for the Powers and Abdul.

The difficulty was overcome by the appointment of Alexander, already Prince of Bulgaria, by the Sultan as Governor of Eastern Rumelia for a term of five years. Thereupon the Prince went to Philippopolis in that capacity.

Austria from the first had disliked the establishment of Bulgaria and disliked still more the increase of its territory by the addition of Eastern Rumelia. Milan, King of Serbia, probably with the consent of Austria, took the opportunity of invading Bulgaria, claiming that Serbia's territory should now be increased at the expense of her neighbour. Suddenly and without warning, on November 13, 1885, Bulgaria was invaded by Serbian troops at four points. Prince Alexander appealed to the Sultan as the sovereign lord of Rumelia for help. None, however, was forthcoming; Abdul Hamid being quite content to see his two lost provinces of Serbia and Bulgaria at war with each other.

The moment was critical for Bulgaria, and that for a reason which no student can safely overlook. No one denies that the liberation of Bulgaria was due to Russia. Her sacrifice of men and money had been great, and, as a result, the Bulgarians were set free from the Turkish yoke. Throughout the whole of the province, the sentiment of gratitude to the Russian Czar was profound. Nearly every Bulgarian house had a portrait of Alexander "the Liberator." But there was another side of the picture. Russian diplomacy has always tended to become domineering and arrogant and has seldom shown itself to greater disadvantage than in dealing with Bulgaria. Russia had undertaken to organise a Bulgarian Army, to officer it with Russians, and to provide a Minister of War. But her tactless agents so mismanaged their task that the alternative soon presented itself to the Bulgarian people of becoming a Russian Province, as some foolish Russians stated was the intention of Russia, or of becoming a really independent State. Many Bulgarians felt that the want of experience in the country was too great to enable it to be governed without foreign aid. Others unattached to party recognised that the contest meant one between those whose cry was " Bulgaria for the Bulgarians " and those who considered that their only safeguard against Turkey was to allow their country to become a second Finland. Undoubtedly the majority of the Bulgarian people cherished the traditions of their race and hoped to see an independent Bulgarian Kingdom.

Several questions tending to make the Russians unpopular had arisen between the Bulgarians and those who had now come to be regarded as their taskmasters. One of the most burning arose from the fact that the Russians would allow no Bulgarian to have a commission in the army beyond the rank of captain. The Minister of War took his own course without reference to the inexperienced Bulgarian Ministers; for Russia had claimed and exercised the right to appoint the Bulgarian Minister of War. Ill-feeling between Russians and Bulgarians became acute. It resulted in a sudden order from Petersburg for the withdrawal and immediate return of all the Russian officers in the army, about one hundred and fifty in number.

It was at the moment when these officers were withdrawn and the Bulgarian Army was without superior officers that Milan invaded the country. The Bulgarian troops had to retreat before the Serbians and fell back upon Slivnitza. On November 15 the invaders attacked them. Fighting took place in the Dragoman Pass, near the source of the river Morava, where an attack was made by 40,000 Serbians. The Bulgarians held their ground and on November 21 and 22, 1885, defeated them. King Milan and his troops fled across the Serbian frontier. Inexperienced, and without trained officers, the Bulgarians had shown a stubbornness worthy of veterans. To add to their difficulties, Prince Alexander was absent from Sofia, probably in Varna, when the invasion occurred. Communications and transport were slow and all the advantages appeared on the Serbian side. The contest at Slivnitza was a soldier's battle, that is, there was apparently no directing head to lead them. The Bulgarians had only one objective, to drive back the enemy. They chased the Serbians across their frontier. Then on November 28 the Austrian Emperor intervened. He gave formal notice to Bulgaria that if her troops advanced further into Serbian territory they would have to deal with Austrian troops.

Once more Abdul Hamid was urged to exercise his right of entry. His refusal was probably due now to the representations of Sir William White, then in Constantinople, who knew Belgrade well and the ways of its King and of Austria. He was indeed more familiar with the politics and people of the Balkan States than any Ambassador England ever had at the Sublime Porte. It was largely due to his influence, first, that England invited all the Powers to request Alexander not to mobilise, informing him that their influence would be exercised in favour of the peaceful union of Eastern Rumelia and Bulgaria, and second, that Abdul Hamid did not exercise his right to send troops for the assertion of Turkish authority in conformity with the Treaty of Berlin.

In 1886 occurred an incident which was more like one out of mediæval Italian history than one in the nineteenth century. Russian intrigue, conducted by the adventurous underlings of her Diplomatic Service, led to a conspiracy amongst certain of the Bulgarian military officers to replace Prince Alexander by a Russian prince. The plot was carefully concealed, and this for obvious reasons, the most important being that the nation was not dissatisfied with its prince. In the third week of August, 1886, the plot was carried out. Prince Alexander was kidnapped by the conspirators and carried off to the frontier. It was an ugly business and greatly discredited Russian diplomacy in the Near East. The inconsiderate withdrawal of the Russian officers and the dictatorial conduct of the chief representatives of Russia looked like mere spiteful interference.

Russian diplomacy made it appear that the Deliverer was determined to treat the people he had rescued from Turkish rule as if they were serfs. It did more perhaps than anything else to estrange the people from a belief in the single-mindedness of Russia in setting the country free. Great resentment was felt against the perpetrators, and Prince Alexander at the popular demand returned in triumph on September 22 of the following year. There is good reason to believe, however, that his return was permitted by Petersburg on condition that on his arrival he should formally abdicate and leave the country. This arrangement was carried into effect, and at the end of September, 1887, Alexander left the country. The Prince was a Battenberg, a brave soldier, a straightforward and not unthoughtful man. It is difficult to know what was the real objection that Russia had to his rule in Bulgaria, though probably the chief one was that she desired to have a Russian prince as being likely to be more compliant with her wishes.

It was consequent on these events that Stambuloff, an advocate who had been educated in Russia, came to the front to play a part in the politics of his country. His clearheadedness and strong will soon indicated him as the Prime Minister in the near future. On the departure of Alexander he had been named one of three Regents to act in lieu of a Prince. A Provisional Government was formed and an election took place to decide what should be done.

The kidnapping of Prince Alexander, and the interregnum during which Bulgaria was without a recognised ruler, were a severe trial for the young nation. Russia had not only withdrawn all her officers but appeared to be doing all she could, short of going to war, to bring the Bulgarian people to their knees. A confusion, little short of anarchy, ensued. The disorder was increased by the rivalries between the Ministers and the Regents, rivalries which reflected the divergence of Bulgarian opinion.

During the next two or three years political interest in the Near East gathers round the conduct of Abdul

Hamid in reference to Bulgaria. The expulsion of Gavril, the prevalent disorder, and the absence of a prince gave the Sultan many opportunities of that intervention in Eastern Rumelia to which he had a clear right under the Treaty of Berlin. Gavril's expulsion was an open defiance of his authority. The disturbance foreseen by the Treaty had commenced and was continuing. Though it was well for the peace of Europe that Abdul did not exercise his right, as some of his Ministers urged him to do, his conduct illustrates at once his weakness and his vacillation.

Stambuloff as the head of the regents, with insight as to what ought to and what could be done, acted very much as a dictator. The people, wholly unaccustomed to political affairs, needed a leader who should lead and recognised in him such a leader. He was determined to carry into effect the policy of "Bulgaria for the Bulgarians" and was not minded that his people should exchange the Turkish yoke for that of Russia. Radoslavoff, the Premier, while claiming as strongly as Stambuloff that he desired to be independent of Russia, acted in opposition to him. Zancoff, leader of an extreme party, was regarded as the mouthpiece of Russia. Amid the excitement of party passion, his friends took the remarkable step of sending him to Constantinople in order to induce the Sultan to exercise his right of interference. Abdul Hamid refused. Russia soon became so irritated against Bulgaria that she herself proposed common action with the Sultan. Had Abdul Hamid accepted her invitation, he could have gone as the mandatory of the Powers and the guardian of European treaty law. What a position before gods and men! Surely the temptation to him must have been great.

The question of the appointment of a successor to Alexander became a burning one. Zancoff openly declared (1) for the reappointment to their rank in the army of the traitors who had taken part in kidnapping Prince Alexander, (2) for a Russian Minister of War, and (3) for the appointment of the Prince of Mingrelia, a Russian subject, as Prince of Bulgaria.

When Zancoff with his companions returned from Constantinople, the garrisons of Rustchuk and Silistria revolted against the regents with the object of supporting Russia's demands. They were defeated, and Zancoff with Karaveloff and others were arrested at the end of March, 1887. The regents put down the revolt and executed some of the rebels at Rustchuk.

The visits to Constantinople had done harm to the Russian cause. The suppression of the Rustchuk and other revolts made it evident that the Russian party were losing influence. They saw that they could not hope to have a Russian prince elected. Thereupon Russia invited the Powers to join "in preventing further bloodshed." The popular sentiment remained loyal to the absent Alexander; and on the anniversary of his birthday, April 6, 1887, a *Te Deum* was sung at Varna, and letters of congratulation poured in for the absent Prince from all parts of the country. Stambuloff had become the popular opponent of Russian interference with the internal affairs of the country. Accompanied by one of his colleagues, he made a tour throughout Southern Bulgaria and was everywhere welcomed with enthusiasm. He had taken the bold step of cashiering 100 officers out of the 700 Bulgarian soldiers who had taken part in the kidnapping.

The great desire of the Powers was to preserve European peace; and the representations of all the Ambassadors in Constantinople, with the exception of that of Russia, were now in favour of non-interference. They supported this policy the more confidently because it had become clear that Abdul Hamid would not exercise his right, under the Treaty of Berlin, to send troops into the country. Even Austria would not be more sultanist than the Sultan.

Meantime a deputation consisting of Stoiloff, afterwards Prime Minister, Grekoff, and Calcieff, all good men, had gone into Central Europe in search of a prince. They had seen Prince Waldemar of Denmark, and negotiations with him and with Ferdinand of Coburg had commenced in December, 1886. Ferdinand consented to become prince, but made his acceptance subject to the approval of the Powers, and especially of Russia. As Austria and Russia were already rivals, it was feared in Bulgaria that upon his appointment Russia, supported by Turkey, would invade the country. The Sobranje was convoked, the elections hurried, and upon the refusal of Prince Waldemar to accept the princely throne Ferdinand was unanimously elected. Stambuloff had hastened to give what legal sanction he could to the choice of the deputies. The Sobranje on July 4, 1887, gave a unanimous vote for the appointment of Ferdinand. Thereupon fresh troubles began. Stambuloff resigned because of disagreement with Radislavoff.

The representative in Sofia of Abdul Hamid, a certain Gadban Effendi, declared that the elections were unfair. In all probability they were gerrymandered, as have been subsequent elections in all the States of the Balkan Peninsula, but no amount of gerrymandering could prevent a real expression of the wish of the country. Russian agents were intriguing in favour of the election of a Russian prince. The Russian Government even sent a fleet to Varna in the hope of increasing Russian influence and of reminding the people that she could effectively interfere. General Kaulbars, who did not represent the best kind of Russian diplomacy, had been sent into Bulgaria. Russian soldiers were landed, and Kaulbars threatened the Bulgarians. Russia had already been unsuccessful in her support of a prince. When the Sobranje found that Prince Waldemar of Denmark refused to act, the Russians, once more finding that Stambuloff and his followers were not compliant, recalled Kaulbars and the Russian Consul. Bulgaria was to be dragooned into acquiescence.

Russia refused to recognise that the unanimous vote of the Sobranje was valid. France and other Powers called attention to the fact that by the Treaty of Berlin the Prince could only be validly elected with the consent of all the Powers signatories of the Treaty. Ferdinand negotiated with Russia; but although he failed to obtain her consent, he learned that no other Power made formal objection to his election. Accordingly he decided on August 9 to accept the princely throne and its risks. Russia, finding that she was unsupported, accepted the *fait accompli* and contented herself for the time with lodging a protest. On August 24 Turkey also protested because the election had been made without her consent, but she did nothing more. After long negotiation Russia persuaded France to join with her in proposing to send a Russian Commissioner to superintend a new election to be followed by the choice of a prince. Abdul Hamid, however, would not consent to the interference of a Commissioner named by foreign States. These Powers, now joined by Germany, added to the confusion by withdrawing their consuls from Bulgaria on August 22, the day preceding that appointed for Ferdinand's public entry into Sofia. On August 23 Ferdinand carried out the programme arranged for his entry. The British Consul, however, remained.

Ferdinand, with the aid of Stambuloff, had triumphed. The impression which he created was not favourable. His manner, stiff and haughty, was always against him. Even five years later the attitude of the Bulgarians towards him pointed to the conclusion that while they considered it expedient to accept his rule, they cared little for him personally. He gave the impression of desiring to make the gulf between himself, the grandson of a French king, and his people impassable. The stories everywhere told of him pointed to the same conclusion. In this respect he compared unfavourably with Prince Alexander, who was always genial and never "put on side." Conduct of this kind was ill placed. The Turks, to whose rule the Bulgars had been subject, are democratic in manner. A poor gardener or shoeblack will speak to a pasha without subserviency, and nothing could be more alien to his subjects than the attempt to introduce into their country the forms and ceremonies of the ancient aristocratic and despotic system of France.

Ferdinand had dissolved the Sobranje on August 24. New elections were held early in October. Russia, persistent in her hostility even to the extent of employing her old enemy to crush the rebellious province, had modified her former proposal, and had come now to an agreement with Turkey that she and Turkey should appoint two Commissioners, and that a new prince should be elected from two candidates named by her. The other Powers disliked the arrangement, and the Bulgarian people were still more hostile to it. Happily for them, Abdul Hamid once more changed his mind. He not only withdrew from his engagement to name a Commissioner to act with the Russian, but refused to call on Ferdinand to leave Bulgaria pending new elections.

The influence of England was steadily used in Constantinople by Sir William White to leave the choice of the new Prince solely to the Bulgarians. Abdul Hamid for once followed British advice, as it coincided with his own desire to remain inactive. Ferdinand, having obtained once more the unanimous vote of the Sobranje, made a tour throughout the country. It took place in the last week of 1888, and was entirely successful, for he was accompanied by Stambuloff, who was immensely popular, and by his mother, the Princess Clementine, a daughter of King Louis Philippe, a woman of great charm, tact, and ability, who did far more to dispel the open and latent opposition to Ferdinand than did the Prince himself.

Once more Russia endeavoured to induce the Powers to join her in getting rid of Ferdinand. They were however not only desirous of peace, but the long agitation had convinced them that the Bulgarian people were quite competent to manage their own affairs. England, Austria, and Italy formally refused to make any further representations against his occupation of the princely throne. Abdul Hamid, indeed, though he had missed many opportunities of intervention, could not relinquish his dreams of again bringing Bulgaria under Turkish rule. As a mark of his displeasure, and, as it was believed at the time, at the instigation of Russia, he imposed 8 per cent. *ad valorem* duty on all exported Bulgarian produce which had to pass across Turkish territory.

The quarrel between Ferdinand and Stambuloff does not fall within the range of this book, but it added to the difficulties of Bulgaria, for Ferdinand's position was not yet secure. He was still not officially recognised as Prince, and the relations between him and the representatives of all the foreign Powers in Sofia were strained. In the autumn of 1889 all foreigners excepting Russians recognised that this position was detrimental to the public interest. In October, 1889, the Austrian semi-official *Fremdenblatt* suggested that the time had come to recognise Ferdinand as Prince. His occupation of the throne had become an accomplished fact, and every Power in Europe wished to see a settlement of the question without war. The struggle had become one mainly between Austria and Russia. Whatever one did the other opposed. Bulgaria wanted loans in order to construct her railways, linking up the Serbian line from Belgrade with the Turkish line from Constantinople. Bulgaria proposed to obtain one from Austria. Russia opposed, taking up the position that, according to the Treaty of Berlin, Turkey alone had the right to sanction the construction of railways in Eastern Rumelia. But Russia stood alone in her opposition. Turkey indeed might once more have chosen to assert her rights, and a serious difficulty in such case would have been created, for the necessary money for the construction of the railways would not have been forthcoming. But as Turkey desired the construction of railways in Eastern Rumelia in the interest of her own line, the loan was issued without opposition and the money for it subscribed six times over. England of course had not opposed a practical proposal for the construction of railways; and the influence of Sir William White, her great ambassador in Constantinople, was constantly used to support reasonable Bulgarian demands. The British Agent and Consul-General in Sofia at this time was Sir Nicholas O'Conor, who heartily co-operated with the Ambassador. He was an exceptionally good man for the position, cool, thoughtful, and conciliatory. He got on well with his colleagues, and was always sympathetic with the Bulgarians, especially when they desired to advance industrial projects. When he had to deal with Balkan statesmen, they found him painstaking, courteous, and cordial, and without the arrogance which sometimes characterises young diplomats when dealing with the representatives of small States. The influence of England in Bulgaria steadily increased because her people believed that England desired her progress. An arrangement was concluded between the British Government and the Bulgarian for the entry of British goods on payment of an *ad valorem* duty of 8 per cent.

The Bulgarian Government had its own serious internal troubles, which, except as to Macedonia, do not concern us here, for Abdul Hamid hardly interfered with them.

The non-recognition of Ferdinand weakened Stambuloff's representations to the Porte on the condition of the Macedonians. Thousands of them had taken refuge in Bulgaria from the anarchy which Abdul Hamid was instigating or tolerating. In June, 1889, Stambuloff drew up a strong letter of remonstrance, addressed by Prince Ferdinand to Abdul Hamid as his suzerain,[1] in which he claimed that Bulgaria had been flouted and neglected. It concluded with a menace unless something was done for the bettering of the Macedonian population. The letter was not without effect on the Sultan.

On March 27, 1881, Stambuloff and his colleague Beltcheff, the Minister of Finance, were fired at in a street in Sofia. Beltcheff fell mortally wounded by three shots which were intended for his companion. The latter, however, died a few days later from his wounds. The evidence at the time—and none has been forthcoming to contradict it—shows that the assassination was not the work of Russian agents. Stambuloff had made many enemies, at home as well as in Russia. He was essentially a strong, but also a violent, man, and while strenuous measures were necessary in the troublesome

[1] The contents of this letter are given in the chapter on Macedonia.

times that ensued after the kidnapping of Alexander, the violent attacks in his own newspaper upon the Russian Emperor and even his family were recalled as an explanation, though not as a justification, of the terrible crime.

After the murder of Stambuloff the history of Bulgaria hardly concerns our present purpose. Her action was bound up largely with that of the Powers in endeavouring to obtain order in Macedonia. Her ideal for that province, constantly put before Europe, was the establishment of an autonomous State.

Ferdinand, looked on coldly by Russia, turned his attention towards Abdul Hamid. He persuaded the Sultan to name him formally as Governor of Eastern Rumelia. He offended Russia by ostentatiously posing as the vassal of Abdul Hamid. The Sultan was flattered, and welcomed the visit of the Prince to Constantinople. But Abdul Hamid was too shrewd and distrustful not to discern that Ferdinand was endeavouring to play him off against Russia. Of course Abdul's Press made much of the visit; but as the great mass of the ignorant Turks regard all foreign princes as necessarily the vassals of the Padisha, the incident of the visit cannot be said to have increased the Sultan's reputation. When, after the revolution in Constantinople of July, 1908, Ferdinand declared himself king, then, indeed, the Sultanic Press came out in the strongest condemnation of the traitor to his Sovereign.

An observer may well ask whether Abdul Hamid's action in reference to Bulgaria indicated able statesmanship. Assuming that he desired to recover the principality and to preserve Eastern Rumelia, as he undoubtedly did, such an observer would note that he had many opportunities of probably successful interference. Had he stood upon his rights under the Berlin Treaty, it would have been difficult for the Powers to have opposed his employment of force, for he would have been acting by their mandate. By declining to act he preserved peace for his country, and in so doing contributed to European peace. No one however can fairly attribute this result to the foresight of Abdul Hamid's statesmanship. From the Turkish point of view he stands condemned for acquiescing in the wrenching from Turkey of the fertile province of Eastern Rumelia. We may agree with the Austrian statesman Andrassy that "every inch of territory taken from Turkey is gained for civilisation," but one cannot expect a Turk to do so. Her Sultan reigns in order to preserve his territory intact; and the Turk had a just cause of complaint against his Sovereign when, having rights recently sanctioned by European treaty, his policy was so vacillating that he declined to take advantage of favourable opportunities to assert them, if need be by force.

Note No. 1.—"Sir Henry Layard must leave Constantinople," All the evidence shows that Sir Henry had an honest desire to ameliorate the condition of the Armenians. Already when a young man bent on his explorations in Nineveh, he had noted that they were oppressed. In individual cases not only of Armenians, but of Moslem Arabs, he had interfered, without waiting for instructions from home, to prevent some of the abominations of the Turkish officials. He received a trustworthy report that a stupid Vali on the Persian Gulf had ordered a forest of date-palms to be cut down because it furnished not only food but comparative wealth to an Arab tribe who exported crushed dates to England. His idea was that the members of the tribe must be kept poor in order that they should be subservient. Sir Henry went to see the Sultan and obtained orders for the immediate removal of the Vali. In spite of the story current in England that Layard could be forgiven for discovering Nineveh, but that Nineveh's discovery of Layard was unpardonable, his sturdy common sense and kindness of character revolted at the treatment of the Armenians and Arabs.

Note No. 2.—In my "Forty Years in Constantinople" I attributed the saying about Layard and Nineveh to Lord Palmerston; I find however that it has been attributed to many others, of whom the witty Lady Morley was one. Perhaps a better claimant might be a sprightly lady, Miss Emily Eden, whose works, and especially her novels, says a correspondent to whose stores of facts I am greatly indebted, are not nearly so well known to the present generation as they deserve to be. In July, 1866, Miss Eden wrote as follows to Lord Clarendon: "About twenty years ago I remember writing to Lord Ellesmere, who was rather *enjoué* with his Nineveh book, that I could forgive Layard for having discovered Nineveh, though I was satisfied to take it as Jonah left it, but I could not forgive Nineveh for having discovered Layard."

CHAPTER VII

ABDUL HAMID'S DAILY LIFE

Abdul Hamid's daily life; enlargement of Yildiz; daily programme; his recreations; reading of *djournals;* private theatre; his loneliness.

It is worth while to interrupt the narrative of Abdul Hamid's reign and to try to realise what was the daily life of the Sultan during the middle period of his reign. He had completely succeeded in getting rid of the party of reformers, in reducing his Ministers to the position of merely executive officers, who were allowed little initiative and whose duty was limited almost exclusively to giving effect to his arbitrary decrees. He had in fact made himself an absolute Sovereign, and henceforth until 1908 the country was in a period of strictly personal government.

He had now made Yildiz his permanent residence. Built by his predecessors on a hill known by that name and signifying "starry," overlooking the Bosporus, and about half a mile behind the palace of Dolma Bagshé, he had enlarged a comparatively small residence. The great palace last named was never liked by him, probably because it was associated with Abdul Aziz, and it was now reserved for State functions. Even before the year 1885 Abdul Hamid had enlarged the garden around the existing building.

He ruthlessly appropriated houses and grounds belonging to his subjects, including two Christian cemeteries. He surrounded the enlarged garden by a high wall and subsequently, in 1898, had a second wall built, so that the enclosure came to be regarded as a fortress. Its position is charming. From various points within it views extend northwards over both sides of the Bosporus. In another direction, Scutari, the Princes Islands, and a portion of Stambul rise from the azure blue of the Marmora. On every point of vantage Abdul Hamid built a chalet or kiosque. Each of these was usually supplied with powerful telescopes, so as to serve as points of observation. Many of them contained accommodation for sleeping and temporary residence, and each was surrounded by a terrace on which trusted guards could keep watch while their lord was within. It was commonly reported that he rarely slept twice in the same building. Lofty walls encircled the enclosure from the first. A French writer speaks of Yildiz, with its commonplace palace, its many kiosques and chalets, as a "Macedoine" (the name given to a salad made up of a large variety of fruit and vegetables). In order to render Yildiz strong against attack, he had cleared away an entire street of houses in the neighbourhood and had removed every obstacle to its defence. One of the stories told at the time is not without its amusing side. Von der Goltz Pasha, then an instructor in the Military School, about a mile distant, in lecturing upon military attack, accidentally put his pointer upon the map on which the hill of Yildiz was marked and asked a question relative to his lecture. The incident was at once reported to the Sultan, who sent for the German Ambassador and caused a strict inquiry to be made, from which he was convinced that no instructions were being given for attack upon the palace in which Abdul Hamid had entrenched himself.

After a severe earthquake shock in 1894 he built another kiosque containing eleven rooms and resting upon an artificial rock, the whole so constructed as to render an occupant safe either from earthquake or fire. Never indeed so long as he was allowed to live in Yildiz did he neglect any means of making it secure against possible enemies. The worst enemy he had to fear was fire, and the precautions he took against it were excessive. In 1898 he built a second encircling wall, and the barracks of his Imperial guard were constructed against it. Not only had he entrenched himself as securely as possible in the great enclosure, but he had made it so self-contained that he had within it a farm, a small artificial lake, stables, workshops, a menagerie, and an aviary. Altogether, including the ladies of his harem and their attendants, there were said to be nearly 5,000 persons resident within the enclosure, while adjoining it there were 7,000 of the Imperial Guard. So far as Abdul Hamid was concerned, it was at once a fortress and a prison which was locked on the inside. Not far from the palace of Yildiz were a *koluk*, that is, a police office, and a prison, and some of the most horrible stories told of Abdul Hamid speak of the tortures and the cruelties perpetrated in that building. There can be no reasonable doubt that many persons suffered tortures for offences committed in and around Yildiz, for the details given of these horrors are too many and too detailed not to have in them a large amount of truth.

Abdul Hamid's habits were fairly regular. Like most of the inhabitants of Turkey, he was an early riser. He usually went into his workroom about eight o'clock and began the day, as most people do in Turkey, with a strong, unsweetened cup of coffee, followed by a cigarette, which was the first of a long series continuing until the day's work was done. After a light breakfast, usually consisting of eggs and milk, the first task, to which he devoted himself with great assiduity, was to read the *djournals*, or reports of his spies. His correspondence was large. He had to examine proposals of army contractors and others, petitions, and accounts of tradesmen. It was remarked that the larger part of his time was occupied with private affairs connected with Yildiz itself. As he had no confidence in those about him, he personally conducted the whole of his correspondence. As the morning advanced his secretaries and chamberlains reported what they had done the previous day. Then came the time for the Sultan to see men permitted to have audiences, for Abdul was not inaccessible to tradesmen or unsuspected persons with whom there was business to be done. The Chief

Eunuch, who was with him on these occasions, had almost invariably before him a pile of applications for contracts or concessions, and of petitions. The Turkish tradition is that every subject has a right to present a demand to his Sovereign, and this was one which Abdul Hamid could not set aside.

About ten o'clock Abdul Hamid took his lunch. He had for many years suffered from dyspepsia and a nervous malady which made him abstemious. Like all Turks, he was particular as to his drinking water, but it was notorious that the Sultan invariably obtained his from a spring at Kiat-hané, a village on the north side of the Golden Horn. The explanation of this preference was that before he was Sovereign a gipsy woman had warned him to anticipate danger to his life from an external source, such as plague or cholera, but had assured him he would be safe if he only drank Kiat-hané water. He was subject to many similar superstitions, and, like the majority of his subjects, believed in the predictions of soothsayers.

After his lunch, which he always took alone and over which he only spent a few minutes, Abdul Hamid received his secretaries and gave them orders to be transmitted to his Ministers. Before the end of the century he had acquired the habit of rarely seeing his Ministers. He transmitted orders and general instructions, and they obeyed them.

In summer and autumn Abdul Hamid took a short siesta. Then followed his time for relaxation and for throwing off the cares of the day. In the early years he had been fond of riding; but though he had always a number of superb horses in his stables, it may be doubted whether after 1890 he rode any of them. He was therefore compelled to limit his exercise to walking, always of course within the limits of Yildiz. Though the palace was surrounded by guards, yet when he walked in his park he was preceded by a eunuch, in whom for years he had great confidence, whose duty was to clear anyone out of the way his Majesty chose to go, and was followed by two of his trusted guards.

Amid his loneliness he found amusement in carpentry and in fretwork, in which he excelled, and in pistol shooting, in which he had become such an adept while yet a prince that it is said he could write his name with shots on a board at a distance of twenty-five paces. One of his guards was often employed to throw oranges into the air, which the Sultan would rarely miss. It struck one at first as curious to learn that after ascending the throne Abdul Hamid dabbled a little in analytical chemistry. Possibly the idea was given him by Lord Salisbury. Such slight skill as he obtained together with his conversations with Dr. Mavrogeni, the chief physician at the palace, had something to do with the favour he showed towards the proposal, which was fully carried out, of establishing a medical school in Constantinople, a school which is the most notable asset to be placed to his credit.

He took interest in an intelligent old Turk who had a talent for mechanics. A small pleasure boat on the lake within the park was propelled by clockwork of which the motive power was a spring, and in this the Sultan often passed a pleasant hour.

Four o'clock in winter and six in summer was Abdul Hamid's time for the evening meal. This meal, like his lunch, he took alone, and occupied only a few minutes over it. He kept up the curious custom of sending the dish of which he had partaken to a favourite. Not seldom he would require the Superintendent of the Kitchen to partake of a dish which he had produced. His food was prepared in a building separate from that known as the palace kitchen. His diet at this evening meal was as simple as that at lunch, for it must always be remembered that dyspepsia and his nervous disease had largely obtained the mastery over him. If the statement be true that he sometimes took a *petit verre de cognac* after his evening meal, no sensible man will blame him.

After dinner came far too often the reading of *djournals*. If disposed for a less irritating pleasure, one of his professional buffoons with two or three favourite servants would be called in. One such buffoon was a man on whom, for the amusement of his Majesty, rough tricks and horse-play were indulged in with impunity, and from whom stories, either simple or coarse, might be expected, for, like all Turks, Abdul Hamid loved a good story-teller.

Abdul Hamid must often have found his evenings wearisome. He had built a small theatre at Yildiz and usually had two companies of actors in his pay, many of them in the early part of his reign being Armenians. He preferred that women's parts should be taken by men. When a French company arrived in Constantinople he generally arranged that it should perform in the small theatre at Yildiz. The company was glad to be able to state that it had played before the Sultan, but it found the performances far from exhilarating. The audience was always extremely small. As the Sultan himself never applauded, no one else ventured to do so. The whole performance was deadly dull. With such a performance Abdul's normal day's work terminated.

In his palace at Yildiz, with its beautiful but somewhat dreary grounds, he was a lonely man without friends, for the men who were around him were neither of good social position nor sufficiently intelligent to invite friendship. Companionship had now entirely ceased between him and his Ministers. He did not want to see them, nor they him. His very servants avoided meeting him, for he had become a terror. Unable to keep up a conversation in any language but Turkish, with which no Ambassador or foreign Minister was acquainted, intimacy with any of them was also out of the question. It is true that he gave dinners occasionally in honour of ambassadors or distinguished foreigners and in the earlier years to a few prominent members of the community and their wives, but anything more frigid, more unlikely to conduce to friendly conversation, could hardly be imagined. The Sultan himself is said to have loathed them. Yet they were served in the best European fashion; crockery, napery, and glass were the best that money could buy; the cooking was unobjectionable;

opposite each guest would be half a dozen different kinds of glasses, though of course everyone knew that, as the Sultan himself did not drink any alcoholic liquor, none of his subjects would do so in his presence. Such dinners were solemn farces, the banalities of Turkish Court life. The absence of women from the table increased their deadly dulness, for while no Turkish lady was ever present, the wives of ambassadors or of persons in his service hardly added gaiety to the function. Moreover, the giving such dinners became rarer with every year which passed. The visitors were honoured by dining with his Majesty, but those to whom the novelty of the honour had passed soon became, like Abdul Hamid himself, bored at the entertainment. The Sultan, with nobody of his own intelligence with whom to talk, with no intellectual tastes and no lofty and ennobling designs for the welfare of his people, and with the constant fear of dyspepsia before him, was unenviable in his great loneliness.

It is impossible to speak with anything like exactitude of Abdul Hamid's harem. Many lady writers have written and have given second or third-hand accounts of it. No male visitor, of course, was ever permitted to enter it. Two remarks may however be safely made: first, that Abdul Hamid was not a sensual man, his harem being very much smaller than that of either of his immediate predecessors; and second, that the accounts given of his innocent delight in the company of the ladies of his harem are to his credit. He never knew however the home delights of an ordinary Turk, with his one wife and family; the sweet companionship of a home was denied to him.

Abdul Hamid had made himself a virtual prisoner in his palace at Yildiz, with the door locked from the inside. In thus secluding himself he was not following the example of any of his predecessors, for the Turkish tradition was of sultans who rejoiced in the active exercise which fitted them for the field of battle, who loved hunting and out-of-door sports, who could shoot further than any of their subjects, or who in the capital went about freely amongst their people, often in disguise, to learn their complaints and desires, to see how they lived, to be better able to render themselves popular, and to spy out the discontented. Abdul Hamid preferred to remain immured and to do his spying by others.

His habits did not conduce to his bodily or mental health. As the years passed his physical ailments increased, and the evidence appears to show that his mental capacity diminished.

CHAPTER VIII

ABDUL HAMID'S RELATIONS WITH FOREIGN STATES

Incident of *Kostroma ;* French land *stationaire's* crew at Ismidt, members of Roman Catholic orders forbidden to enter Turkey; settlement of claims by some European States for damage done to their subjects in Armenian massacres; attack on European post-offices; Abdul Hamid seizes land unfairly; change in appointment to British consular service in Turkey.

A PARABLE often related in Moslem coffee-houses gives the popular notion of how the safety of Turkey, and especially of Constantinople, has been secured. The carcase of a sheep was suspended in a Han at a height sufficient to be beyond the reach of the village dogs. Nevertheless each of them tried to snatch a mouthful. Sometimes they succeeded, but each and all had failed to detach the carcase, and the combined attempts usually ended in quarrels in the village pack. The suspended carcase represented Turkey; the pack of wolf-like dogs stood for the European Powers. It was the genius of Canning, afterwards Lord Stratford, which first recognised that in dealing with Turkey, especially in compelling her to do justice to her Christian population, Europe ought to be united. Mr. Gladstone acted upon Canning's idea, and "the concert of Europe" was the ideal cherished by him for compelling Turkey to do justice to the Christian races of the Empire.[1] Lord Salisbury, without adopting the phrase, acted upon it. Hence in writing on Abdul Hamid's relations with foreign States the Salisbury policy will be best seen when he is acting with the other Powers in block. In the many questions which arose out of

[1] See note at end of chapter.

Abdul Hamid's treatment of the subject races in the Empire, the Powers, as we shall see, generally acted together. But there were other questions where separate States had no common interests, and the most important of these must be noted. From 1890 to his deposition there was no year in which Turkey had not to treat with some Power on a question which more particularly concerned it than Europe generally.

By the Treaty of Paris and by earlier international agreements Turkey had been made the guardian of the Straits, and no vessel of war had the right to pass the Dardanelles if carrying more guns than were necessary for firing salutes. Merchant vessels however were free to pass. Russia, after the Treaty of London in 1871, had constructed a number of armed merchantmen, forming her "Volunteer Fleet." Although armed, they carried the Russian commercial flag. In April, 1891, permission for one of these vessels, named the *Kostroma*, to pass through the Dardanelles was refused by Abdul Hamid. Russia protested that she was within her rights; and notwithstanding Abdul Hamid's protest and actual refusal the difficulty was arranged, Russia consenting, in order to be agreeable to the Porte, that she would notify it when one of the Volunteer Fleet proposed to pass through the Straits. The right of Russia was by no means clear; but Abdul Hamid acted impulsively, first in protesting, and then in as hastily surrendering.

During the Armenian massacres, 1894–7, Frenchmen in the capital had not attempted to restrain their indignation at the Sultan's treatment of his Armenian subjects. French steamers had received refugees and had refused to give them up. When the Turks entered a monastery, under French protection, near Ismidt, on which the tricolour was flying, this had been torn down by a too officious Turkish official, and the monks, who also were under French protection, had been expelled. The French Ambassador protested against the insult. The Porte proposed negotiation, which, had it been permitted, would have lasted long and probably would have been useless. The French Government demanded an immediate apology. The Sultan hesitated. The French *stationaire*, in spite of the protests and prayers of Abdul Hamid when he learned that the captain would not discuss the insult to his flag, went from the Bosporus to Ismidt, and her captain marched his crew with fixed bayonets and the tricolour flying to the monastery and again hoisted the French flag in its usual place. This and other similar incidents aroused the anger of the Sultan. He wished especially to strike at the French Christian missions for having been the cause of what he, not incorrectly, called a violation of Turkish territory. He waited his time, and in May, 1901, issued an iradé forbidding French members of the Roman Catholic orders to settle in Turkey without special authorisation. Now, no right was more firmly established by a series of capitulations beginning in 1535 than that of the entry of the religious orders. It had remained undisputed until the time of Abdul Hamid. The iradé caused great irritation to the Catholic portion of France. At the same time a French financial group could obtain no satisfaction from the Porte in reference to its claim on account of the quays in Smyrna. A group of local French bankers had in vain sought also for settlement of their claims founded on judgments in the Turkish courts. The Sultan's obstinacy led in the month of August to diplomatic relations being broken off between the two countries. Negotiations went on for some weeks; then on November 5, 1901, France sent ships of war to Mitylene and took possession of the Custom House. Straightway the Porte proposed to settle the financial claims, but France, having been compelled to use force, now insisted upon a settlement of all outstanding questions. Among the new demands the most important was the recognition of the rights *ab antiquo* of all French religious and scholastic establishments in Turkey and their exemption from taxation as in past years. On November 9 Abdul Hamid agreed to everything. The incident was one more illustration of his policy of refusing just demands, making objections, and finally surrendering everything.

Abdul Hamid's conduct in reference to the Armenians led to the presentation of many claims by American citizens and by British subjects and those of France and Italy. During the massacres in the Armenian provinces the Moslem mobs, notwithstanding orders not to do injury to the property of any foreign subject, did not discriminate. Houses and shops were plundered belonging to Christians, and the mob did not stop to inquire whether the owner was Greek, Jew, or Armenian. So long as he was not Moslem they plundered without distinction. Hence the belongings of many foreign subjects were stolen or destroyed. Some Armenians when they had become American citizens returned to Turkey, still retaining their newly acquired nationality. Indeed, the number of such men in the Turkish Empire ran into hundreds. Other Armenians had brothers or fathers settled in France, England, or Italy who had appointed their relations in Turkey as agents, for many of them had established flourishing businesses. When the shops or houses of such men were plundered, the respective Governments of the owners protested and claimed compensation. The Sultan absolutely refused, alleging that foreigners must suffer the damages which resulted from internal disorders, just as Ottoman subjects suffered. But the Powers knew that these outrages had been ordered by Abdul Hamid and supervised by his subordinates. They therefore persisted in their demands and spoke of the employment of force to obtain satisfaction. A curious idea occurred to someone and was at once adopted by the Sultan. He called the American Minister, Mr. Griscom, and requested him to procure the attendance of the agent of the celebrated American firm of shipbuilders named Cramp. Negotiations were entered into; the style of ship was fixed upon, the price duly stipulated, and the order arranged. Then the agent was informed that to the price he must add the sum of so many pounds, being the amount claimed by the American Minister as compensation for the damage done to Americans. This sum was to be paid to the Minister. He of course could do what he liked with it. In this way the Sultan judged that he had avoided the admission of the validity of the American claims. He had of course satisfied the American Minister. The arrangement was to be kept secret. It naturally became public after a few days.

A like procedure took place with Armstrongs in reference to the British claims and with the French builders. As to those put forward by Italy, the proceedings were slightly varied. One of the old ironclads was sent to Ansaldo's, at Genoa, to be repaired and refitted, and the Italian claims were added to the price. In this way the various ambassadors were satisfied and the claims got rid of. These new ships took their place in the Golden Horn.

When it was decided to send a ship to Italy for repairs, the one chosen was one of those which had been sent to the Dardanelles. Before leaving a transport went to take out all the guns on board the other ships which had gone to the same place except a small one for signalling. In this way three ships, the only ones outside the harbour of the Golden Horn, were rendered incapable of being used against the Sultan. Abdul Hamid had thus shown his knowledge of international law and of statesmanship, and had added three powerful vessels to the Turkish fleet.

Having got rid of government by Ministers and thus rendered himself an absolute ruler, Abdul Hamid was often tempted to act in an arbitrary manner towards foreign States. He never understood the value of *quieta non movere*. In an old-established government like Turkey, especially in one which was hardly half civilised, practices had been adopted and welcomed by his own subjects and by all foreign Powers which had been forgotten in European countries. One such practice was to allow foreign nations to have their own post-offices. Its origin is easily understood. When, especially after 1535, treaties or capitulations had been made with France which shortly enured to the advantage of every important European country, trade and commerce took a considerable development. The traders were always under the protection of the country of which they were subjects. No Turkish post-offices or mail service existed, and the merchants received their letters in the Ambassador's bag. For convenience, each Great Power established a post-office, which was always attached to its embassy. Sometimes, though rarely, some of the Powers founded post-offices in a few of the chief towns in the interior. The practice worked well for centuries, but it had its inconveniences; and when after the Crimean War Turkey entered officially into the rank of the European Powers she wished to have the Post-offices in her own hands. Most States recognised that her claim should be admitted as soon as she had shown her capacity to manage them so as to secure the regularity which characterised the foreign post-offices. But Turkish Ministers as well as all classes of foreigners saw Turkey fail in every successive attempt and acquiesced in the old arrangements. Abdul Hamid however wanted to extend his spy system to them, to learn who were his disaffected subjects and to control the correspondence of all. Accordingly in 1901 he determined in his own impulsive and arbitrary manner to abolish the privileges of the European Powers in having post-offices.

It was in May of that year that he ordered the letter bags of the foreign post-offices in Constantinople to be seized on their arrival. Already letters which arrived in the capital by the Turkish post-offices from the interior were delivered ostentatiously open. He now sent messengers who upon the arrival of the tri-weekly trains from Paris, London, and other European cities, seized the mail bags although they were sealed and addressed to the British and French post-masters, carried them off to the Turkish Post-office, opened them, and took possession of those which were addressed to Turkish subjects. The foreign post-masters, acting on the instructions of their embassies, refused to take delivery of the rest, on the ground, amongst others, that they could not control the number of postal orders which had been received. Great turmoil arose in the foreign community, and within a week Abdul Hamid had to give instructions that there should be no more violation of the postal rights of the embassies. His action was one more illustration of his impulsive and ill-considered action and of his having to climb down.

Abdul Hamid came into conflict with the British and other ambassadors through his efforts at land-grabbing.

During the years 1882–90 the Civil List, acting under the orders of Abdul Hamid, dispossessed hundreds of peasants, occupants of lands throughout the country, in order to add such lands to the private domain of the Sultan. It was remarked that these attempts were first made in places where there were no foreign consuls, and upon Ottoman subjects only. The intention was to prevent publicity to what in many cases was nothing short of robbery. Wherever the officials of Abdul Hamid had reason to believe that the official copies of the *hodjets*, or title deeds, were lost, Circassians or nomads would be settled upon the property as tenants of the Sultan and would be furnished with new *hodjets*. It was in vain that the neighbouring proprietors and villagers of all races and creeds testified that the dispossessed peasant or his grandparent had held undisputed possession to the knowledge of the oldest inhabitant, or that they could show that in one of the many fires common in Asia Minor villages their *hodjets* had been destroyed. They were told by the iniquitous agents of the Sultan that they had no right in presence of the new-comers, who had obtained *hodjets*. After a while the creatures of Yildiz became bold enough to seize land belonging to foreign subjects, and by 1890 there was probably not an embassy that was not troubled with complaints from its own subjects of attempts to steal their land with the buildings upon it. The British Embassy protested strongly in many such cases. By the Turkish law of 1869 foreign subjects were for the first time permitted to hold land in Turkey.

The condition however was attached that they should be assimilated to Turkish subjects in everything regarding the ownership of such property. The result was that legal redress was impossible in the Turkish courts of law. These courts gave such judgments as they were ordered to give, and a foreigner had no redress except through his embassy; indeed, it was the number of complaints from the embassies that mainly put an end to this wholesale theft on the part of Abdul Hamid, mainly, though not exclusively, because the Finance Minister and the leading Turkish notables justly complained that the new occupants, being tenants directly of the Sultan, were exempt from taxes which went into the public treasury. The action of Abdul Hamid in the matter helped to contribute to make him unpopular. Moreover, it soon became recognised that where the old occupant was a well-to-do Moslem he was not disturbed by the planting of new-comers upon his land, whereas his poorer neighbour, and especially if he were a Christian, suffered without redress. Abdul Hamid always loved money, and his private income had become enormously increased by his employment of those who were ready to augment it at the cost of the public treasury, but his achievements as a land-grabber from his Christian subjects greatly assisted to make him hated.

There are other incidents which would furnish illustrations of Abdul Hamid's relations with foreign States. Such, for instance, is the expulsion of Fehim Pasha, which was due to the representation of Sir Nicholas O'Conor and Baron Marschall. Such also is the incident of Tabah, on the Gulf of Suez, where the Sultan attempted to change the boundary of Egypt. It is more convenient, however, to treat these in other portions of this book.

Note, p. 115.—Before leaving Const· ntinople in January, 1877, after the failure of the European Confe ɔnce, Lord Salisbury caused it to be known that he was far from s .tisfied with the information regarding what had passed in various parts of the Turkish Empire. The British Embassy, and therefore the British Government, had not been furnished with anything like adequate news of the movements that had taken place in Bulgaria and elsewhere. While in Constantinople he had seen Mr., afterwards Sir William, White, Sir William Holmes, and several other consuls from different parts of the country. With the exception of the two mentioned and one or two others, he was dissatisfied with their conduct as public officers and with their ignorance of the country. Many of them were not British subjects, and were placed in circumstances which made it unlikely that they would be acquainted with what was going on in their own district; and many were engaged in business where their private interest required that they should be on good terms with the Turkish officials. On his return to England he organised a plan for the appointment of student dragomans, who were to be young men of British birth, who should undergo a special training in one or more languages of the country and in elementary law. They were to be selected after a competitive examination. The inducements held out were high, the greatest being that not only would the consular service of the East be in the main reserved for them, but that men who proved capable in such service should pass into that of diplomacy. The result has on the whole been fairly successful. It has been marred by the fact that the promise that exceptional men should pass into the diplomatic service has not been kept. The British service has been the loser. Various instances have occurred in which men with quite exceptional experience, qualifications, and knowledge of the country would have been of great value if they had been diplomats. With the sole exception of Sir William White, none have been so named.

CHAPTER IX

ABDUL HAMID'S RELATIONS WITH EGYPT

Egypt; story of deposition of Ismail, Khedive of Egypt; disturbances caused by Arabi; riots in Alexandria in June, 1882; battle of Tel-el-Kebir; France declines to join with England in occupation of Egypt; Sultan requested to send troops as symbol of his authority; negotiations through Lord Dufferin; Baker Pasha endeavours to persuade Abdul Hamid to accept British invitation; Sultan delays until occupation takes place; Baker leaves capital; Sir Drummond Wolff appointed envoy in 1885 to arrange for departure of British troops; signs an Agreement with Grand Vizier, accepted by Lord Salisbury, repudiated by Abdul Hamid; Wolff Convention becomes dead letter, in 1882 attempt made to foist new Firman upon Egypt changing boundaries of Egypt, discovered and withdrawn; another attempt to change boundary in 1906; defeat of all Abdul Hamid's designs regarding Egypt.

Notes, on the Caliphate; is Sultan of Turkey Caliph?—statement of opposing views; on attempts to create disaffection in India; on Pan-Islamism; on liberal Moslem sects.

In this chapter are related the various dealings of Abdul Hamid in reference to Egypt. They include a series of attempts on his part to change the order of succession to the Turkish throne, to create and employ Pan-Islamism as a weapon against Great Britain, to oppose European, but especially British, influence in Egypt. England and France succeeded in getting rid of the rule of Khedive Ismail. All Abdul Hamid's Pan-Islamic intrigues failed. His fatuous refusal to join England in sending troops into Egypt to co-operate with the British led to its occupation. His desire to coerce England into an immediate withdrawal of our troops and his gross breach of faith in rejecting the Wolff Convention, which his own Ministers had signed and doubtless he himself had approved, had convinced England that his word could not be trusted. Lastly, his desire to encroach on the boundaries of Egypt not only failed in its direct object, but compelled him for the first time to recognise formally that England had occupied the country.

Abdul Hamid, like his predecessors, always attached great importance to the suzerainty of Egypt. It was the "brightest jewel which he possessed." It was especially valued by him because from his accession he emphasised more than any of his predecessors his claims to be Caliph.[1]

Ismail was the reigning Khedive when Abdul Hamid became Sultan. He had succeeded in the lifetime of Abdul Aziz in obtaining a Firman changing the order of succession from the Asiatic to the European mode. He had accomplished this by paying heavy bribes in Turkey to the Sultan and all round. It is unlikely that Abdul Hamid, who had already children born to him, ever made any objections to this change in the law of succession, because he hoped from the first to succeed in making it applicable to the Turkish throne and therefore to his own son. Egypt, after the Firman in question, remained under the Sultan's suzerainty. Ismail was a typical Eastern monarch, who regarded the principal use of a Ministry as a means to furnish him with an unlimited supply of money. He spent what he had lavishly. He had a large and unusually extravagant harem. Egypt had already incurred many debts; and the holders of Egyptian Bonds, most of which were in France or England, were alarmed at his extravagance. The peasants were overburdened with taxation but voiceless. Roads which had been good were allowed to get out of repair; forced labour, with an extensive use of the *kurbash*, was constantly exacted; and the great mass of the population were oppressed. The French

[1] For a discussion of the history of the Caliphate see note at end of this chapter.

and English bondholders became alarmed for the safety of their investments. Already in 1859 the Khedive had had to surrender the power of imposing taxes and of contracting loans, but the Firman which changed the order of succession made him virtually independent, the only practical limitations being that he must not build ironclads, make treaties, or coin money. Ismail had encouraged the slave trade, and Sir Samuel Baker had been appointed at the request of the Powers to head an expedition into Central Africa to suppress it. He returned in 1873; and Gordon, afterwards of Khartum fame, was appointed as his successor. Comptrollers had been named by England and France with the object of keeping down the expenditure in Egypt and of effecting reforms. One of the most important of these reforms was the introduction in November, 1875, of International Courts. The Mixed Courts, that is, those which have to deal with questions between Egyptian subjects and Europeans, followed, and were formally opened on January 1, 1876. It was in November, 1875, that a bold economic measure was taken by Mr. Disraeli. The opening of the Suez Canal had greatly affected the economic situation. A large number of shares in it belonged to the Khedive personally. Ismail was always in want of money, and when these were offered for sale, they were purchased in November, 1875, by Mr. Disraeli for the British Government. The purchase gave the British shareholders a majority of voting power. In September, 1878, Sir Rivers Wilson was appointed Finance Minister; and a few weeks afterwards M. de Blignières was named Minister of Public Works. Both these representatives remonstrated with the Khedive on account of his extravagance. A financial scheme had been prepared by a commission of inquiry of which M. de Lesseps, the builder of the Suez Canal, was president and Sir Rivers Wilson vice-president. With them were four Commissioners of the Public Debt. The Comptrollers, who at that time were Mr. Romaine and Baron de Malaret, were purposely kept outside the commission. Its report was drawn up by the present Lord Cromer, then Sir Evelyn Baring, who had gone out to Egypt as a Commissioner of the Egyptian Public Debt in 1877 and became Comptroller-General in Egypt in 1879. Lord Cromer was assisted by the other Commissioners, and notably by his French colleague, M. de Blignières.

The work of the commission was well done, and is notable as the first attempt to deal seriously with Egyptian finance. It laid down the basis of a composition with the creditors of the Government, but it also showed that the real debtor was the Khedive himself, who had not only spent his own money, but had borrowed on the Khedivial estates. It was, therefore, necessary to limit his Civil List. The day previous to the publication of the report, namely, April 8, 1879, the Khedive dismissed the European Ministers. This action embarrassed the European Powers. It meant that Ismail would not consent to any control over financial administration. In May England and France demanded the appointment of European Ministers. The Commissioners proffered their resignation, which was accepted. Ismail tried at first the policy of bluff. He increased his army, but a few days later he found that he could not trust it. The popular sentiment, already strong against him, was increased. Apparently he had relied on discord among the Powers, but when the German Consul-General declared that the Khedive must be held responsible for the payment of a judgment debt levied by the international tribunal, to the establishment of which Germany had been a party, Ismail apparently considered his case hopeless. Probably also the representatives of England and France felt that Prince Bismarck's action in ordering the German Consul-General to put forward the small German claims indicated the desire on the part of Germany to take a hand with England and France in the settlement of Egyptian affairs, a desire which was regarded as inopportune and likely to cause trouble. However this may have been, both Governments decided that the deposition of Ismail was necessary, and they lost no time in taking action so as to avoid interference. On June 19

Sir Frank Lascelles sent a communication to the Khedive, by order of Lord Salisbury, to the effect that the French and British Governments "officially advised his Highness to abdicate and leave Egypt." The communication added that if he accepted this advice the Powers would recognise the validity of the Firman which had changed the order of succession and allow his son Tewfik to succeed; in addition he would receive a substantial pension, an amount subsequently fixed at £40,000 per annum. If, on the contrary, his Highness refused to abdicate and thus compelled the Cabinets of Paris and London to address themselves to the Sultan, his Highness would not be able to count on the Civil List or on the succession of his son. On June 21 Ismail asked for time and stated that he had referred the question to the Sultan, on whose interference he built great hopes. The agent whom he sent to Constantinople was instructed to attach importance to the fact that this was an attempt by France and England to disregard Abdul Hamid's sovereign rights. It was believed in Egypt while these negotiations were going on that the claims of Prince Halim, the Crown Prince *de jure* if the Firman was disregarded, were favoured by the Sultan. But in truth Abdul Hamid, who had followed the events in Egypt with great interest, apparently never dreamed that the Powers entertained the idea of a deposition without his consent. Although he favoured Halim, he was unwilling to consent to the revocation of the Firman which Ismail had obtained. Indeed, from the first, and throughout his reign, Abdul Hamid hoped to obtain the change in the order of succession to the Turkish throne. He seems to have had no objection to the deposition of Ismail, taking it for granted that his rights as suzerain would be respected and that he would be applied to in that capacity by England and France.

Meantime the demand for abdication made on June 19 required a prompt answer; the request for time for consideration was on June 21. Probably neither of these facts was known in Constantinople earlier than forty-eight hours before the time fixed for the announcement of the abdication or deposition. When Abdul Hamid learnt the arrangement he was greatly alarmed. Egypt was the greatest of his possessions, the brightest jewel in his Crown. His loss of reputation would be enormous, especially among his own subjects, if the Powers changed the ruler of Egypt without his consent. Probably nothing that had happened since his accession had so greatly alarmed him. He immediately called together all his Ministers, who all recognised that such a step, without their Sovereign's consent, was to be avoided if possible. The discussion lasted till after midnight. The ablest man amongst his Ministers was Alexander Caratheodori, who had been Minister of Foreign Affairs at the Congress of Berlin, and whose clearsightedness was evident to all who knew him. After all others had given their opinions, Caratheodori, who had incurred some disrepute amid the Moslems because he had had to consent at Berlin to the sacrifice of territory, was appealed to by those of the Ministers who knew his capacity. He boldly declared to his Majesty that this was a case in which audacity and celerity furnished the only remedies. But Abdul Hamid, always vacillating, suggested negotiations for delay. Caratheodori urged the Sultan himself immediately to depose Ismail and to appoint Tewfik his successor. By so doing he would assert his rights over Egypt, and prevent England and France being credited with the deposition. Delay would risk the sacrifice of Egypt. The proposal was a startling one and was hotly discussed, but time was short, for on the following day, as Caratheodori reminded his Majesty, with or without his consent, the deposition would be proclaimed. Finally, it was recognised that audacity was the safest course in Abdul Hamid's interest, and thereupon, in the early morning of June 24, Caratheodori drove from Yildiz to the telegraph office at Pera with full powers and dictated three despatches. The first was to Ismail. Telegraphing on behalf of the Sultan he declared that his Majesty, recognising his extravagance and violation of his duty towards his Suzerain, found he had so misconducted himself that he herewith issued a Firman deposing him. The second telegram was addressed to Tewfik, the son of Ismail, notifying him that he was appointed by Abdul Hamid, and advising him to avoid the faults of his father. The third was addressed to the Turkish Minister in Paris and informed him of the two previous despatches. By this stroke, although Abdul Hamid had not defeated the designs of England and France, he had at least saved his reputation among his subjects as Sovereign Lord of Egypt.

Ismail left Egypt and took his £40,000 a year, and went, accompanied by his harem, to live in Naples. No privileges were granted to him beyond the two mentioned, of receiving a handsome pension, and of securing the recognition of his son as his successor. He was, however, allowed to keep one or two palaces, which he chose to consider as his private property, though they had really been bought out of public funds, and were afterwards sold by him.

Before he left Cairo Ismail collected all the jewels belonging to the ladies of his harem, and had in a number of jewellers from the town, who were stripped naked and who took the stones out of their settings. These he wrapped up in a towel and took away with him to Italy.

Tewfik became Khedive on June 24, 1879. Abdul Hamid claimed that he had obtained a diplomatic triumph in deposing Ismail and appointing his son. It was generally recognised, however, in Constantinople that if triumph there were, it was on the part of England and France. One indeed wonders how the Sultan could have been kept in ignorance of the intentions of the Western Powers. That their conduct was wise under the circumstances can hardly be doubted. Had they commenced negotiations with the Sultan as the Sovereign Lord of Ismail, they would have been involved in a long controversy; for Abdul Hamid, and indeed all his Ministers, attached great importance to lengthy negotiations, and Germany might possibly, even at that early stage, have considered it in her interest to pose as the defender of the rights of the Sultanate. By adopting a bold course with Ismail, England and France carried through their project without great difficulty, and without intervention. They treated the Sultan almost as a negligible quantity. Abdul Hamid knew that he had been so treated, and resented the action of England and France, and when at a subsequent period these two nations disagreed as to the policy to be pursued in Egypt, his resentment fell almost solely upon our country.[1]

The Khedive Ismail was deposed in June, 1879. England and France, which had hitherto acted in harmony in Egypt, continued to do so for nearly two years. Then there arose a certain tension between the two countries which resulted in separate action. A military revolt by troops who had received no pay broke out in 1880. France and England acted together in giving their advice to the new Khedive in order to put an end to the revolt, which at one time appeared very serious, and the advice and efforts of Sir E. Malet, the British Minister, and of Baron de Ring, succeeded in preventing its spread. A Military Committee was formed, headed by Ahmed Arabi and Mahmud, whose aim seems to have been chiefly a demonstration against Turkish officers and foreigners. In August, 1881, Ahmed Arabi with his followers surrounded the Khedivial palace at Cairo and made a demand for higher pay. In February, 1882, they forced on the Khedive an administration, at the head of which was Mahmud, while Arabi was Minister of War. Thereupon the European Concert was invoked and a Conference was held in Constantinople. It was alleged that there then occurred a conspiracy to assassinate Arabi and to dethrone the Khedive, but evidently Lord Cromer believed that such conspiracy never existed, and that it was merely a creation of Arabi's craven imagination. Forty-five persons, mostly Circassians, were arrested. Serious

[1] The most complete and trustworthy account of the deposition of Ismail and of other events of this period in Egypt is given by Lord Cromer in his "Modern Egypt," Vol. I., Chapter viii.

rioting took place at Alexandria and Cairo. The former of these cities was fortified, and England and France united in protesting against the fortification, the misgovernment, and the continuance in office of Arabi. A detachment of the fleet of each nation arrived in Alexandria at the end of May, 1882. Arabi refused to resign, whereupon England and France sent an ultimatum calling upon Arabi and the other Ministers to give up their seals, in order that the Khedive's authority might be re-established. On the last day of May the Ministry yielded. Thereupon great alarm existed in Alexandria. The Arab mob, which had followed the lead of Arabi, rioted. A great many Europeans left the city, and it is said that 5,000 Egyptian soldiers were killed. The mob attacked the European population, the great day of rioting being June 11, 1882. On July 10 Admiral Seymour destroyed the forts at Alexandria. Arabi was declared a rebel by the Khedive and, in reply, on July 24, proclaimed a Jehad or Holy War.

France withdrew her fleet from Egyptian waters on July 30. England had now to take the pacification of Egypt into her own hands. On September 13, 1882, Sir Garnet Wolseley, who had landed at Alexandria and assumed command a few days earlier, advanced with 11,000 infantry, 200 cavalry, and forty guns from Ismailia, and fought the battle of Tel-el-Kebir. On the 14th the victorious British Army, led by Sir Charles Watson, entered Cairo. The back of the rebellion had been broken, and on September 25 the Khedive himself made a triumphant entry into his capital.

The separate action of England led to the abandonment of the Anglo-French control, notice having been given on November 9 that it would cease on January 11, 1883.

The agents of Abdul Hamid kept him well informed of what was going on in Egypt, and he was unable to conceal his delight on seeing the difficulties which had arisen between England and France. He was fond of telling a story, the moral of which was that Turkey would always be preserved by the conflicting interests and struggles of the giaours. Here was a striking illustration of this divergence and its results, due largely it was believed to the secret instigation of his agents. He was satisfied with their action.

The British Government had decided that the temporary occupation of Egypt was necessary to secure its future good government. The idea, however, fully shared both by Lord Salisbury and Mr. Gladstone, was that the occupation should only be temporary. Each of these statesmen expressed his conviction that it was undesirable in the interests of Great Britain that anything should be done which would tend to render the occupation permanent. Apart from the immediate question of Egypt, both these statesmen, but especially Mr. Gladstone, retained the traditional conviction that it was in the interest of England to support the integrity as well as the independence of the Turkish Empire. Mr. Gladstone and the Foreign Secretary, Lord Granville, apparently never wavered from the opinion that it was their duty to request the Sultan to take part in the proposed occupation. Even had the French consented to act with us, the British statesmen would still have requested Abdul Hamid to send some troops, if only to show that the Sovereign of the country, under whose name they proposed to act, was a consenting party. He was to be invited to send troops in order that his rights as Suzerain might not even appear to be evaded.

The tension between the two Western Governments, however, had become more acute than during the earlier troubles. France was urged to join her forces to our own. Nearly all the French officials in Egypt considered that it was in the interests of their country that there should be a joint occupation. They believed that England's conduct at Alexandria and the expedition of Tel-el-Kebir showed that, whether France joined her forces or not, England would occupy the country. Unfortunately, an opposite view prevailed amongst many of the French residents in Egypt, and especially in Cairo. From the moment of the withdrawal of their fleet an attitude of hostility arose amongst this section of the community, and telegrams strongly in opposition to joint action were sent to M. Gambetta, who was then the most important man in France, stating that the occupation was not necessary and that England dared not attempt it without the co-operation of France. Their effect, according to one of the most intelligent Frenchmen then resident in Egypt, was to completely override the despatches and letters sent from French officials and the better informed men of the French community in Egypt. The delight of the Arab mob, which included the partisans of Arabi and of all who wished to put an end to the financial reforms which the joint control had inaugurated, was intense when France definitely refused to join in the occupation of the country. Such delight was heartily shared by Abdul Hamid. He had already been informed that his co-operation would be requested by England. This placed him in a dilemma. To accept would be to recognise the right of interference of the British in Egypt, which was an integral part of his Empire ; to refuse was dangerous, because he did not know whether England would venture on the occupation without his consent. He soon learned that the desire of France was that he should refuse, but there was always a lingering fear that England might choose to act not only without France, but without him, and so he commenced the policy to which he always attached great importance, of making delays.

What was done in the capital became of prime interest. The negotiations between Abdul Hamid and the British Government were conducted by Lord Dufferin, who, on his arrival, for various reasons, was curiously considered to entertain friendly feelings not only towards Turkey, but towards the Sultan personally. Lord Dufferin was an Irishman, and Ireland was not believed to be loyal to Britain. His friendship with Mr. Disraeli was well known and much talked about. In several small but really important matters the British Ambassador had complied with demands of the Sultan which the representatives of the other Powers had refused. One of these was to give effect to Abdul Hamid's wish that no foreigner should be permitted to display any flag for decorative purposes except a Turkish. For this and other inadequate reasons it was believed that on this Egyptian question Lord Dufferin would be equally complacent in reference to demands which Turkey or England might make. The leading statesmen of both political parties had often spoken of the necessity of doing nothing to impair Turkish sovereign rights. Abdul Hamid could not make up his mind what to do. The one thing of which apparently he had become certain was that England would not occupy Egypt unless his troops co-operated.

Finally a formal invitation was given to him to send such a detachment of troops, small or great, as would enable the British Government to state that in occupying Egypt they were carefully respecting Abdul Hamid's suzerain rights, and were acting in accord with him.

Lord Dufferin had by this time come to know the Sultan and his ways. He was the first Ambassador to recognise that the Porte, meaning by the term the Turkish Ministers, on important subjects had no will of their own; that the Government was not only nominally but really in the hands of the Sultan. After having given his message, anticipating that he would be worried morning, noon and night by communications from the Palace, he took somewhat unusual steps. He had a beautiful little yacht in which with Lady Dufferin he often ran down for a week-end to the Prince's Islands, and anchored in a small bay behind the point of the Glossa, or tongue. His despatch boat brought him communications daily, but otherwise he had no intercourse with the Sultan or his agents. At that time on the same island lived Baker Pasha, who was now in active service under Abdul Hamid. He went every morning to the Palace, returning in the evening. He recognised from the first the friendliness to Turkey of the British proposal, but, having taken service with the Turks, he continued staunchly loyal to them. He urged Abdul Hamid and his Ministers to lose no time in consenting to act with the British. At first he was confident that Abdul Hamid would comply with the British demands, but every day his confidence decreased. The Sultan, and those who reflected his opinion, were convinced that England would not and dared not attempt the occupation of the country without his co-operation. They believed that their refusal to co-operate would be a great blow to Mr. Gladstone and the Liberal Government then in power, and they were foolish enough to believe that if they continued to refuse they would have the support of the Conservative Party. During an eventful week, Baker combated Abdul Hamid's confident opinion that England dared not attempt the occupation of Egypt without his consent and co-operation. He stated that he had urged that England having declared that she was about to make such occupation, neither the non-acquiescence of France nor the refusal of Abdul Hamid would turn Mr. Gladstone from his purpose; that he and other Liberal statesmen could not, and dared not, in their own interest, retreat from the decision they had taken. It was even amusing to hear that Baker was declared to be a supporter of Mr. Gladstone. He found it vain to explain that his sympathies had always been with the opposite political party, and that the advice he was giving was that of a strong Conservative speaking in the interest of the Sultan of Turkey.

As the time drew near for an occupation, Baker, who was kept daily for hours at Yildiz, became intensely anxious, and spoke of the supreme folly which reigned in the counsels of the Palace. At the end of a full week Lord Dufferin was sent for by the Sultan and returned to Pera. He had a morning interview with his Majesty in which the Sultan proposed new negotiations. The reply was that he was without authority to enter upon them. He was kept at the Palace during all the afternoon and evening, the Sultan expressly sending word that he wished him to remain to dinner. Lord Dufferin, however, was aware, though probably no one else in Constantinople was, that the very day on which he was sent for by the Sultan was to witness the entry of the army of occupation into Egypt. For him it was one of great anxiety, and when he left the Palace late in the evening he was surprised that no secretary or other messenger had arrived from the Embassy giving telegraphic news from Egypt. On his way homewards he met the long-expected messenger. To his anxious inquiry whether a telegram had come the answer was that it had arrived, but had taken a long time to decode. It conveyed the news that the occupation had taken place. This was a Saturday night. The state of mind of Abdul Hamid when he learnt the news could only be described as one of fury. He found that the statements made by Baker Pasha were true and that the great leader's word had been kept. British troops had entered without his co-operation or consent.

On the following day Baker, the loyal servant up to that time of Abdul Hamid, left Constantinople in a steamer bound for Alexandria and shook off the dust of his feet from a country which he ever afterwards spoke of as hopeless so long as it was under the rule of Abdul Hamid.

When the Sultan heard of his departure his anger found vent against him. The Turkish newspapers were instructed to attack him. He was denounced as a traitor. Any more ridiculous statement could hardly have been made. He had served him faithfully, had urged him to common action with Great Britain in order to save his rights in Egypt; but he had seen the imperviousness of Abdul Hamid to any argument which ran counter to his desire. In the interest of Turkey Baker had told the disagreeable truth, but he had done his utmost to save him until this last gigantic blunder.[1]

[1] Baker Pasha fled to Egypt, was welcomed there by the Khedive and his Government, and was shortly afterwards made commander-in-chief of a new army formed under his supervision. His career there, however, was an unhappy one. The Egyptian army under Hicks Pasha had been entirely destroyed by the followers of a Mahdi. Thereupon the new army under Baker was sent to resist the same enemy, but the men were poor fighters, and, in spite of the drill through which they had been put incessantly under his orders, had not stuff in them to resist the attacks of the Arab tribes in the Sudan. His army was also defeated. Baker was so upset that it was with difficulty he was prevented from committing suicide. He, however, lived on a few months longer.

The history of Abdul Hamid's dealings with Egypt during the next few years was one of intrigue with the Khedive and with disaffected Egyptian Ministers in order to interfere with British rule. Meantime, both in Parliament and out, the leaders of both political parties professed their intention to withdraw British troops from Egypt; and no one acquainted with the facts can doubt the loyalty of their intention and their desire that Egypt should continue under Turkish rule and under a good native administration. Lord Dufferin drew up a scheme for introducing a measure of self-government for the country. Intelligent foreigners, however, concluded from the first occupation that England could not relinquish Egypt, however much her statesmen desired it. The American Minister at Constantinople paid a visit to Egypt and on his return to Constantinople openly declared that, England being in, he did not see how it was possible that she could get out, however much she desired it.

Nevertheless England, not so much to comply with the desire of Abdul Hamid as because the leaders of both parties had stated that the occupation was only temporary, took a very important step in concert with Abdul Hamid in order to fix the period of British occupation.

The Wolff Convention.

A Conservative Government had succeeded to that of Mr. Gladstone, and it was Lord Salisbury who took the next step. He had been an equally ardent advocate for the entry of Turkish troops with ours, more as a symbol of Turkish authority than for any assistance they could render, and now took up the task of executing the promises made by himself and his predecessor of limiting the time during which the British troops should remain. It was under these circumstances that on August 3, 1885, the Right Hon. Sir Drummond Wolff was sent as Envoy Extraordinary on a special mission to Constantinople with reference to the affairs of Egypt, and he was undoubtedly the right man to send for such purpose, for he was experienced in diplomacy and statesmanship. Every step in the arrangement was watched with jealousy by Abdul Hamid. The Envoy took the matter very coolly, pointed out the absurdity of many of the suggestions made by the Ministers on the Sultan's behalf, but finally, in October, 1885, came to an arrangement, which was modified in January, 1887, by which the last British soldier was to leave Egypt within seven years after its confirmation by the two Sovereigns. There was in it also a proviso that if at the end of the term reoccupation became necessary, British troops should be called in to aid the Sultan in preference to those of any other Power. It was an arrangement absolutely friendly to Turkey, an arrangement which any clear-headed man, with a knowledge of the circumstances, might have considered even a triumph for Turkish diplomacy. The relations, however, between England and France were still strained. The French Ambassador in Constantinople, the Comte de Montebello, most unwisely in French interest, is understood to have advised the Sultan to reject it. He carried the Russian Ambassador with him. In spite of their opposition, the Convention was agreed to and signed *ne varietur*. Most people in Constantinople thought that the question of the occupation by British troops was finished. Englishmen generally regarded its provisions as equitable and expedient, for the political leaders of both parties had pledged themselves that the occupation should be temporary. It was therefore with surprise that the world learned that, after the English Government had given their confirmation of it, the Sultan refused to give his. It was a supreme act of folly on his part, as many of his subjects and even Ministers acknowledged. He however, with his limited vision and ignorance of European politics, considered that he had won a great diplomatic victory over England. Abdul Hamid's view was reflected in the Palace, which was exultant. All wondered what would be the attitude of the British Government. Probably to their surprise, it was found that Lord Salisbury was not in the slightest degree disturbed. He was annoyed at the bad faith of Abdul Hamid, but it was a case of *beati possidentes.*

Within a year it dawned upon Abdul Hamid that he had blundered, and that the advice given him by France and possibly Russia was not in his interest. He therefore sent instructions to the Turkish Ambassador in London to see Lord Salisbury and ask for the reopening of negotiations. The Prime Minister declared that he had no wish for further negotiations, and that, after the rejection of the Wolff Convention, he had no proposal whatever to make. Lord Salisbury, as everybody knew, could give a short answer when necessary, and no British statesman who visited Turkey sooner took the measure of Abdul Hamid's ability than did he. The reply he gave to the Turkish Ambassador probably lost nothing of its undiplomatic character in transmission. It greatly annoyed Abdul Hamid. The British Minister had forgotten apparently that the request came from the Sultan. The Turkish Ambassador was ordered peremptorily to demand the reopening of the negotiations without delay. It was near the end of the parliamentary session. Lord Salisbury replied that he was tired and must rest; moreover, the Egyptian question was not pressing and might perfectly well stand over. He would do nothing.

It was generally believed that when France and Italy came to an arrangement in 1896 in reference to Tunis an understanding was arrived at to the effect substantially that France would make no further difficulties about our occupation of Egypt, and we should make none about Tunis. Indeed, in 1904 France recognised the dominant position of England in Egypt. The Wolff Convention in fact became a dead letter. Abdul Hamid was hoist with his own petard.

In 1892 Sir F. Clare Ford was appointed British Ambassador in Constantinople, and questions arose in reference to Egypt, when once more Abdul Hamid's designs were defeated. The question of most importance was that of granting a new Firman for Abbas Hilmi, the new Khedive, successor of Tewfik. Abdul Hamid thought he saw his opportunity of endeavouring to obtain possession of a portion of the Sinai Peninsula. He in fact wished to draw a boundary line from El Arish to Suez. The Firman had been prepared, but before promulgation had to be examined by Lord Cromer. He knew the Sultan sufficiently well not to express his approval of it until he had seen the full text, but neither he nor Sir Clare Ford could persuade the Sultan to disclose it. Sir Clare went on leave, and the negotiations were successfully conducted in his absence by Sir Edward Fane. He was able to secure communication of the text for Lord Cromer a few hours before the time fixed for the Firman to be publicly read in front of the Khedivial Palace at Cairo. Lord Cromer instantly countermanded all the orders that had been given, and delayed matters about forty-eight hours until the Sultan had sent a telegram annulling the objectionable parts.[1] Abdul Hamid's intrigues had been again successfully defeated.

Yet once again, though after the expiration of the century, the Egyptian question came up, and Abdul tried the same trick in 1906 of endeavouring to change the boundaries between Turkey and Egypt. Sir Nicholas O'Conor, then ambassador and a most painstaking and careful diplomat, had to deal with the question. Izzet Pasha, who was at that time the chief secretary and favourite of the Sultan, had constructed under his orders a railway intended especially for the use of pilgrims from Damascus to Hedjaz. A small body of Turkish troops sent down from Damascus over a portion of this line already constructed occupied the village of Tabah, on the western side of the Gulf of Akaba, one of the two which form a fork at the northern end of the Red Sea. The village beyond doubt was in Egyptian territory and south of the recognised boundary between Turkey and Egypt, which runs through Akaba Rafia to a point a little to the north of El Arish. The village was so evidently in Egyptian territory that Sir Nicholas

[1] Lord Cromer in his work on "Modern Egypt" touches lightly on the subject, but Lord Milner deals with it fully.

was confident that the occupation was a simple blunder on the part of the Turks which would be at once recognised after examination of the official maps. Three months passed in negotiations. The Ministers jestingly spoke of Tabah as occupying Egyptian territory, while one even boasted that it was a try-on by the Sultan. Sir Nicholas patiently continued the negotiations, pointing out in various ways how beyond doubt Tabah was not Turkish. In May, 1906, Sir Nicholas gave formal notice to the Turks that they must evacuate Tabah, and they then might join a commission of Egyptians and Turks to draw a boundary line between the two points which had long been shown on the official map. Meantime our Mediterranean fleet had assembled at the Piræus, and Sir Nicholas now gave the Turks ten days' notice to evacuate Tabah. Then Abdul Hamid saw that he had once more blundered. His Ministers endeavoured to obtain some concession which would save the Sultan's face. But Sir Nicholas refused to give way. Finally, ten hours after the time which had been given in which the Turks were to clear out, Abdul Hamid consented to the British demands. It was a triumph for British diplomacy for two reasons: first, because the place was acknowledged to be within Egyptian territory, and second, because for the first time England's right to act on behalf of Egypt was definitely recognised by the Sultan.

Abdul Hamid's dealings with the Egyptian question afford an answer to the claims of persons who have chosen to attribute to him statesmanship. On every occasion of his dealings with Egypt he had been compelled to give way and to recede from the position which he had taken up. In the matter of Tabah he plumed himself upon the fact that he had allowed the term of the ultimatum to pass by ten hours and had thus obtained a diplomatic victory. No Englishman could doubt that when Mr. Gladstone and Lord Salisbury declared that England would evacuate Egypt they were not only sincere, but had the majority of their countrymen behind them. In rejecting the Wolff Convention,

Abdul Hamid showed at once his bad faith and his want of statesmanship. When, still earlier, he had refused to send troops with ours into Egypt, he should have recognised as a statesman that it was a grand opportunity offered him by England to assert his sovereign rights. Even at the earliest period of his reign, when England and France, acting together, deposed Ismail, a statesman would have seen that the question was largely whether such deposition was approved by the majority of his subjects. A witty French statesman during the period of our occupation declared that the cry of France for the departure of the British troops was obviously hollow, because whenever there was an announcement that they were about to leave Egypt down went the value of all Egyptian securities. Indeed, in no part of his reign is his want of statesmanship more conspicuous than in his dealings with Egypt.

Note on the Caliphate.—Before speaking of Abdul Hamid's dealing with Egyptian questions, it is well to give an account of the various opinions held by Mahometans on the Caliphate, so far at least as they bear on the claim of the Sultan of Turkey. The question is of importance to the British Empire, for within its ambit are included nearly one hundred million Moslems, out of whom some ninety million acknowledge the title of the Sultans of Turkey to what may be called the pontifical office of Islam.

The Sultans of Turkey derive the title of Caliph from the assignment made in 1518 by the then Abbaside Caliph to Selim I., the second Sultan in succession to Mahomet II., the conqueror of Constantinople.

Mahomet, the founder of the Islamic faith, with the object of preserving the integrity of his religious community, had made an arrangement by which his authority passed to a successor. His ancestors had long been guardians of the sacred shrine of the Kaaba, from which Mecca derives its sanctity, and of Medina, which contains his mausoleum, and which is held in equal veneration. It is believed among all the sects of Islam that these cities can never pass under non-Moslem guardianship without convulsing the Moslem world. Next come in order of sanctity the cities of Irak, or Mesopotamia, where lie buried the holy Imams, and Stamboul, sanctified in Moslem eyes by the remains of the holy men and the champions of the faith who lived and died there.

The four Caliphs who succeeded the founder of Islam were men of ability, and in various mosques their names are still inscribed in great letters for the veneration of the faithful.[1]

Islam is divided into two great sects, the Sunni and the Shiah, each of which, however, has many sub-sects. Out of the three hundred to three hundred and fifty millions of Moslems the Shiahs in all probability do not exceed thirty millions. They are mostly in Persia, where the State religion is Shiahism. About one-third of the population of that country are Shiahs. Both the great divisions agree that the religious efficacy of the rites and duties prescribed by the Sacred Law, and in fact the validity of Islam, depend on the existence of a vicegerent and representative of the Prophet, who as such is the spiritual head of the faithful. This spiritual head is called the Imam, or Caliph. His office is the Imamate, or the Caliphate. The great difference between the two sects consists in the fact that whilst the Imam of the Shiahs, owing to the disappearance of the last Apostolic Imam, is only spiritually present at the prayers of the faithful, the Sunni insist on his actual physical existence to preside and officiate, where possible, at the devotions of the congregation, and to impart validity to the official acts[2] of the "minor" Imams, who are his representatives or delegates among the people.

The term "Shiah" is applied exclusively to the followers of the twelve apostles of the house of Mahomet. The Shiah Imams are descended from Fatima, the daughter of the Prophet, "Our Lady of Light," as she is reverently called by the faithful, who was married to the fourth Caliph, named Ali.

The followers of Ismail, a son of the sixth Apostolic Imam who had died in his father's lifetime, broke away from the true succession and gave their adhesion to the son of Ismail. They formed a sect with doctrines which have no place in orthodox

[1] A valuable historical sketch of the history of the development of the Caliphate is given in the *Contemporary Review* of June, 1915, by the Right Hon. Syed Ameer Ali, who, besides being a Moslem himself, occupies a high position in what we may call the hierarchy of Islam.

[2] The word "officiation" would best express my meaning, but I do not find it in any dictionary.

Islam. A descendant of Ismail, Obaidullah, rose to power in Northern Africa in the tenth century, and his successors formed an empire, which became flourishing, with its capital at Cairo. They assumed the title of Caliph, and are spoken of as the Fatimide Caliphs. Their doctrines spread largely both in Asia and Africa, but their right to the Caliphate was never recognised beyond their comparatively limited number of followers. The last Caliph of this dynasty died in 1171 in Egypt, when Saladin restored Sunni orthodoxy in that country, which has since remained faithful to that form of Islam.

The Sunnis, like the Jews, believe that the Messiah is yet to come, that the Saviour of Islam is still unborn. "The Sunni Religious Law insists that the Imam must be actually present in person to impart religious efficacy to the devotions of the faithful, and that, where it is not possible for him to lead the prayers, he should be represented by persons possessing the necessary qualifications directly or indirectly representing him."[1] Such teaching reproduces to some extent the Christian notion of Apostolic Succession, but the line, so far as leading the congregation in prayer is concerned, is much less distinctly marked. As the Caliphate is believed to be ordained by divine law for the perpetuation of Islam and the perpetual observance of its laws and rules, there must therefore always be a Caliph, the actual and direct representative of the master. Syed Ameer Ali is careful to point out that, while there exists a spiritual tie between the Imam and the congregation, there is no inconsistency between this dogma and the statement that there is no priesthood in Islam. The Caliph must lead public prayers unless it is physically impossible, and this rule has long been followed by the Ottoman Sovereigns.

It was when Mahomet was stricken by his last illness that he deputed Abu Bekr to lead the prayers in his absence. On his death the master's nomination was accepted by the congregations, and Abu Bekr thus became the first Caliph. He was installed by the unanimous suffrage of the entire congregation of Moslems, and in theory this has been the universal practice ever since.

Amongst his qualifications it is necessary for the occupant of what we may call the "pontifical seat" that the Moslem chosen should be a Sunni, capable of exercising supreme temporal

[1] *Contemporary Review*, June, 1915, p. 685.

authority and independent of outside control. Syed Ameer Ali affirms that Moslem law does not insist upon his descent from the Koreish, the Arabian tribe to which Mahomet belonged, provided that he be free from personal defects, a man of good character, possessed of the capacity of conducting the affairs of state and of leading prayers. It is true that the institution of the office was when the tribe of Koreish was the most advanced and powerful in Arabia, and the one to which the Prophet himself belonged. It is admitted also that the early doctors of Moslem theology accept the authority of the "Sayings" of the Prophet, which declare that the Caliph should be a Koreish by birth, but the opponents of this view claim that the condition was due to the special needs of the time, that the Prophet was thinking only of the immediate future rather than laying down a hard and fast rule of succession for all time, and that, as a qualified and capable ruler at that time could only be found among the Koreish, the recommendation was given that the Caliph, who was also the chief Imam, should be chosen from among them.[1]

The first Caliph, Abu Bekr, nominated as his successor Omar; and the appointment was accepted by the Moslems. Omar died from the effect of a wound inflicted on him by an assassin. Before his death he had appointed an electoral committee consisting of six members. Their choice fell on Osman, who was accepted by the people. On Osman's death, Ali, the son-in-law of the Prophet, who, according to the Shiahs, ought at once to have succeeded the Prophet, was now proclaimed Caliph and Imam. Ali united in his person hereditary right and election. Revolt was made however against him. He himself was killed by the hand of an assassin, and with him ended what Moslem theologians speak of as "the perfect Caliphate," because in each case the title to the rulership of Islam was perfected by the universal suffrage of the Moslem community or nation. In 661, on Ali's death, a certain Muawiyah obtained the assignment of the Caliphate from Hassan, the eldest son of Ali and hence belonging to the Koreish. Great rivalry commenced at once between two offshoots both of which belonged to the Koreish, the most powerful of which were known as the Ommeyads. Muawiyah was the first Caliph of that house.

[1] At one time it was affirmed by some Moslem jurists, apparently to give force to the sanctity of the Abbasid Caliphs, that the Caliphate was the monopoly of the Koreish.

The Ommeyad dynasty was overthrown in 756 and was succeeded by the Abbasid, who held temporal and spiritual sway over Islam for five hundred years from their seat at Bagdad, then the most important Moslem city, the centre of its intellectual activity. It was there that the rules relating to the Caliphate were systematised. Since that time it has been generally held amongst the Sunni that the Caliph is not merely a secular Sovereign, but is the spiritual head of what we may call the Moslem Church and the actual divine agent for its government. The general rule came also to be admitted that the Caliphate is indivisible, and that there cannot be two Caliphs existing at one and the same time. Election to the office of Caliph was recognised as essential, and this usually took place with great ceremony.

The Bagdad Caliphate lasted until the destruction of the city by a Tartar-Turcoman invasion in 1258. The then Caliph, with his son and the principal members of his family, perished in the general massacre. The havoc and ruin caused by this terrible invasion, serious as it was to the Greek Empire, was still more destructive to the Moslems. When Ghengiz Khan, the "scourge of God," appeared in Asia Minor, there existed great intellectual activity under the rule of the Bagdad Caliphs. Literature, arts, and crafts of every kind were cultivated; the neighbouring cities were populous, and Islam was shown at its very best. When his successor, Hulaku, reached Bagdad, he inveigled the Caliph into his camp and then ordered the sack of the city. From Bagdad he proceeded to attack the Crusaders, who were aided happily by Baibars, the Sultan of Egypt, and for the first time met with a great check, which enabled the latter, named henceforth as "champion of Islam," to rid Syria and Mesopotamia of the Tartar horde. For a while no Caliph existed, and Syed Ameer Ali states that, according to the Sunni doctors, the devotions of religion were devoid of that religious efficacy which is imparted to them by the presence of an acknowledged Imam.

The right to the Caliphate had become vested by five centuries of Moslem prescription in the house of Abbas, and an escaped member of the house was invited to Cairo to be installed as Caliph. The ceremony is described as imposing and sacred. When his descent had been proved before the chief judge, he was acknowledged as Caliph under the title of As-Mustansir b'Illah, that is "Seeking the help of the Lord." This was in May, 1261. The new Caliph's name was impressed on the coinage and recited in the daily prayers. Thereupon he proceeded to invest the Sultan of Egypt with the Black Robe and diploma which in the eyes of the Orthodox were the essential symbols of legitimate authority.

The Abbasid Caliphate thus established in Cairo lasted for over two centuries and a half, from 1261 to 1518. Each sultan on his accession received his investiture from the Caliph of his time and professed to exercise his authority as a descendant and delegate of the Caliph. The appointments of ministers of religion and judges were subject to his formal sanction.

Selim I., the second successor of Mahomet, the conqueror of Constantinople in 1453, was girt with the sword of Osman in 1512. Egypt during the previous thirty years had been the scene of anarchy under the later Mamluk sultans, and a section of the population invited Selim to enter the country. He early overthrew the incompetent Mamluks and incorporated Egypt in the Ottoman Empire. According to the Sunni records, Selim at that time was recognised as the only Moslem Sovereign who could restore the historic character of the Caliphate and discharge effectively the duties attached to the office. Accordingly the then Caliph of Cairo in 1517 by a formal deed of assignment transferred the Caliphate to the Ottoman conqueror. In the same year Selim received the homage of the Sharif of Mecca and acquired the right of the guardianship of the Holy Cities. Solemn prayers offered in Medina and Mecca were claimed to have given finality to the right of Selim to become Caliph. Henceforward Constantinople, his seat of government, became the Dar-ul-Khailafat and began to be called by Mahometans "Islambol," "the City of Islam." Thus the Caliphate became the heritage of the Ottoman house.[1]

[1] I have followed in this notice of the Caliphate the learned and valuable essay of Syed Ameer Ali referred to on p. 144.

It is the more valuable because the Syed belongs to an ancient division of Mahometans known as the Mutazalis, whose doctrines approach somewhat more closely to those of the Shiahs than to those of the Sunni. They have constituted a distinct school of Moslem thought since the eighth century A.D. It may be added that the Syed's judicial habits of thought, great learning, and high character led to his being appointed to the position he now holds as one of the judges of our highest court of appeal.

I entirely agree with him and emphatically endorse his opinion that the question of appointing a Caliph or of interfering in the question is one which ought to be left solely to Moslems. It would be as impertinent for us as Chris-

The Syed's view is emphatically that the Turkish Sultan is Caliph. But while many Moslems would support it, others come to a different conclusion.

It is well therefore to see what other observers have said on the subject. The Rev. Dr. T. P. Hughes, an Anglican clergyman who has spent many years in India and is the author of a "Dictionary of Islam" and of an excellent summary of the Mahometan faith entitled "Notes on Muhammedanism," states that he has "not seen a single man of authority who has ever attempted to prove that the Sultans of Turkey are rightful Caliphs," and he gives a number of quotations on the subject from Mahometan writers.[1] A similar opinion is expressed by the Rev. Edward Sell.[2] Dr. Hughes, writing eight years ago and alluding to his long residence in India, says, "After a careful study of the whole subject for thirty years, twenty having been spent amongst the mosques of the Moslems, I will defy anyone to produce any reasonable proof that any Moslem school in India acknowledges Abdul Hamid as the rightful Caliph."

In the early years of Abdul Hamid, the chief mosques in Stamboul contained extracts from the Sacred Books of the qualifications required in the Caliph. About 1890, by Abdul Hamid's commands, these were ordered to be taken down, and a considerable amount of discontent was thus created amongst the Ulema. One of them asked my informant, "Does Abdul Hamid consider that we are fools, that we do not all know the extracts by heart, and does he think that because they are taken down we shall cease to teach them in the ordinary course of study?"

Having given the opposing views on the question, the reader must be left to form his own judgment.

Note on Pan-Islamism.—It is to the credit of the great body of the Ulema in Turkey that they refused to support any of the

tians to interfere in the question as it would for Moslems to interfere in the appointment of the Archbishop of Canterbury or the Pope of Rome.

With the Syed's valuable contribution may be compared a learned and impartial article in the *Quarterly Review* of July, 1915, by Mr. Stanley Lane Poole, who subjects the Caliphate to historic treatment in which he points out that the popular opinion that there is only one Caliph is incorrect. "There are in fact at the present time six." The article is full of valuable suggestions, and ought not to be overlooked by anyone desiring to form an independent opinion on the subject.

[1] Hughes, "Notes on Muhammedanism," 2nd ed., pp. 152—154.

[2] "The Faith of Islam," p. 85,

projects of Abdul Hamid when they varied from what they regarded as the precepts of their faith. As an illustration, the following will suffice: About the time when Abdul Hamid ordered the taking down of the notices of the qualifications of the Caliph he sounded the Ulema on the question whether he could rightly decree a change in the order of succession to the Ottoman throne. The result of this inquiry led him to take no further steps in what he evidently wished to do, namely to bring the law of Turkish succession into line with that which prevails in Egypt.

During the course of his reign Abdul Hamid made some attempts to create disaffection amongst the Moslem population in India. Lord Dufferin found that he had established a press at Yıldiz, and that notices and pamphlets had been published intended for distribution amongst Indian and Afghan Moslems. He interviewed the Sultan and told him very emphatically that none of these must be sent, and that any attempt made in such direction would be regarded as an unfriendly act by the British Government; that Great Britain granted and would always grant the utmost freedom to the Mahometans of the Empire. Happily they recognised the justice of our conduct in regard thereto, but the British Government would not tolerate any outside interference with the religious faith of the Moslems in the Empire. Nevertheless Abdul Hamid sent messengers to Afghanistan and elsewhere to endeavour to stir up disaffection.

All attempts in the direction of Pan-Islamism made by Abdul Hamid completely failed. Many Indian Moslems during the last forty years visited Turkey. Some of them were barristers-at-law, and the impression generally left was that, while they went to Constantinople as the pious Jew of old time might have gone to Jerusalem, they left it with far other feelings. They hoped to see Islam at its best; they went away greatly disappointed. They were often kindly treated and made much of by good Moslems, but the longer their stay in Islambol the more completely did they realise the maladministration of government, and especially the disgraceful condition of the courts of law.

Even in Turkey itself Pan-Islamism as a living force can hardly be said to have existed during Abdul Hamid's reign, for Pan-Islamism in the sense in which the term is usually employed means a fighting force in favour of the faith. However much the religion of Mahomet may have been aided by the sword in the early centuries of its progress, its spread was much more due to its ideas and its opposition to the corrupt practices of some of the degraded Eastern sects of Christianity than to violence. The time has long passed since Turks were ready to fight simply for the spread of their faith. The Senussi and some of the Mahadis and the followers here and there of individual Mahometans have caused considerable expansion of Mahometanism in Africa, Arabia, and elsewhere, but such expansion, according to the judgment of outsiders, has been due usually to their desire to bring back the simplicity of the early Islamic faith.

The real simple life and spiritual life of Islam is to be found in Turkey amongst various sects of Dervishes, such as the Mehlevis and the Bektashis. Englishmen generally are unaware how highly developed is their spiritual life. Phrases are used, prayers are recited, which recall the language of Christian mystics. The Mehlevis, the most important of the Dervish sects, have always been distinguished by their spirit of religious toleration.[1] The community is an ancient one, whose head has resided for many centuries at Konia, the ancient Iconium, is known as the "Chelibi," and has the right to gird the sword of Osman on a new sultan.

The Bektashis are not less tolerant in religious matters. The influence of these two great communities has been a humanising one on the Moslems of Turkey, and it is largely due to the wide dispersion of their members that the spread of Pan-Islamism of an objectionable character entirely failed in the Turkish Empire. The only Pan-Islamic movement which has existed is a purely religious one. The great missionary efforts that Mahometanism has made in Africa and Asia are not due to a political Pan-Islamism, but to the leaven of the sects mentioned, who understand that if missionary efforts are to succeed, they must be made by spiritual and not by temporal forces.

[1] The present Sultan, Mehmet V., is reported to be one of the members of the community.

CHAPTER X

INTERNAL ADMINISTRATION OF EMPIRE

PART I.—RAILWAYS.

First direct railway communication between Constantinople and London; the Bagdad Railway; German aspirations; general design; monopoly of railway; Russian demand; Abdul Hamid's resistance fails; Kaiser's two visits to Constantinople; declares himself protector of Moslems; the Hedjaz Railway for pilgrims to Holy Cities.

BEFORE the accession of Abdul Hamid only three lines of railway had been constructed in the Turkish Empire. A concession for the oldest, from Smyrna to Aidin (the ancient Tralles), was granted in July, 1856, and the railway was forthwith constructed. Smyrna is the principal outlet for commerce from the western part of Asia Minor, and the railway built and still held by a British company, running at its opening only as far as Aidin, helped to develop agriculture along the Mendere valley and the district to the south-east of Smyrna. In 1888 permission for extension to Dinair was granted, and in 1906 to Lake Eghirdir. In 1883–1884 a French company obtained a concession from Smyrna and built the Smyrna and Cassaba Railway. The railway built, shortly before the accession of Abdul Hamid, from Haidarpasha, on the Bosporus, to Ismidt, had already been commenced. Another line to Adrianople had also been constructed shortly before his accession, the concession having been granted to Baron Hirsch. All these lines played a useful part in the economic development of Turkey. The last-mentioned, however, stopped at Adrianople because at that time no railway existed in Bulgaria.

When Abdul Hamid ascended the throne the best routes from London to Constantinople were either by railway to Marseilles and thence by steamer to the Bosporus, or by railway to Berlin, thence to the Russian frontier, Podvolocheskoff, on to Odessa, and by steamer across the Black Sea to Constantinople. The first took a week, and the second four and a half days. Bulgaria from the establishment of the Principality saw the importance both of roads and railways, and when her line was linked up with that which the Serbians had built from the Bulgarian frontier to Belgrade, Turkey recognised the desirability of linking up her Adrianople line and thus having a direct railway communication to Belgrade, from which place already by the Austrian line the journey could be made to Vienna and Western Europe.

It was in 1888 that direct railway communication was opened between Constantinople and Paris. A steady increase in traffic took place in each succeeding year, and especially after the institution of an international train known as the Orient Express. It is sufficient to say that during the last quarter of a century the service by this train was one of successful management.

The Bagdad Railway.

The idea of constructing a railway from Constantinople to the Persian Gulf had long been entertained both in England and Germany. All agreed that such a line would be the main trunk road for the Empire. Before the opening of the Suez Canal several British engineer officers had gone over the ground and had prepared general plans for a railway. When, however, direct water communication was established between the Mediterranean and the Red Sea, a railway connection between Constantinople and Bagdad did not appeal to Great Britain. Our merchants and statesmen recognised that, so far as the Far East was concerned, the improvements already made and being made in steamer communication caused the road through the Suez Canal to be more useful and profitable than the best railway.

Their prognostications have proved correct, and it now seems more unlikely than ever that land carriage across Turkey can compete economically with that by sea. It was of the trade to and from the Far East that British engineers were mainly thinking.

Germany on her side had other views. She thought from the first of Asia Minor as a field for colonisation by her own subjects, a dream which Great Britain had never shared. German writers and thinkers had long hoped to find a place in the sun for their country in the Turkish Empire. Hemmed in by other States, Germany found her people emigrating in large numbers to the United States, to British colonies and elsewhere, and sought to find territory in which her surplus population might settle. As far back as 1830 Moltke, the great German strategist in the Franco-German War of 1870, who had spent two years in Turkish service, advocated the foundation of a German Principality in Palestine. It is doubtful whether (as is sometimes asserted) he contemplated the settlement of his countrymen elsewhere in Turkey. He probably knew the country too well to advise their entry on so serious an undertaking. In 1846, Lizt proposed the construction of a railway to Bagdad. In 1848, Rosher claimed that the heritage of the Turkish "sick man" ought to fall to Germany. In 1886, a German Oriental scholar, Sprenger, described Babylonia as "the most remunerative field for colonisation and as the only country not yet occupied by great Powers." Many German writers advocated the establishment of a Protectorate in Asia Minor. Dr. Seton Watson has traced the growth of the idea in Germany of a domination over all the territories between Berlin and Bagdad, and has shown how Germany's thinkers gave the nation a conception of a world policy that would aim at such a result. It would be out of place to attempt to repeat what he has said.[1] It may be remarked, however, that Prince Von Bismarck did not share the opinion that the future of Germany lay in the countries

[1] See "Pan-German Aspirations in the Near East," by R. W. Seton Watson, D.Litt., in *Journal of Royal Society of Arts*, March 31, 1916.

between Berlin and the Persian Gulf. Even the prospect of possessing Constantinople did not appeal to him. His ideal was of a Germany which should be closely united with Austria and which should keep on good terms with the people of the Balkan States. After the defeat of Austria at Koeniggrätz, he did not attempt to obtain from Austria any indemnity or an inch of territory. He recognised that the interests of the two States were bound up together. At a later period when the late Kaiser had allied himself with the Czar and the Emperor of Austria, and when the interests of Austria and Russia were in conflict, he threw in his influence on the side of Austria. On the accession of William II. in June, 1888, and the dismissal of Bismarck shortly afterwards, the idea of a Greater Germany which had been spread by a number of writers apparently took possession of the new Kaiser. Already the German Embassy in Constantinople had been working to secure from Abdul Hamid and his Ministers an apparently unimportant railway concession in Turkey. A short line of about forty miles long between Haidarpasha (a village adjoining Scutari, on the Asiatic side of the Bosporus and immediately opposite Constantinople) and Ismidt had been built by the Turkish Government. Such line was the natural head of a road of any kind to Bagdad. Since the time of the Emperor Justinian, in the middle of the sixth century, a considerable portion of trade between the East and the West had been diverted by the great Emperor from the Persian Gulf through Mesopotamia, Cilicia, and Konia, into two great roads, the chief of which went to Ismidt or Nicomedia. The city indeed is at the head of a great natural highway to the central tableland of Asia Minor which had been used for many centuries. The Turkish Government decided that owing to the changed circumstances of the times the termination of this great road should not remain at Ismidt, but be at the nearest point to the capital, namely Haidarpasha. This line was leased for working to a British group in 1872. In violation of the stipulation in the lease, the Turkish Government seized the railway in 1883, and after a few months handed it over to a German group. In 1889 the Anatolian Railway Company was formed in Germany to take over the line. The latter thus became possessed of the terminus of a line which constitutes the most valuable, if not the only practical, terminus of a railway from Constantinople to Konia and Bagdad. The Turks probably surmised that this was the German idea and insisted that before extending it from Ismidt in a south-easterly direction towards Konia they should build a line eastward to Angora. This extension was at once taken in hand and executed.

During the following years little or no progress was made in railway development.

In 1889, a year after his accession, the Kaiser visited the Sultan in Constantinople. The event was of importance and marks the commencement of a series of incidents which enabled the Germans to obtain a preponderating position in Turkey. From that time until the Revolution in 1908, the first care of German diplomacy was to obtain influence over the Sultan and his Ministers in order that Germany might carry out her designs in Asiatic Turkey. The most pressing of these was to obtain the right, that is, the monopoly, of constructing a railway to Konia, thence across the Taurus Range to Adana, thence to Alexandretta, and through the Amanus Range, *viâ* Aleppo, to the Euphrates, and onward to Bagdad. The visit of the Kaiser in the autumn of 1898 secured the promise of the extension of the Anatolian Railway from Ismidt to Konia, the concession for which was formally given in 1899.

On November 7, 1898, when at Damascus, the Kaiser proclaimed himself the protector "for ever" of the three hundred millions of the Moslem world. From the time of the visit to the Sultan two years later, Germany had entirely her own way with Abdul Hamid. From the capital the Kaiser went to Jerusalem, and on the anniversary of the day when Luther nailed his famous thesis on the church door of

Wittenberg he repeated the Reformer's declaration "to maintain this field."

In February, 1893, the Anatolia Company had been authorised to extend from Ismidt to Konia. This part was nearly finished in 1896. When in 1898 the Kaiser visited the Sultan, he was promised the extension to the Persian Gulf, and this was granted in March, 1903. This is the basis of the Bagdad Railway enterprise.

About this time (May, 1903) some kind of agreement was made between the Kaiser and the Emperor of Austria by which the latter was to have Salonika.[1] The first proposal of Germany was that France and England should be joined with her in supplying the capital for the construction of the Bagdad Railway, and that on the board of directors of the company to be formed for carrying out the project there should be British and French representatives. The representation proposed, however, was inadequate, as the German members could always outvote the combined British and French. Nevertheless, it was generally recognised that the construction of a railway from Constantinople to Bagdad would be of great economic value for the development of Turkey. Mr. Arthur Balfour in the House of Commons supported the enterprise, though after four or five weeks he came to take a different view, and the Bagdad Railway was recognised to be a powerful German, and not international, undertaking.

The German people expressed their delight at the prospects of the construction of such a railway, and spoke of establishing colonies of Germans all along the line. The undertaking was seriously taken in hand. The line from Ismidt to Konia and, indeed, to the Taurus Range was completed before the deposition of Abdul Hamid. Instead of crossing the Taurus through the Cilician Gates, the route chosen was to the east of that pass. The Taurus presented serious obstacles, the rocks being mostly of a friable nature, so that cuttings had to

[1] Sir Valentine Chirol is my authority for this statement. Such an agreement would explain much of the conduct of Austria during the six years preceding the Revolution of 1908.

be deep and the tunnels long. The projected line terminates on the south of the range about fifteen miles west of Adana.

A short railway between Mersina through Tarsus to Adana had already been constructed and was in working order. Fifty-five per cent. of it was owned by British subjects, the remaining forty-five by Frenchmen. The Germans negotiated with a small group which held all the French shares and purchased them in block. Having quietly bought British shares in the line whenever offered for sale, they succeeded in obtaining a dominant voice in the direction of the railway, so that it became and is now under German management. Its advantage to the Germans was that it prevented the necessity of constructing a line from the north of the Bay of Alexandretta for the purpose of carrying materials for the construction of the proposed railway. Thence it had to pass east from Alexandretta through the Amanus Range. That range is of harder rock and has not yet been completely pierced. Thence the railway proceeds through Aleppo to Jerablus (the Carchemish of the Bible), which is on the Euphrates. From the latter place to Bagdad no engineering difficulties of importance occur.

In order to provide the money for the construction of the line the German Embassy succeeded in persuading Abdul Hamid to grant heavy kilometric guarantees which the Turkish population justly regarded with suspicion.

One of the disagreeable aspects about the German railway development in Asia Minor is the suggestion of a desire, deducible from many facts, to exclude all other nations from taking part in railway development in Asia Minor. They have already acquired one of the two important lines in Turkey which terminate in Smyrna, namely that which runs to Cassaba. A strong American group, of which the heads were Mr. Chester and Mr. Colt, made a series of proposals for railway construction from Alexandretta in a north-easterly direction. They stood no chance of being accepted because they were opposed by the Germans.

Seeing that Germany had obtained the promise of the concession of a railway to Bagdad, and was opposing the grant to the subjects of other States of railway concessions in Asia Minor, especially towards the north-east, Russia grew alarmed and made a formal demand through her Ambassador that Turkey should grant no concessions in her north-eastern provinces except to Russian subjects or with the consent of the Russian Government. The demand was undoubtedly a stiff one, but it appeared to Russia, as, indeed, it did to most observers in Turkey, that Germany was doing her utmost to obtain a monopoly of railways in the Empire. She had already made much progress in securing such a monopoly. She had evicted the lessees of the line from Constantinople to Ismidt, had acquired preponderating influence over the Smyrna and Cassaba line, and had virtually annexed the Mersina, Tarsus and Adana Railway.

Russia's alarm was natural. The demand, however, was so serious that Abdul Hamid took very unusual means to have it withdrawn. He wrote to the Czar of Russia complaining of the proposal and declaring that, in presence of the friendship which existed between the two Sovereigns, it could never have been put forward with the consent of his Majesty, and he, therefore, brought it to his knowledge that it might be withdrawn. The answer he received was a curt one, to the effect that no servant of Russia dare put forward such a proposal without his Sovereign's consent. Simultaneously the Sultan addressed letters to his "friend," the Kaiser, and to Queen Victoria. The Kaiser was evidently in a difficulty. In a semi-official paper which on this occasion was believed to have been directly inspired by him, the proposal was mentioned with the remark that though the Kaiser was always ready to oblige his friend the Sultan, it must be remembered that the Czar was also his friend, and that, therefore, the case was not one in which he could interfere. The Sultan's letter to Queen Victoria was presumably handed over by her to Lord Salisbury, whom the Turkish

Ambassador in London was ordered to visit. The Ambassador's instructions were to call special attention to the provision in the Cyprus Convention by which England undertook to defend Turkey in case of any aggression made by a foreign Power. He claimed that the demand was such an aggression. Lord Salisbury, however, knew the Treaty and pointed out to him that the undertaking to defend Turkey was conditioned, among other things, by the obligation on the part of the Sultan to introduce reforms for the Armenians. Instead of carrying out this obligation, his Majesty had been murdering them.

Repulsed by all three sovereigns, Abdul Hamid conceded the demand of Russia.

The design of Germany to have the monopoly of railway traffic and of other great industrial undertakings in Asia Minor took so strong a development after the Kaiser's second visit to the Sultan that foreign residents in the country concluded that an arrangement had been made between the Courts of London and Berlin by which Germany was to be allowed a free hand in Asia Minor even to the extent of blocking British proposals. It was at a time when the relations between England and France were strained, and when the outrages in Armenia led to the belief in England that the best plan of giving security to Armenians was that the provinces in which they were numerous should come under foreign rule. To allow Germany a free hand had the advantage of suggesting that, having invested most of her capital in Asia Minor, she would take upon herself to prevent the capital falling into Russian hands.

The dreams of German colonies along the Haidar-pasha-Bagdad line had already before the Revolution of 1908 proved illusory. No German colonies in the Empire exist, except small ones, mostly of Second Adventists, in Palestine. It is as unlikely that they ever will exist as that colonies of British settlers will ever establish themselves in India. Climatic conditions count for something, but the great obstacle is that already the line is surrounded by sufficient inhabitants who cannot and ought not to be dispossessed by those belonging to any foreign race.

It is useless to predict what will be the immediate future of the Turkish Empire, but whoever may be the possessors of the territories through which the line from Constantinople to Bagdad and the Persian Gulf may pass, it should be placed under international management. Assuming that Turkey is to remain in possession of the country, she is too hopelessly incapable of managing so great an undertaking. The only departments or undertakings in Turkey which have proved successful are those which are managed by foreigners. If, therefore, no satisfactory arrangement is arrived at by which the Bagdad Railway should have an international administration, it would be well to place its management under the Department of the Public Debt, if that institution should survive the present cataclysm.

Serious complaints were made by the people of Turkey on account of the large kilometric guarantees which were assigned to the railway company to be paid from the revenues of the districts through which the line passes. But the development of the country made by the railway will probably amply cover the guarantees necessary and will benefit the peasants. It may be added at the same time that it was only the great influence which the Germans had acquired over Abdul Hamid, which could have induced him to resist the popular outcry against the apparently excessive guarantees.

That the Bagdad Railway will be completed is certain. Whatever Power or Powers are in possession of the country through which it passes, its importance for commercial purposes will be recognised. Its construction has gone on slowly but steadily during the last ten years. The engineering difficulties in the Taurus are being rapidly overcome. Those encountered in tunnelling through the Amanus Range are more serious, but are already vanishing. Already in 1916, by far the larger portion of the line is constructed. These, once overcome, the road to Jerablus, on the Euphrates, is clear. The desert beyond only presents difficulties in crossing the rivers.

In reference to the project generally, it may be safely observed that every inch of railway built in Turkey is a gain to the population. Crops rotting in the fields, fertile land practically uncultivated, the absence of means of communication between one town and another or between the towns and the sea contributed largely to increase the poverty to which nomads and misgovernment had reduced Turkey. The returns made to the Department of Public Debt, which may always be taken as trustworthy, show that wherever a railway has passed through any given province its revenues have been largely increased.

Germany had sacrificed much to obtain the Bagdad concessions. She had spent money lavishly. Above all, had declined to aid the other Powers in obtaining good government for Crete, for Armenia, and Macedonia for fear of losing influence with Abdul Hamid. The interest of the resident inhabitants was sacrificed to the economic interests of Germany. At a time when English and French residents in the capital incurred the enmity of the Sultan by sheltering Armenians from his cruel clutches, Germans, evidently acting under orders, refused to render any similar aid. Germany had sold her soul for the Sultan's favour.

The Hedjaz Railway

The most important outcome of Abdul Hamid's Pan-Islamism was the execution of a project which was carried out by his ablest Private Secretary Izzet Pasha, namely, the construction of a railway from Damascus to the Hedjaz. The Secretary was a man of great intelligence and possessed exceptional knowledge of questions connected with the internal condition of the Empire. A Syrian Arab by birth, he went to Constantinople as a young man and shortly afterwards obtained an appointment as a Judge in Macedonia. Even while in that Province he formed a very poor opinion of the Turkish Ministers and others in the immediate *entourage* of the Sultan. After some years he succeeded in getting himself transferred to the capital where he was promoted to be a Judge in the most important Commercial Court which deals with cases between Turkish subjects and foreigners. His chance came after interviews with the Sultan, who recognised that he had not only an exceptional knowledge of what concerned Syria and Arabia, but also of Macedonia, with which the European Powers were continually troubling his Majesty. Before long he acquired possibly more influence with the Sultan than any other subject. He continued to be his Private Secretary until the Revolution in 1908 and then fled from the country.

The pilgrimage to Mecca is one of the four requirements or "pillars" of Islam. At all times there has been a steady number of Believers who have made their way to the Moslem Holy Land. In the absence of statistics of any value, it may be said generally that the number of pilgrims had fallen off during the first years of Abdul Hamid's reign. Of late years, however, and largely owing to the conquests of Russia in Central Asia, the number of pilgrims had steadily increased. The men usually bring with them considerable sums of money to meet the expenses of the long route. In the early days of Abdul Hamid many died on the way. The pilgrimage was always a trying one for the pilgrims, but was regarded as a gold mine by the tribes of Bedouins, especially in Northern Arabia to the east of the Jordan. In the autumn of 1876, the British Consul declared that the common form of dowry among the Bedouins was the share of booty which should fall to the bridegroom when the next annual caravan for the Holy Places was plundered. It is not too much to say that at that time and down to the construction of the railway, every caravan had to pay outrageous sums of blackmail either to Bedouin chiefs or to the Turkish Governors. Hence it is not necessary to suppose, as was commonly alleged, that Izzet Pasha in advising the construction of the Hedjaz Railway was seeking to serve his private ends. The Sultan, who was for the moment ready to engage in any scheme which would increase his influence as Caliph, readily fell in with the plan of his Secretary, and, accordingly, in the summer of 1900 Abdul Hamid commenced the construction of a railway from Damascus to the Hedjaz. Already a line had been built from Haifa to the Horan and Damascus. A few years before the Hedjaz Railway was opened Abdul Hamid had made one of his spasmodic efforts to increase his reputation as Caliph and to spread Mahometanism. He had founded or rebuilt a certain number of mosques and had sent many preachers into Africa. Yet it cannot truthfully be said that in building the Hedjaz Railway he had no other reason for favouring the project than that of facilitating pilgrimage. His hold upon the Arabs around Yemen was always slight, and a railway would be of value for keeping them in order. The undertaking was a difficult one, and the difficulty was increased by his desire to show the Moslem world that a railway for a religious purpose could be constructed entirely by Moslems. Its cost was almost entirely met by contributions from Mahometans in all parts of the world. Although the designs and the supervision of the construction had to be entrusted largely to foreigners, the idea was never lost sight of that the railway was intended for Moslem pilgrims. It is probable also that Abdul Hamid hoped that the railway would enable him to recover his influence in Egypt. Nevertheless, the railway was one of public utility, and Abdul Hamid deserves credit for having encouraged so useful an undertaking. It is now complete as far as Medina.[1]

Besides the railways mentioned, five short ones deserve notice. One is from Mudania, on the Sea of Marmora, to Brussa. The line had been planned and partly completed before Abdul Hamid's accession. Locomotives and a certain amount of rolling stock had

[1] In a later chapter it will be seen that one of the charges brought against the Sultan was that a large sum collected for the construction could not be accounted for.

been provided. All were allowed to remain unused for years before permission was granted to complete the line. The second also started from Mudania and runs to Smyrna. The third, about forty miles long, is between Jaffa and Jerusalem. In connection with Damascus are two lines; the first, running on an old coach road, built by a French company from Beyrout across the two ranges of Lebanon, and the second, from Haifa.

The amount of railway development during Abdul Hamid's reign was small. It was small owing mainly to the rotten condition of his administration. It is true that the Sultan disapproved almost every kind of public works. Probably, so far as he held any convictions whatever on the subject, he agreed with one of his early Ministers who expressed his distrust of railways, and claimed that so long as the Turks had only their camels and horses they were prosperous and happy. But in spite of the fact that Abdul Hamid told Mr. Joseph Chamberlain and other Europeans that he wished to see his country covered with a network of roads and railways, he was himself the great obstacle to their construction. After he had got rid of the reformers, his employees were allowed a free hand in obtaining bakshish. It was the price paid for their sycophancy; no concessions could be obtained without it. One of the members of a British firm, which up to his arrival in Constantinople had had the largest experience in the world in railway construction, was sent for by the Grand Vizier, on the occasion of his visit to the Bosporus, and asked whether he would not apply for a railway concession. His answer probably startled the Minister. He would not apply; because his firm did only clean business. He had carefully looked into what had been done in Turkey, and found that the only way to carry out public works was to distribute bakshish freely and his firm had refused to fall in with such practice. When this was promised, bad work was passed; extra charges allowed, and peculation of every kind tolerated. Abdul Hamid is responsible for making no attempt to put an end to the practice. Indeed in popular belief—which may be admitted in such cases to be of doubtful value—he himself shared in some of the large sums paid for all important concessions.

CHAPTER X—*continued*

INTERNAL ADMINISTRATION OF EMPIRE—*continued*

PART II.—THE TURKISH PUBLIC DEBT

Story of the Turkish Department of the Public Debt. Turkey practically bankrupt on accession of Abdul Hamid; paper money; proposal to cede revenues from six different sources to be collected and administered for holders of Turkish bonds; proposal by Porte discussed with Mr. Robert Bourke on behalf of British and other bondholders; results in Decree of Muharem, December 20, 1881; formation of Council for the administration of the Ottoman Public Debt; successful from first; illustrations of good management; unification; proposal to manage collection and apportionment of revenues for payment of kilometric guarantees; Department never officially recognised by British Government: Why? Ameliorations in financial service introduced; formation of Tobacco Regie; silk industry re-created and viniculture assisted by Department; a Department which made for progress.

Story of the Turkish Department of the Public Debt

OWING to the extravagance of Abdul Aziz, which, as already mentioned, led to his deposition, Turkey on the accession of Abdul Hamid was on the verge of bankruptcy. New loans were contracted with local bankers, and outside Turkey, to pay the interest on debts. The financial administration was utterly rotten, and probably not more than 40 per cent. of the taxes collected found its way into the Treasury. The Public Debt outside the Empire amounted to 190,750,000 Turkish pounds (the Turkish pound is equal to 18*s.* 2*d.*). During 1875-6 expenses rapidly increased from various causes. The amount of revenue fell. The Turkish Government were forced to recognise that some remedy must be found. They were unable to float more loans or otherwise borrow more money. They were, in fact, living from hand to mouth, mostly upon small loans obtained from Galata bankers.

On September 11, 1875, Turkey had committed what in a private individual would have been an act of bankruptcy. She ordered the suspension of the payment of one-half of the interest and sinking fund from the following month, with the exception of those on the Egyptian Tribute Loans, and of one made in 1855 guaranteed by the British and French Governments. Then came many makeshifts to obtain money. Paper currency, locally known as *caismes*, was issued. The Turkish sovereign or lira (the equivalent of 100 gold piastres) was the standard. The Government in issuing *caismes* declared that the one lira note was equivalent to 120 silver piastres, the usual rate of exchange being 108. The promises made by the Government were so alluring to the ignorant of the community that many of them brought forward their savings and converted their gold and silver into paper money. Gradually and rapidly its value depreciated so that within a few weeks, the happy possessor of a gold lira could exchange it for 160 paper piastres, and the poor peasants thought that the operation of their paternal Government was for their benefit. To such an extent did this fiction prevail that even the tradesmen in Constantinople made but slight advance in their prices, evidently believing that the fall in the value of the paper was a rise. When the war with Russia broke out, they began to realise their mistake, for suddenly Turkish gold rose from 160 to 300 piastres the lira, and finally no one would take the paper money, except at an outrageously low value. When the Russian War was over, the leading financial establishments in the country, of which the Imperial Ottoman Bank was the most important, refused further advances unless those which they had previously made were secured. They made a practical suggestion that six revenues paid to the Government, known as the "Six Indirect Contributions," should be handed over to a committee of local bankers to be collected and administered by them. After considerable negotiations this condition was accepted in principle on November 22, 1879. The "Six Contributions" were the total revenue derived from tobacco, salt, wines and spirituous liquors, stamps, fisheries, and silk, subject to a reduction of one million sterling, but plus the contribution of Eastern Rumelia and Cyprus and the tribute of Bulgaria. All these were to go to bondholders.

The Porte and Abdul Hamid still found the difficulty of borrowing money serious. It was indeed impossible, except by the consent of the Ottoman Bank and of the local bankers who acted in accord with it. They were determined in their own interest and in that of the foreign bondholders, that so much at least of the income of the country as was necessary to meet the interest upon the bonds, should be set apart from the general revenue for their benefit and that of the bondholders whom they represented. In order, moreover, to obtain new loans from abroad, it was equally necessary to satisfy the bondholders that old and new loans should be secured by a sound administration. The original scheme required enlargement and amendment. It could not be left in the hands of local bankers.

The stoppage of payment of interest on the bonds already mentioned had been a terrible blow to Turkish credit. In England and France, Turkish securities had been favourably regarded because they offered 1 or 1½ per cent. more interest than could be obtained on British or French Government securities. This was a tempting bait to numbers of middle-class investors, to whom the difference between 3 per cent. and 4 or 4½ meant great difference in comfort. Moreover, it was well known that Englishmen in high positions who had had experience in Turkey, had believed in the solidity of Turkish guarantees. It was notorious that even the great Ambassador who became Lord Stratford de Redcliffe, had made large investments in Turkish funds. It was therefore not wonderful that such funds constituted a favourite form of investment. The same observation applies to France, but an additional inducement had made French small investors eager to hold Turkish bonds. Owing to different arrangements on the French Bourse from those in England, they were a favourite form for that kind of gambling which is known as "buying and selling differences," the simplest form being the purchase of a large amount of bonds to be delivered at a later date, which both buyer and seller recognise that the buyer would probably be unable to take up, that is, to pay for. If in the interval between the purchase and the date fixed for delivery the market price of such securities had risen or fallen, one or other of the parties pocketed the difference. The fluctuations of the market during the period between 1875, when the first decree was issued reducing the amount of interest to half, and the end of 1879, were enormous, and affected not merely Government securities but the shares of the various banks and other establishments doing business in Turkey, and of the institutions which had business operations with the Government. Thus, for example, the shares of the Ottoman Bank fell for two or three days to about £2 15*s*., and rose within two years to about £25. This was mainly due to speculation in Paris, and dismay arose, because it was recognised by the directors themselves that the latter figure was above their actual value. All concerned, including the Turkish Finance Minister, recognised that in such a fluctuating and unsteady market, it was impossible to obtain new advances from Europe. The bankers' project must be modified. Accordingly, when on October 3, 1880, the Porte addressed the Embassies, suggesting that the foreign bondholders should appoint delegates to proceed to Constantinople to come to an understanding, the invitation was accepted. The English and French bondholders had already commenced to act together, but now they, as well as the Dutch, Austrian, German and Italian bondholders, formally elected delegates.

The Right Hon. Robert Bourke, M.P., represented the British and Dutch. The first idea was that the delegates should form an International Commission, but

Mr. Bourke found the plan open to two objections; first, that the delegates were unlikely to agree among themselves, and second, that the Porte would not entertain a proposal by which it should be left out. The case would be one of "reckoning without your host."

The Dutch, who held a considerable number of Turkish bonds, wisely placed their interests in the hands of the British Council of Foreign Bondholders and decided that its delegate or delegates should act also for them. The Imperial Ottoman Bank and its group acted for the French bondholders, the chief place of business for such bank, though nominally in Constantinople, being really in Paris. A few German bondholders were represented by Herr S. Bleichröder. In Italy also there were Turkish bondholders, and these were represented by the Italian Chamber of Commerce. Negotiations took place between the delegates and a Turkish Commission of six members, and between them and the Porte. The result was that an agreement was come to which resulted in the promulgation of a law known as "The Decree of Muharem." Such decree bore date of December 20, 1881, or in Turkish, the 28th day of the month of Muharem. Mr. Bourke had arrived in Constantinople at the end of August, 1881. His report presented to the bondholders is dated January 10, 1882.

The issue of this decree was an event of high importance for Turkish finance. Thereupon the Council for the Administration of the Ottoman Public Debt became a Turkish Institution, commonly known as the Debt or the Public Debt. The largest amount of foreign bonds being in English and French hands, it was decided that the United Council of Foreign Bondholders should be under an English or French President, each of whom should hold office alternately for a period of five years.[1]

The British representatives always played an important, perhaps, indeed, the most important, part on the Council of the Public Debt, and were successively, Sir Hamilton Lang, Sir Edgar Vincent, Sir Vincent

[1] Article XV., Decree of Muharem.

Calliard, Sir Edward Fitzgerald Law, Sir Henry Babington Smith and Sir Adam Block.

This is not the place in which to give the history of the development of the Institution which took in hand the management of the conceded revenues for the benefit of the bondholders. But every year that passed increased its efficiency, satisfied the bondholders, and, what is of more importance, reduced into order the administration, collection and application of the public funds. Nor is this the place to speak of the unification of the Turkish Debt, and of the various manipulations of the same which were mutually beneficial to the Turks and their creditors. The revenues collected by the Public Debt, greatly increased from 1882 to 1903. In the latter year the increase became more rapid, owing probably to the unification (on September 1, 1903), by which the Turkish Government itself obtained an interest in the revenues, since three quarters of the surplus after the payment of the interest and sinking fund of the Debt went to it directly, whilst the remaining one quarter was utilised for sinking fund purposes.

In 1889 the Turkish Government, which, after some hesitation, had come to recognise the utility of the Public Debt for its own purposes, joined with certain railway companies to which the Government had granted kilometric guarantees in requesting the Department to take over the administration of revenues outside those conceded by the Decree of Muharem for the payment of such guarantees. Whether it was a good or a bad thing from the bondholders' point of view, is a moot question, but there is no doubt that it was to the advantage of Turkey. In subsequent years further revenues were specially assigned for collection by the Public Debt. These steps meant better administration, that is, a greater approach to justice for the taxpayers and more revenue for the Turkish Treasury, and for the foreign bondholders. In the last few years the Turkish Government showed an increasing desire to hand over their revenues for collection by the Public Debt, and if events had pursued a normal course, the Department would probably have been made collectors of the revenues for the whole of the Turkish Empire.

When the Revolution of July, 1908, happened, the Young Turks recognised that the Department could administer the finances of the Empire better than they could; that native officials, trained by it, were not only more efficient, but less open to corruption, and that there was a regularity in the Debt's administration which had never been attained under Turkish management.

The Members of the Council of the Public Debt, acting under a succession of able Presidents who held office until the outbreak of the present war, succeeded in making the Ottoman Public Debt Department certainly the most efficient and best organised administration in Turkey, and one which would bear comparison with any corresponding administration elsewhere. It is tempting to enter fully upon the services which this Turkish Department, officered by Europeans, has rendered to Turkey as well as to its constituents, the bondholders. Some details of its achievement, especially in later years, may, however, be noted. Its gross receipts during the year 1903-4 were £T2,971,984. The corresponding receipts of 1911-12 had steadily risen to £T5,061,335, or, deducting new Customs dues, to £T3,910,150. This was an increase during the interval, of nearly one million Turkish pounds, a proof at once that the revenue of the country was increasing, and that the administration of its finance had greatly improved. Taking an average during the thirty years in which the revenues were administered by the Public Debt, there is an increase during this period of 79·07 per cent. The tables published in the Special Report on the Public Debt by Sir Adam Block in January, 1914, show that this increase in the revenues administered by the Council of the Public Debt had been steadily progressing during each of its three decades.[1]

Provision had been made in the Unification Scheme for redemption. In 1904-5 (which is taken because redemption only took place in six months of the previous

[1] Sir Adam Block's Report, pp. 17-19.

year, 1903) £T222,398 represented the value of debts redeemed. In 1912–13 £T621,610 was devoted to redemption. During the years from 1903 to the end of 1913, including the six months of 1903-4, no less a sum than £T4,329,028 had been applied for that purpose, the whole representing 10·24 per cent. of the Public Debt. Bondholders as well as everybody who wished well for the financial situation of Turkey, must have recognised that this was a brilliant result. In addition, the effect of dealing with Turkish Lottery Bonds, which, though not quoted on the London Exchange, are a favourite form of investment on the Continent, must be noted; on September 1, 1903, the date of the Decree of Unification of the Turkish Debt, the nominal capital of the Lottery Bonds was £T13,448,789. Between 1903 and the end of 1913 bonds for the nominal value of £T509,604 were cancelled. As mentioned in the case of the conceded revenues in the period between 1903-4 and 1912-13 these Lottery Bonds were as usual drawn for cancellation, the number drawn being proportionate to the amount which the Public Debt had at its disposal for dealing with them. In 1904-5 the nominal value of drawn bonds was £T41,663; this steadily increased until in 1914 £T79,755 were drawn. Provision had been made also for a Reserve Fund of two million pounds sterling. This Reserve Fund still exists and, according to the latest information, is intact.

Considerable sensation was created in Constantinople at the time of the unification when it was stated that a secret understanding had been come to between the French and the Germans, by which the three-quarter surplus of the conceded revenues should be assigned as a guarantee for the payment of the loans issued for the construction of the Bagdad Railway. The work of collecting by the Council of the Debt for railway guarantees was of course not contemplated in the Decree of Muharem, and though public opposition was marked against such guarantees, especially to the Bagdad Railway, the collection and administration of a portion of the tithes, which were set aside for such guarantee, were taken over with general satisfaction by the Public Debt. Here, as in other matters, there was a steady and rapid improvement in the gross receipts under its administration. The totals published in Sir Adam Block's Report (p. 64) are valuable, because they suggest that there is reasonable hope that heavy though the payments were which had to be made for kilometric guarantee on the railway, the increased produce of the districts through which the railway passed, produced increased revenues, and this with the result that a smaller amount of guarantee was necessary. Thus, for example, the total of guarantees paid in the year 1908 was £T771,509. This went on steadily decreasing until in 1912 (the last year for which we have returns) the amount of guarantees paid was only £T341,388.

That the Public Debt Department has been a great success and promised much for the financial regeneration of the Turkish Empire, is admitted by everyone acquainted with the country. Curiously enough, and unlike the delegates of all foreign States, the British delegate was never officially recognised by the British Government. Nor indeed was the Department itself. Its delegate was in consequence at a disadvantage in comparison with his colleagues. The latter were representatives of their Governments, which took great interest in their doings, and in the economic progress and financial reforms which the Public Debt Department was slowly but steadily carrying out in the Empire. In this respect, British diplomacy did not compare well with that of some of the other Powers. The attitude too often taken even by our Ambassadors was that they had nothing to do with trade or economic questions. Their example was contagious, and affected the British Consular Service. One British Consul-General was deservedly snubbed by an Ambassador who took exceptional interest in trade questions, because he stated that he knew nothing and cared little about tariff questions on Turkish railways. Germany's influence in Turkey during the last fifteen years was largely due to her keen interest in such questions, and to the support which she gave to her business men. Whether greater collaboration and co-operation between the Government and banking and commercial interests, with the object of assisting bankers and traders to obtain and do business, is a good policy or not, it is one which England in the Near East has not followed. The refusal to recognise the Department of the Public Debt is possibly due to the same antiquated aristocratic contempt for anything that has to do with commerce or shopkeeping. The Department of the Public Debt was not to be recognised because it was only concerned with matters of finance. But in Turkey and the Near East generally, political and financial interests are always closely allied.

The many reforms accomplished by the Public Debt, and especially during the administration of Sir Adam Block, and in spite of the non-recognition of that Department by the British Foreign Office, redound greatly to his credit. In one important respect Sir Adam had an enormous advantage over his predecessors in that he knew Turkish as well as he knew his native tongue. He had been the Embassy First Dragoman, but abandoned that position because he could rise no higher in the Consular Service to which he belonged and, by the practice of our Foreign Office Service, could not be taken into that of diplomacy. The Turkish Public Debt gained; but our Diplomatic Service lost by his transfer.

While what has been said will give an idea of the progress and general utility of the Public Debt Administration, it conferred other advantages on Turkey which are deserving of notice. The collection of the revenues of the country became more regular. The terrible leakage was greatly lessened. The collectors and inspectors, who were at first mostly foreigners, showed neither fear nor favour. The amount paid in to the Treasury steadily increased. Assessments for the purposes of taxation which were found in disorder were corrected. Wealthy men had been able to bribe the assessors so that they should pay less. Poor men had no redress when assessed beyond the value of their property. Great care was taken by the Public Debt in the appointment of the first inspectors, and as they and their successors, Turkish subjects, were well paid, fairly treated and supported by the Council in just demands, men of excellent character were forthcoming.

It was interesting and hopeful to see the reform that was made in assessment; interesting because it showed that the general belief in the corruption of the old officials was well founded; hopeful because it demonstrated that the revenues of the country might be largely increased without unfair pressure on the peasants. During the early years of the Public Debt, the inspectors and the chief officials were partly foreigners and partly natives. The Department was rortunate in obtaining a few foreigners who spoke Turkish well, and who could deal with the proprietors without the necessity of native interpreters. A strong and proper desire existed in the Council to employ natives wherever possible. They soon found, especially amongst the Armenians, trustworthy and efficient servants, who, once they recognised that the pilferings and even wholesale robberies of pervious years would no longer be tolerated and that they would be protected, lent valuable aid to their employers. Indeed, on many occasions the Council of the Public Debt have borne testimony to both the sagacity and knowledge which were displayed by the native contingents of assessors. It was shown for the first time in recent Turkish history, that the country could produce as efficient public servants as any other, once it was recognised that honesty was the best policy, as under the Public Debt it soon proved itself to be. Every year increased the efficiency of the Department.

Looked at with a certain suspicion and never recognised officially by the British Government, regarded with anxiety by Abdul Hamid, and not entirely trusted either by Russia or Germany, the influence of the Public Debt steadily increased until the outbreak of the world-war.

Abdul Hamid and his Ministers saw that the collection of the conceded revenues was made fairly and that, without getting into serious conflict with his Government, the Department every year had an increase of revenue in which his country participated. Germany so completely abandoned her distrust that it was she who suggested that the collection of the revenues from which her kilometric guarantee was to be paid should be taken over by the Public Debt.

The Department was a success because, though nominally Turkish, its direction was in the hands of foreigners. But, at the same time, it was training up a new generation of native public servants, whose influence was gradually spreading to other departments of the State and leading to honest habits. Fears, indeed, were entertained during some years that Abdul Hamid would either abolish the Department or claim to make such modifications in the Decree of Muharem as would largely diminish its value. Such fears proved groundless.

The extent of smuggling, especially of tobacco, induced the Department to approve a project which met with no opposition from the Turkish Government, of separating tobacco from the list of the "Six conceded revenues." A company was formed, mainly with French capital, to purchase the rights of the Public Debt Department, to deal with tobacco. The formation of such a company, which was to work in co-partnership with the Government, had been anticipated during the visit of Mr. Bourke. In return for these rights the company was to pay £T750,000 per annum to the Public Debt. The company itself was officially described as "Co-interested with the Ottoman Government," and as a company "*en regie*," literally, "in trust." The Regie Company, as it is usually described in Turkey, was never greatly approved by Abdul Hamid. Under the provisions of its constitution it had the right to appoint "coljies," or officers, to preserve the rights of the Regie. For some years the conflicts which took place between them and the native smugglers were almost constant in every part of the country, the worst offenders being ill-paid soldiers. Abdul Hamid probably for this reason never entered cordially into the plans for suppressing smuggling.

The Department had a long fight in order to suppress smuggling. It would probably be difficult to find a smoker in Turkey who has not had offered to him packages of Turkish tobacco at a price less than half that of the same quality sold by the agents of the Department of Public Debt, or its present substitute the *Regie Ottomane de tabac*. The smuggling of tobacco, indeed, in the early years of the Department was general throughout the Empire.[1]

The notice of the Public Debt Department may be concluded by mentioning other incidental but important services which it rendered to Turkey. Among its active members was Sir Vincent Caillard. To him, acting for the Department, probably more than to any other person, is due the revival of the silk industry in Turkey. In 1880 that industry was practically dead. In the 'seventies of last century it had been flourishing about Nicaea, in the neighbourhood of Brussa, and in a wide stretch of country south of the Marmora. Tens of thousands of mulberry trees had existed, furnishing the leaves on which the silkworms feed. Nearly all had been cut down because there were no silkworms to be fed. A fatal disease had appeared amongst them, which had destroyed the industry even more completely than the terrible "phylloxera" had done that of the wine trade of France. Sir Vincent took advantage of the results of modern science. The French chemist, Pasteur, had found a remedy both against phylloxera and the silkworm disease; a small school of sericulture was established by the Department, which resulted in the re-establishment, under happier conditions, of the silk industry in Turkey. Pasteur had found that under the microscope the eggs of the silkworm moth, when they were black, indicated that the mother moth was

[1] Even as late as June, 1914, on a visit to Marsovan, two days' carriage journey inland almost due south of Sansoun, it was difficult to buy cigarettes which had been made by, or under the Ottoman Regie. Unless the buyer were suspected of being a spy, the seller would volunteer the statement that he had better tobacco at a lower price, which was, of course, smuggled.

diseased. The question, therefore, was of finding out which were the moths free from disease and of keeping only the eggs, or, as they are technically called, the "seed" of healthy moths. The sight in the school was an interesting one. In one corner was a great heap of small muslin bags, each about three inches square, the muslin being of the thinnest and cheapest variety. In each was a dead moth and her eggs. Upon a table were several microscopes, each magnifying 1,200 times. The process of selecting healthy seed was a simple one. One of the bags was opened, the dried moth placed in what looked like a toy mortar; a toy pestle with a glass of water was at hand and a few drops poured into the mortar and stirred rather than beaten with the pestle and then a drop was placed under the microscope. The observer could see at once whether there were any blacks seeds or not. If there were any, the bag was thrown into a receptacle to be burnt; if there were none, the mother was pronounced to have been free from disease. In this way healthy silkworm seed was placed on the local market. The most interesting feature was to see peasant boys of thirteen or fourteen who took great interest in learning the simple process. The villagers united to subscribe the £12 necessary to buy a microscope amongst them and soon learnt how to select the healthy seed. The movement spread with great rapidity. Peasants, Moslems and Christians, alike, knew the value of the industry and did their part well. So successful indeed were they that two years after the introduction of the school of sericulture a cartload of mulberry leaves was selling at twenty times the former price, when the enormous number of mulberry trees existed.

A somewhat similar service was rendered to the country in connection with viniculture. Phylloxera, which had devastated France, made its appearance in Turkey. It was curious to see how irregularly and yet how steadily it spread. Vineyards within three or four miles of Constantinople, which had manifestly been stricken by the disease, were within half a mile of others which were entirely free from it. Here again the Public Debt Department came to the aid of the peasants. It had been found that a native American vine had sufficient vitality to withstand the attacks of the phylloxera, and that other vines when grafted upon the American were also able to withstand it. The Department established a school of viniculture. Thousands of American vines were planted and were sold to the cultivators at little more than cost price. In other ways the Public Debt Department proved a benefit to the country.

The administration of the Public Debt has been dealt with at some length because it is the one Department under the rule of Abdul Hamid which made for progress. The Turk has never had an aptitude for business or commerce, that instinctive aptitude for business which has for many centuries characterised the Jewish, the Armenian, and certain other races. The accounts of a wealthy Turkish pasha are usually in a muddle, and his absence of power of control causes him to fall an easy victim to men of other races. His ability as a soldier is no match for the cunning of the stranger in the economic struggle. His extravagance is often limited only by his inability to borrow more money. The transmitted habits of centuries suggest an explanation. The nomad Turk had little regard for the property of others, and his modern representative reproduces this trait. He never acquires a fortune by thrift. The Turkish peasant always has been poor: a simple industry like that of silk-making or of viniculture appeals to him and is within the measure of his capacity. To have assisted him to overcome the difficulties created by what he regarded as Kismet was a service useful to him and to the country.

The improvements in Abdul Hamid's reign connected with financial administration, with collection of taxes, the stoppage of leakage, especially of the portion that should find its way into the public Treasury, and in a dozen different directions, were due to the admirable administration of the Department of Public Debt.

It furnished hope to the country for the future, not so much because it largely increased the revenue going to the bondholders and the Treasury, as from the fact that it had become a moral influence under whose example a large number of employees were being trained to be honest and efficient. The Department itself was presenting a model to the public of an administration in which the heads were bent upon introducing changes which would benefit the country as well as themselves. As the one great healthy institution which was created and developed during Abdul Hamid's reign it will always be remembered.

CHAPTER X—*continued*

INTERNAL ADMINISTRATION OF EMPIRE—*continued*

PART III.—ARMY-NAVY GENDARMERY

1. Army becomes demoralised. 2. Navy remains idle. 3. Gendarmery projects. 4. Postal service by Turks fails. 5. Establishment of School of Medicine.

1. *The Turkish Army's Degeneracy under Abdul Hamid.*

ABDUL HAMID's treatment of the fighting forces of Turkey merited and obtained the condemnation of all classes of his subjects, but especially of the Moslems. The Turks have always formed a military caste. They know little of agriculture except in its most primitive form. They have always looked upon commerce with the contempt of ignorance. Trades and industries, except in such simple forms as keeping small village shops, are left to the giaours who profit by Turkish dislike of such occupations. There are, indeed, a few village industries, such as carpet weaving, in which men and women work, but it is rare, indeed, that they are not superintended by Christians. But soldiering is the real business for which the Turk has an aptitude. Its alternate demands for energetic service and periods of lethargy suit his temperament. On many a battlefield and during long centuries he has proved himself a valiant soldier. In the Turco-Russian War of 1877-8 he fought well both in Europe and Asia Minor. All the glories of his race were won on the field of battle. The sieges of Rhodes and of Belgrade in carrying out the policy bequeathed by Mahomet II., in which those places were captured, and that of Plevna in which the Turk lost, all bore witness to his value as a fighter. The battlefields of Maritza in which the South Slavs were defeated, and that of Kossovo-pol in which Northern Serbia was reduced to slavery; the bloody field of Mohacz, the siege and capture of Buda-Pest, all attest his competence and endurance. It is true that all the battles had been won mainly by Janissaries, and that they were to a man, Christians of origin, but the Janissaries had been absorbed into the population and furnished good fighting blood to the nation. The second Mahmud, during the first quarter of last century, had introduced Western drill into the Army, and in the Crimean War the Turk did not make a bad show. After that war, French officers were introduced into Turkey, and did their best to improve it.

When Abdul Hamid was girt with the sword of Othman, or Osman, the army was a fairly good fighting machine. The reform in it made by Mahmud II. and the experience of the Crimean War had been beneficial. He, however, knew of the French debacle of 1870-1, and within four years of his accession obtained German officers to replace those from France. But already the demoralisation, which was largely due to his opposition to all reforms so long as he could secure his own personal safety, was working like a venom in all the body politic. Just as he obtained British officers to make England believe that he wished effectively to police the country, and having obtained them did not allow them to work, so he wanted German soldiers to persuade Europe that his army would be in line with European armies. No blame can be justly attributed to the officers sent from Germany; yet from General Von der Golz downwards they effected few beneficial changes in the army and this because the Sultan only wanted a show army. The troops around Yildiz made a goodly appearance each Friday when Abdul Aziz left his palace for the weekly prayer in the new mosque he had built outside the gates of Yildiz. But while they were gaudily and well clothed, their comrades in every other part of the Empire were in rags. Those who have seen European armies in any other country can hardly believe the wretched appearance which the Turks presented in the provinces. Their pay, usually one piastre a day (2*d.*), was usually months in arrear. They were ill fed, ill shod, and ill housed. Little *esprit de corps* existed among the officers. They had no common mess, and, indeed, it was generally stated that Abdul Hamid regarded anything like intimacy among the officers with suspicion. In the Greek War of 1897 they gained an easy victory under German leadership, for the Greek Army was as much demoralised as their own. But when the real hour of trial came after the formation of the Balkan League in 1912, the result of the neglect of the army became immediately visible. The Serbians defeated a large army at Komanovo. The Bulgarians swept the Turkish Army before them at Lulu Burgas, and would probably have captured the lines of Chatalja if the Russians had not intervened. Their organisation so completely broke down that Mr. Ashmead Bartlett, describing what he saw and admitting the bravery of the ordinary Turkish soldier, declared that the Turk had not a capacity of organisation sufficient to enable him to run a village circus. Never probably during the whole of Turkey's history was the Turkish Army so utterly demoralised. That demoralisation was due to Abdul Hamid.

2. *The Fleet under Abdul Hamid.*

Turkey has rarely distinguished herself at sea. Her naval strength was destroyed by Don John of Austria at Lepanto in 1571, when the legend became current among the Turks that while Allah had given dominion over the land to the believers, He had left that over the seas to the giaours. Nevertheless the Turkish fleet on Abdul Hamid's accession had so far developed that she was held to possess one of the great European fleets.

His treatment of it shows the injury he inflicted upon the Turkish nation and illustrates his character. When he commenced his reign, his fleet compared favourably even with that of France. The ships were fairly up to date; many of the officers had been trained in our navy.

There existed at the Turkish arsenal on the Golden Horn upwards of two hundred British subjects from Scotland and the north of England who were skilled engineers, and who were engaged in repairing ships or building new ones. The crews until the accession of Abdul Hamid had been kept in good training. The fleet had taken an important part in the revolution which deposed Abdul Aziz and placed Murad on the throne. Abdul Hamid, after the short and inglorious reign of his brother, kept the ships bottled up in the inner harbour of the Golden Horn. Until his day it had been the habit to send them for practice on short cruises and for the rest of the summer to keep them at anchor in the southern end of the Bosporus. Abdul Hamid changed all this. The two hundred British workmen at the Turkish arsenal were gradually paid off and returned to England. Within three years of his accession all but half a dozen had been discharged. Thereupon the ships became ill kept. It was no secret that their boilers were not attended to, and that they were deteriorating rapidly from neglect. Until the Greek War in 1897 Abdul Hamid never allowed any war vessel to come out of the Golden Horn. On one occasion indeed during that war four ironclads, two cruisers, and five smaller boats were sent to the Dardanelles in order to threaten the Greek fleet in the Piræus, or wherever they could find it; but they never got any further than the Dardanelles. It was even reported that small essential parts of the machinery were carefully retained in Constantinople. The larger vessels were unable to steam more than six knots an hour.

The additions which Abdul Hamid made to the fleet consisted of twenty torpedo boats, which were built in France, and of three large ironclads. The popular belief in Constantinople was that the torpedo boats, which were duly bought and paid for, were never intended to be used. Such belief arose from the fact that they were allowed for years to remain idle in the Golden Horn during the remainder of Abdul Hamid's reign. Some persons were alleged to have gained huge commissions on their purchase, and perhaps therefore they had served the purpose for which they were bought.

The story of the addition of the three largest ironclads to the navy has already been given,[1] and illustrates the limits of Abdul Hamid's intelligence. It is sufficient to say that they are powerful ships and do credit to their builders; one was from Armstrong's, of Newcastle, a second from Cramp's, an American firm, and the third was built in France. Why were they ordered? How did it dawn upon the Sultan between 1896 and 1904 that, having neglected his fleet, he must have ships of the latest date? The explanation has been given.

3. *The Gendarmery and Abdul Hamid.*

Before the conclusion and failure of the Conference in 1877, when Lord Salisbury left Constantinople, he had urged the Porte in its own interest to institute two reforms which appealed to the Turks generally. In addition he determined that England should effect reforms in the consular service in the Levant. The two reforms urged upon the Sultan were the development of a system of gendarmery and the improvement of the post-office service in Turkey. Colonel Valentine Baker arrived in the country and took service in the Turkish Army before the declaration of the Turco-Russian War on April 24, 1877, and was shortly afterwards made pasha. He had had a not undistinguished career in the British Army, and had attained to the rank of colonel of the 10th Hussars, and took pleasure in pointing out the spot where he, then a subaltern, had encamped with his regiment near Feneraki Point. His reputation as a fine cavalry officer and an excellent organiser had preceded him. He took part in the war against Russia, held a command under Suleiman Pasha, and became a general favourite with the Turkish troops. The talk at this time in Turkey turned largely on reform and the constitution of a body of gendarmery to replace the venal, underpaid, and altogether incom-

[1] In Chapter VIII., on Abdul Hamid's relations with foreign States.

petent guardians of the peace in town or country known as zaptiehs. When the proposal for establishing gendarmery was explained to the Sultan by Sir Henry Layard, Abdul Hamid suggested that the new force should be at once constituted and placed under the command of Baker Pasha. With the impulsiveness which characterised him in many of the crises of his reign, Abdul Hamid sent for Baker himself and arranged that he should select twelve British officers who should be stationed in different parts of the country to organise the new force. The plan was to be executed immediately. Could he not telegraph to the officers? "Impossible," was Baker Pasha's reply. It would be necessary to select men fitted for the task. Accordingly he was instructed to select them and to spare no expense in bringing them out to Constantinople speedily. Baker would have liked a reasonable time in order to see the men who were to be charged with so important a task, but the Sultan's impatience was so great that at the time he would have had them all brought out by telegraph if it were possible. Twelve officers, however, were selected, and subsequently one was added, so that it was natural that the body should be spoken of as "Baker's dozen." It is sufficient to say that nine or ten of them were excellent men for the purpose. In the Turkish papers their qualifications were lauded, and the populace hoped that they would be able to inaugurate a body of police which would secure the protection of life throughout the Empire. As, however, the war was now going on, some of them took part on the side of the Turks. By the time it had come to an end the desire on the part of the Sultan for gendarmery had passed. It was the usual story, so often repeated in Turkish history, of short-lived feverish energy followed by continuous lethargy. It is fair to the English officers to say that they disliked their enforced idleness. Three or four were sent into various parts of the Empire, but were never allowed to do anything. Colonel Briscoe, a cavalry officer, fretted under inaction, and was sent to Aleppo to keep him quiet. Colonel Blunt in similar fashion was sent to Adrianople. Both these men would have liked nothing better than to have been given a body of gendarmes to instruct in their task. They were both genial men, and got on admirably with the Valis and other officials, but the Sultan would not allow them to do anything for the carrying out of the purpose for which they were chosen. The circumstances under which Baker Pasha quitted Turkish service and entered that of the Khedive of Egypt have already been related. He had had no quarrel with the Turkish Ministers, but was personally popular with them, nor had he any private reason to take offence with Abdul Hamid himself. The only work in connection with the gendarmery that he had been permitted to do was to draw up a report on the subject. Thus the project on which the country had been building came to an end. Gradually every English gendarmery officer left the service in disgust with the exception of General Blunt.

4. *Post-offices.*

The second reform suggested by Lord Salisbury, that of the post-offices, was welcomed not merely by the Sultan, but especially by the Moslem population. Even before the Conference of 1877 the reformers among the Turks had determined to make a radical change in this department. The situation was anomalous. Several nations had their own post-offices in the Capital and principal cities of the Empire, where they received letters from abroad and from whence, always under the stamps of their own country, they forwarded letters to every other country. The situation had grown up in consequence of the negligence of the Turkish Government in every matter relating to commerce. Until the Crimean War the Turks had no post-offices whatever. Letters for the members of the various colonies were received by the ambassadors of the countries they represented, and were distributed by the Embassies amongst their own subjects. This had been practised from 1535, and probably from the time of the capture of

Constantinople The ambassadors found, however, at an early stage that this department of their work could readily be separated from that which related to diplomacy, and hence it came about even in the fifteenth century that the republic of Venice had a post-office in Constantinople, which took care of letters coming from Venice, and despatched those which went thither. When in 1535 the French obtained capitulations similar to those which Venice and Genoa had obtained, they established a post-office of their own, always nominally part of the Embassy. All the great nations followed suit. After the Crimean War the Turks determined if possible to take over the whole system, moved thereto particularly by the reports they received from England and France as to the profits which accrued to the nation from having a monopoly of postage in the country, but moved also by the desire of having the opportunity to examine the letters. When it was announced in 1875 that Mr. Scudamore, who had been one of the secretaries of the General Post Office in London, had been selected, with the approval of the British Government, to take charge of the General Post Office for the Empire of Turkey, there was a belief freely expressed on the part of the foreign population that, though the Turks had not shown themselves competent in corresponding matters, it was only just that they should be given a fair chance to see if they could organise a postal service which would work with the same regularity which characterised those of England, France, and other Western countries.

The effort failed, and its failure was due to two causes, first the sheer incompetency of the Turkish administration, though under the direction of Mr. Scudamore, to secure the same regularity in the despatch of mails from even Constantinople which was supplied by foreign post-offices. Time after time the mail-bags which were sent by steamer to Constanza, or, as it was then called, "Kustenje," were not ready when the steamer started, and had to wait for the next. The result was that everybody complained, and sent letters by the foreign posts. The second objection, which ruined the chances of a

Turkish monopoly of postage, was the well-grounded fear that the letters would be opened. Incompetency was the mark of every department under the rule of Abdul Hamid. This state of things continued until the Revolution of 1908.

5. *Establishment of School of Medicine.*

It is a pleasure to turn from Abdul Hamid's failures in order to record one most useful public work which will be associated with his name, namely, the establishment of a medical school at Scutari.

The attitude of the Turks towards sickness and medical men is a curious one. On the one hand, the fatalism of the Turk tends to make him believe that nothing which medical men can do will prevent kismet from working its way; on the other, the experience of centuries has convinced him that medical treatment may be of use. Apparently during all historical time the city on the Bosporus has been a believer in fate, destiny, or kismet. At Chalcedon, on the side opposite to the new Rome, many ancient finger rings have been unearthed, usually of iron, containing a stone in which is inscribed the single word "Tyche," destiny. When the city received its name, the Christian party was sufficiently powerful to justify Constantine in ordering the destruction of all the images adored by the pagan party except the two great figures of "Tyche" which stood on the hippodrome which had been commenced by Severus. These he did not venture to disturb.

Nevertheless at all times surgical treatment came to be recognised by the early Constantinopolitans, as it is by the present occupants of the city, as desirable and permissible. More doubt existed amongst them as to the treatment of diseases. A distinguished medical man who spent his life in the East has declared that probably the introduction of "Jesuit's Bark," better known by the name of "quinine," has done more to reconcile Eastern peoples to the value of medicine than has anything else. Throughout Turkey malarial fever, due mainly to bad drainage, was and is almost everywhere present.[1]

Medical science, however, in Turkey thirty years ago was very backward. Dissection was absolutely forbidden. A number of men calling themselves doctors successfully competed against men properly trained. The latter succeeded without much difficulty in persuading the Turkish Government to allow them to be formed into a guild, and, needless to say, they have steadily waged war against unqualified practitioners. Abdul Hamid saw no objection to the increase of medical men, but it was represented to him that the most competent were foreigners, and that his own subjects, if properly trained, would become equally competent. A few Turkish subjects indeed, including Moslems, but more commonly Greeks and Armenians, had gone through medical training in Vienna, Paris, or England. Their influence, exerted mostly through the society which they had formed, induced the Sultan to establish a great medical school. The building intended for their use is a large and prominent one, occupying a site between the Selimia Barracks, the site of Florence Nightingale's labours during the Crimean War, and the British cemetery. Every well-wisher of the people of Turkey rejoiced at its erection, and credit must be fairly given to Abdul Hamid for encouraging its construction.

Note.—The value of drainage in reference to malarial fever may be illustrated by the following: On a first visit to Nicæa the writer attended the famous Easter Eve services in the only church remaining in the "City of the Creed." Every member of the crowd which attended the out-of-door service had malarial fever clearly written upon his features, and the only medical man in the place, an old Sicilian, declared that there was not a person in the town who was not suffering from it. On a subsequent visit to the city, in company with Mr. and Mrs. Theodore Bent ten years later, no malarial fever whatever existed. The explanation given by the old doctor was that they had had as local governor an engineer who had brought about the trans-

[1] See note on Malarial Fever at end of this chapter.

formation. The city stands at the end of Lake Ascanius and was famous, as far back as 325 A.D., the time of the meeting of the General Council, for its excellent water supply. A group of springs where the water welled up as high as the girths of the horses is still in vigorous action. In course of time a broad rim of sand and gravel had been formed around the lake. Such rim was probably on an average about two feet above the level of the lake. The result was that between it and the foot of the neighbouring hills a large stagnant marsh had been formed, from which the excellent water could only escape by evaporation. The Engineer-Governor cut many deep and narrow channels through the rim, with the double result of getting rid of the water which became stagnant notwithstanding that the springs were constantly flowing, and of putting an end to malaria. Such stagnant waters exist in hundreds of places throughout Asia Minor and malarial fever is in consequence widespread. The commonest demand upon all European travellers in Asia Minor is for quinine.

CHAPTER X—*continued*

INTERNAL ADMINISTRATION OF EMPIRE—*continued*

PART IV.—PRESS. ATTACK ON CHRISTIAN CHURCHES. ESPIONAGE.

Attempts to control local and foreign press; illustrations of ignorance of Turkish officials; certain news forbidden; newspapers subventioned; fulsome adulation exacted. Ancient privileges of Churches attacked; Churches closed; Sultan becomes alarmed; invites intervention of Russia. Espionage; public and private meetings forbidden.

IN his endeavours to make himself an absolute ruler Abdul Hamid tried to obtain control over the foreign as well as the Turkish press. It may safely be said that he was the first Ottoman ruler who had had any such design; for the ignorance which prevailed regarding foreign newspapers even amongst the Turkish governing class is almost incredible. On an occasion when a well-known publicist was sent for to the Palace, His Majesty's private secretary, a respectable and respected Turk, who was probably as much in the confidence of his Imperial master as anyone ever was, afforded a curious illustration. A conversation took place in Turkish between him and the interpreter of the publicist, and the secretary remarked that he supposed the newspaper, a well-known London daily, was published in Galata. When the interpreter expressed astonishment at the question, the secretary asked: "Is any European newspaper allowed to be published in Stambul?" The answer was that London was the place of publication, and not Stambul. He confessed that while he had often heard of the newspaper, he had always assumed that it was published in Galata, a suburb of Constantinople, where newspapers not printed in Turkish are published.

A strict censorship was established in reference to everything printed in Turkey. Nothing was allowed to be published that did not meet the approval of one or other of the censors. The penalty for disobedience was the suspension of the paper or the entire withdrawal of the licence for printing. Abdul Hamid's subjects were to know nothing of any question of which he considered they ought to be ignorant. Certain words were absolutely tabooed. The use of the word Macedonia, of Armenia, and of certain other places, was strictly forbidden. A story was current at the American Bible House about the translation of the message of St. Paul in the Acts of the Apostles, "Come over into Macedonia and help us." "There is no place called Macedonia," said the censor. "But we are translating what was written 1,800 years ago and the name then existed." "We cannot and will not have it mentioned. You must substitute one of the provinces which exist in the place from which the message was sent." It was only after considerable difficulty that the message was permitted to appear in its original form. Indeed, more amusing stories are told of the mistakes of the censors than on any other subject. As some of them throw light on Abdul Hamid's methods of government, they will bear repeating. A Greek gentleman and his wife had educated a boy as a journeyman printer. He had arrived at the age of eighteen or nineteen, when his Greek protector sought advice. The boy had been in prison for several days under the following circumstances: The working printers in Constantinople had formed a Mutual Benefit Society and had published their rules or *Canionismos*, naturally in the Greek language. On the back of the pamphlet containing the rules there was printed in Greek, "While there is time let us do good unto all men but especially to those of the household," and then followed in Greek "Paulos *ep. e. t* Galat," meaning, of course, "St. Paul's Epistle to the Galatians." The boy had been in the printing office where the *Canonismos* had been printed. He was asked to state where was the residence of Paulos. He declared that he did not know. On his arrest he was taken before the police authorities and again declared his ignorance, adding that Paulos, he was told, died some 1,800 years ago. They were indignant and declared that they could read enough Greek to see that he was resident in Galata. Then the boy managed to get into communication with his patron, who informed the authorities in Turkish, which he spoke well, that the statement was true; that Paul was a Christian Apostle who had long been dead. They expressed doubts at this statement and became still more sceptical when he affirmed that the epistle was not to the inhabitants of Galata, but to the Galatians, a people who had lived in Asia Minor centuries before the Turks came into the country. They would not be persuaded until two well-known men were produced as witnesses and formally declared that they had no doubt whatever that the Paul quoted on the title page was long since dead. Then they were persuaded that their ignorance was making them the objects of ridicule. The boy was released and the matter allowed to drop.

Out of the many other stories illustrative of the folly of the censorship, two may be selected. In the early days after the establishment of the Principality of Bulgaria, the printing of books and pamphlets in Bulgarian relating to Christianity was mostly conducted in Constantinople. The MSS. were usually terribly cut about by the censors, and amongst other emendations was one omitting in the Lord's Prayer the petition "Thy Kingdom come." This was regarded as an attack upon the sovereignty of the Sultan. The Empire was good enough for all loyal subjects. It was a subordinate official who had struck it out. The vice-president of Robert College at that time, who was justly regarded as a master of the Bulgarian language, was appealed to, and went to see the chief censor to whom he was well-known and held in respect. He explained that the prayer was not an aspiration for a kingdom or princedom in the earthly sense, but was one uttered by Christ Himself and had been said by millions of Christians all down the centuries. The chief censor replied: "I like and respect you, and if you assure me that it is not intended to be an attack on the Sultan's rights I will let it pass."

Another illustration is the following:—A translation of hymns was made by American missionaries into Bulgarian, and as usual was sent to the censor before being printed. When the copy came back the collection was so cut about that doubt existed as to whether they should print any of it. Lines like "Hail, Prince of Peace," "Onward, Christian Soldiers," "Jesus, the name high over all," and the like, were ruthlessly cut out. Once more the services of the vice-president of Robert College were invoked to overcome the difficulties. The friendly chief censor remarked: "Leave it to me; I will see what I can do." A few days later the censor pointed out that he had allowed many of the hymns to remain which had been objected to, but added: "You Christians take us to be greater fools than we are, for here is a hymn which says 'Shall we gather at the river?' We know what that river is just as well as you do. It is the Maritza."

The events which happened in Egypt from 1879 until the deposition of Abdul Hamid in 1909 were never mentioned in any newspaper published in Turkey. Contemporary history could never be gathered from the files of Turkish newspapers. It was impossible to prevent foreigners receiving newspapers or telegrams, but only those could be published which were approved by the censor. If an emperor or other royal person were killed, it was stated that he "had died somewhat suddenly"; for Abdul Hamid never permitted assassination to be mentioned in regard to them. If bombs were thrown nothing was said on the subject. When Armenians or Greeks or Bulgarians revolted, a paragraph would sometimes appear stating that in such and such a district a band of brigands had appeared but was speedily dispersed by the troops and the usual tranquility prevailed. More usually the event was not even alluded to. Anyone reading the local newspapers, for example, of the Armenian massacres of 1894-8 would conclude there had been nothing extraordinary in the country except that the bands of brigands were rather more numerous than usual. Macbeth, Hamlet, Julius Cæsar, and other plays, English or French, which introduced the death of a prince by violence were altogether banned.

A curious objection was made by Abdul Hamid to the introduction of books into the country published before the year 1700 in any language. Knowles' "History of the Ottoman Turks," Sandy's "Travels," and many others in English, French or Italian were confiscated whenever the authorities could find them. The only explanation ever suggested was that they misrepresented the religion of Mahomet and showed the diminution of the Empire.

As a compensation for not being allowed to publish matters of general interest and to render them devoted to his Majesty, all local papers received subsidies from Yildiz. They had in return to belaud the Sultan. Flattery laid on with a trowel was the rule. When his Majesty's name was brought in, his qualifications were spoken of in superlatives. He was not seldom described as "recognised to be the wisest ruler in Europe"; "the greatest Sovereign who ever girded on the sword of Osman"; "a model ruler, one whose good actions were so numerous that if those performed in a single day were all printed, the columns of the paper would be insufficient to report them." Europeans laughed, but the local papers were not intended for their edification, but for Abdul's subjects.

Abdul Hamid had learnt the power of the foreign, and especially of the British, press in consequence of the attention aroused by the Moslem outrages in Bulgaria. His instructions to his ambassadors abroad were that they should use all their influence, first, to obtain the support of foreign newspapers, and second, to keep him informed of articles unfavourable to himself, so that he might prevent their entry into the country.

Many foreign newspapers, as well as all local ones, were regularly subsidised. Proofs of articles were sent to Yildiz Palace, sometimes by his diplomats, more usually by others, with a notification that if a certain sum were not forthcoming the article would be inserted. Many such sums were forthcoming. Groups of censors examined the leading journals of every European country. The censors were themselves censored: for two sets existed, one at the Porte, the other at Yildiz, and if either overlooked an important passage, an inquiry was held.

Espionage.

Between 1885 and the end of Abdul Hamid's reign, each year witnessed a steady growth in the number of the reports of spies, locally known as "*Djournals.*" Devised at first to inform the Sultan of what his subjects were plotting against him, the system of espionage developed to such an extent that, in popular belief, if three Turkish subjects were seen together one at least would be certain to be a spy. In meeting places, even in clubs and hotels, Turkish subjects were afraid to be seen conversing. It was at once painful and ludicrous to see respectable men conversing and instantly ceasing conversation when a third person drew near. In the hotels kept by Turkish subjects, the hotel-keeper for his own safety had to be on good terms with the police. Not only had he to furnish the usual particulars required in continental hotels from each visitor, but the contents of their luggage, and especially information as to the business which had brought them to Constantinople, and the subject-matter of their correspondence had to be furnished by him. In the larger hotels kept by foreigners there were always resident spies, men and women. Many instances occurred where European travellers, objecting to the obtrusiveness of these creatures, and recognising that they were spies, complained to the manager. His usual reply admitted that the person complained of, though apparently conducting himself or herself like an ordinary travelling visitor to the hotel, was yet employed by the Turkish police, and frankly declared that he could not help it. He would dismiss the spy, if the visitor insisted, but the result would be that he would have to receive another from the police who might be even a greater nuisance than the one dismissed. The spies, male or female, usually paid about one-seventh for their board and lodging of what a traveller would pay.

Probably nothing did more to disgust the Turkish population of the better class with the Government of Abdul Hamid in his later years than did the general practice and extension of espionage. The Turk above the peasant class has the virtues and faults of a dominant class. He is accustomed to be outspoken, to criticise the acts of the Government, and even the Sultan himself. When such men learned that reports of their conversation were largely sought and sent directly to the Sultan, they ceased to have respect for him, and declared more confidently than ever that he could not be a real Turk.

Meetings Prevented.

As part of the same policy the Sultan endeavoured to repress any meeting together of a number of his subjects. Even on the occasion of a family gathering, as at a wedding, spies were constantly present and sent in a *djournal* to the Palace. Anything in the nature of a public meeting of Turkish subjects was strictly forbidden. Abdul Hamid even attempted to forbid evening parties in the houses of foreigners. When the latter, relying on the immunity of their houses granted them under the capitulations, refused to cancel invitations to such gatherings, police were stationed outside the house and warned any Turkish subject that should he enter he would be reported.

On account of these restrictions, and in dread of espionage, many leading Turks on learning that they had been reported, escaped from the country. In doing so, however, they were always faced by the obstacles that no one could leave without a passport, and that passports were steadily refused to any Turkish subject against whom an unfavourable report had been made. The Sultan's own sister bitterly complained to Abdul Hamid that by his injustice he had compelled her husband to flee the country taking with him her two sons. Such fugitives from Turkey became the emissaries of revolution.

There was not an Ambassador who was not annoyed by requests to prevent gatherings of his countrymen because they were alleged to give Turkish subjects the opportunity to meet and conspire together. On one occasion Sir Nicholas O'Conor, British Ambassador, was requested by two emissaries from the Palace to forbid a Christmas gathering of the small British colony at Moda, a village opposite Stamboul. The community had its own church, its own Institute, and an Anglican chaplain who was greatly respected. During three or four years the chaplain had taken great interest in the education of both boys and girls, and had organised a Christmas entertainment of the kind which take place in every British town, and in which children played the most important parts. The emissaries requested Sir Nicholas, on his Majesty's behalf, to forbid the repetition of a performance which had already been given on one or two occasions. His Majesty had been informed that such entertainments were of an immoral character. Sir Nicholas, greatly indignant, replied that they did not come from the Palace because the request was impertinent, and told them to return with that message. Thereupon he immediately sent round to his colleagues, collected a number of children belonging to the different Embassies and took them in the Embassy Despatch Boat to see the show at Moda.

Abdul Hamid had so contrived that there was not a respectable Turk or European who did not loathe the attitude of suspicion and espionage so dear to him. It was notorious that the Turkish Ministers were forbidden to give their consent to the installing of telephones or electric light in the capital, though both Smyrna and Salonica had acquired these conveniences.

Nor did his Ministers themselves desire the telephone. Such means of communication had existed in Bulgaria before 1885; but no telephone was allowed in Constantinople until after the Revolution of 1908, the explanation of refusal given by one of the Ministers when the request was made for permission to install them being, that his Majesty's servants were already liable to be disturbed at any hour of the day or night by messengers from the Palace, but that if telephones were permitted no Minister would ever dare to leave his home or office.

Attacks on Privileges ab antiquo *of Christian Churches.*

Wider spread espionage, the hindrances placed upon travel in the interior and on granting passports for leaving the country, the prevention of sociable or other gatherings, all tended to make Abdul Hamid ridiculous in the eyes especially of his Moslem subjects and to annoy them. Taken together, they constituted a reign of tyranny which the Turks, a long-suffering and essentially good-natured people, loathed. Abdul Hamid knew from his spies that the dissatisfaction was unusual among Moslems, and fell back upon the plan of arousing ill-feeling against the Christians by appealing to Moslem prejudice. The aim, to which he was constant, was to make himself an absolute ruler. He would be the sole ruler in his own kingdom. The Christian Churches had privileges. No man or community ought to possess them, and the Moslem mob and, as he probably hoped, Moslems generally would support him in taking away those privileges. By the mischievous clause which his agents had succeeded in having inserted in Article IX. of the Paris Treaty, no foreign State had the right to interfere between himself and his subjects.[1] He believed himself to have a free hand.

Mahomet the Conqueror, in 1453, and the ablest of his successors, recognised that there were essential differences between Moslemism and Christianity, which

[1] See note at end of chapter.

rendered it necessary that the Christians should have their own laws and customs in reference to ecclesiastical affairs and to many other questions. The mention of bigamy is a sufficient illustration. Moslem law allows a man to have four wives. No Christian community could accept such legislation. It was for this and similar reasons that the privileges of the Churches were, and have always continued to be in the Ottoman Empire, an important part of Ottoman legislation. The Churches had continued to have the right, enjoyed before the Moslem conquest, to deal with their own adherents in matters of marriage, testamentary disposition, and generally of all matters relating to what jurists call Personal Statute. Abdul Hamid, possibly at the instigation of some of the more fanatical Moslems, but more probably with the hope of gaining popularity among them, seems from the first to have determined to get rid of the ancient privileges of the Churches. All the Churches, and especially the Patriarch and officials of the Orthodox Church, dealt with the attacks upon them with moderation, but also with firmness, and with a knowledge that they had the implicit support of every European nation. They met the attacks with remonstrances, and in the last resort with passive resistance. In December, 1893, the Orthodox Patriarch, acting on the advice of his Council, ordered all the churches in his jurisdiction to be closed, because of the Sultan's attempt to abrogate the ancient privileges. This was the signal for the passive resistance of a large and important section of his subjects throughout the whole of his dominion. The Sultan became alarmed when he found that he had irritated not only the Christians and the best men of the Ulema class, but all European States. His own Moslem subjects, or those of them who dared express their opinion, spoke with disgust and abhorrence of his attack, and declared that it was in flagrant violation of the tenets of Islam. He learnt not only that his attempt had failed, but that there was a talk of foreign intervention. He was driven to the great humiliation of having to request Russia to intervene in his favour, a task which the Czar undertook. When the Sultan had given formal promises to respect the immunities *ab antiquo*, the churches were re-opened.[1]

[1] Until the Treaty of Paris, 1856, the Powers had exercised the right of protecting the Christian churches. Our Ambassador Canning, afterwards Lord Stratford de Redcliffe, and others had often usefully exercised such right. The great triumph of Lord Stratford's diplomatic career in Turkey was the obtaining from the Sultan the famous Hatti-hu-mayun, the *Magna Carta* of liberty for the Christians. Imagine therefore his annoyance when he learned that at Paris in 1856, the following Article (IX). was proposed to be inserted in the Treaty. After stating that the Sultan had "decided to communicate to the Contracting Powers the said Firman emanating spontaneously from his sovereign will," the article continues. "It is clearly understood that it cannot give to the said Powers the right to interfere either collectively or individually in the relations of H.M. the Sultan with his subjects or in the internal administration of his Empire."

Lord Stratford wrote to Lord Clarendon, who was charged by the British Government with the conduct of the negotiations in Paris: "There are able and experienced men in this country," meaning presumably himself, "who view with alarm the supposed intention of the Conference of Paris to record the Sultan's late Firman of privileges in the Treaty of Paris and at the same time to declare that the Powers of Europe disclaim all right of interference between the Sultan and his subjects. They argue that the Imperial Firman places the Christians and the Mussulmans on an equal footing as to civil rights. It is believed that the Porte will never of its own accord carry the provisions of the Firman seriously into effect. The Treaty in its supposed form would therefore infirm the right and extinguish the hope of the Christians Despair on their side and fear on that of the Turks would in that case engender the bitterest acrimony between them and not improbably bring on a deadly struggle before long." ("Life of Lord Stratford de Redcliffe," Vol. II., p. 442.)

Nevertheless the objectionable clause became part of the Treaty.

The above is an excellent illustration of the mischief that can be done at a Conference when men inexperienced with the conditions in the country treated of, do not take the trouble to consult those who have such experience The blundering at the Congress in Berlin in substituting the clause for the treatment of Armenians for that which had been inserted in the Treaty of San Stefano is another illustration of the same folly of our diplomatists.

CHAPTER XI

ABDUL HAMID'S TREATMENT OF SUBJECT RACES

PART I.—IN CRETE

Condition of Crete on accession of Abdul Hamid; Christian Governor appointed in 1885; hostilities between Christians and Moslems; Mahmud appointed Commissioner, 1886; insurrection, July, 1889; Christian villages burned; agitation in Greece; Mahmud Jelaleddin, Governor; replaced by Alexander Pasha; Abdul Hamid intrigues in favour of Moslem Party against plans of Powers; Alexander Pasha recalled in 1896; replaced by Moslem; new insurrection; all Powers try to persuade Abdul Hamid to adopt reforms; Christians refuse to lay down arms; Moslem Governor replaced, but Moslem Party with aid of Turkish troops attack Christians; agitation in Athens; clamour for war; war declared April, 1877; Greeks defeated. Subsequent history.

Preliminary

THOUGH the population of Bulgaria and Eastern Rumelia had been definitely emancipated from the yoke of Abdul Hamid he was still the ruler of masses of subject races. The most important were the Cretans, the Armenians, and the people of mixed races in Macedonia. Certain general observations should not be lost sight of. The Turk, whilst possessing many military virtues, has never shown himself a successful ruler of subject races. He is a brave soldier, a kindly host; his long centuries of freedom have made him self-respecting. He gets on well with his friends and with the subjects of most foreign Powers, the latter of whom he regards as his equals. Against them in warfare he proves a fair fighter. His history and his religion, however, have led him to believe that he has a divine right of dominancy over races he has conquered when they belong to a faith other than that of Islam. He is almost entirely devoid of race or colour prejudices. Probably nowhere is the negro, whether bond or free, treated so completely on an equality with himself as in Turkey. But the negroes whom he knows are Moslems. The subject races in Turkey are Christian, and ever since they were conquered, the Turk has never ceased to rule them harshly. We have already seen how the Christians of Bulgaria fared.

Although Abdul Hamid was in no way responsible for the misgovernment of Bulgaria which led to the loss of that Province, the only noteworthy conclusion which he drew from the events leading to such loss was that Europe must be prevented as far as possible from finding out how he treated the races still subject to his rule. He was too ignorant and short-sighted to recognise, as did several of his Ministers, that a policy of even-handed justice would have been wise; that the execution of the provisions of the famous Hatt would have gone far to reconcile the subject races of the Empire to his rule. Such traditions or convictions as he possessed, and a certain vindictiveness in his own character, made him opposed to a policy of reconciliation, and threw his influence on the side of the most ignorant and fanatical section of his Moslem subjects. In his dealings with all the subject races of his Empire we see him at his worst. He answered complaints of oppression by worse oppression. We see his efforts to conceal oppression by subterfuge, lying and intrigue. We see him pretending to yield to the request of the Powers desirous in their own interest, and on humanitarian grounds, of maintaining the integrity of his Empire, and secretly plotting to intensify the evils against which the Powers were striving.

The people of Crete had been restless under Turkish misrule ever since Greece had acquired her independence. The population, virtually all Greek speaking, was 303,000 in 1914, and probably has varied little during a century. Of these only 34,000 were Moslems.

Probably thirty years ago Cretan Moslems were slightly more numerous. The Moslems of the island have long had the reputation of being amongst the most turbulent, fanatical and lawless among the Turkish population on the coasts of the Levant and Southern Mediterranean. Hence many revolts against Turkish rule occurred within a generation before the accession of Abdul Hamid, the latest being less than two years before that event. In the first seven years of Abdul's reign Crete was comparatively quiet. But with the disparity in numbers between Christians and Moslems, it was impossible that the enormous Christian majority should remain content under the Moslem minority. The Christians had been kept down by a series of heartless massacres. Their fellow Greeks in the kingdom had shaken off the Turkish yoke and they were now more unlikely than ever to willingly submit to it.

During 1885 Crete came again into public notice. With the object of satisfying the Christian inhabitants of the island, Photiades Pasha had been named, in 1884, Governor for the period of five years. One must not be surprised to learn that Abdul Hamid sympathised with the Moslem minority in their opposition to the appointment of a Christian Governor. Photiades endeavoured to act justly towards Moslems and Christians alike, but the hostilities between the two sections of the community rendered his position intolerable, and in 1885 he resigned. In 1886 Abdul Hamid sent Mahmud as a Commissioner to Crete. He did his best to bring about a settlement of the continuing difficulties, and on July 19, 1887, made concessions which for a time satisfied the Christians. He reduced taxation, and gave to Moslems and Christians alike a larger share of local government. The Christian majority, however, concluded that they could never obtain justice until they were under Christian government, the government of their choice being naturally that of Greece. They asked for the recall of their Governor, a certian Sartinski Pasha, and demanded annexation to Greece. The Greek people sympathised with their co-religionists, but the Greek Government feared to encourage the cry of annexation, lest doing so should produce war with Turkey, and lest the Cretans, who though divided in religion were a homogeneous people, should become a turbulent element in the Greek electorate. They therefore gave no encouragement directly or indirectly to the Cretan claims. On July 11, 1889, insurrection broke out in the island. The Governor was recalled to Constantinople, and his departure was followed by disturbances throughout the whole of the island. Six Cretan delegates were sent to Constantinople by the Moslems. Several Christian villages were burnt, and a great emigration of the Christian population set in to Greece. Thereupon the Greek Government was compelled by public opinion to act. It issued a circular explaining its position, and claiming justice and better government for the Christians of the island. The Sultan gave no attention to the demands and the irritation in Greece increased. Indeed, it looked as if Abdul Hamid refused to act on the absurd ground that having recently granted certain Bulgarian demands he was now justified in refusing concessions to other Christians. He was foolish enough in January, 1890, to forbid the use of the Greek tongue in the Law Courts even at Janina; for, that city being but a few miles from Greek territory, the restriction in the use of the common language brought home to their neighbours the desire of the Sultan more completely than if it had been limited to Crete.

Nevertheless, such a restriction was quite in accordance with Turkish tradition. Many orders had been issued in former times and in different portions of the Empire, especially in Armenia, forbidding the use of the native language under penalty that the offender should have his tongue cut out. Unfortunately old Turks thought, as young Turks did after the Revolution of 1908, that a nation can be unified by forcing upon it a foreign tongue. In the case of Janina, the prohibition was purely mischievous, for the attempt to enforce it aroused dangerous irritation, made Greeks outside the Kingdom hopeless of just government from the capital, and increased the hostility in Greece towards Turkey.

Abdul Hamid's unopposed oppression of the Armenians at this time encouraged him to attempt a similar treatment of the rebellious Cretans. He sent Mahmud Jelaleddin, a Governor after his own heart, to reduce Crete, as he already believed Armenia had been reduced. The Cretans were, however, a fighting race, and during 1893-4 stoutly resisted all aggression. The disturbances became so serious that in consequence of the remonstrances of the Powers the Governor was changed and replaced by Caratheodori, usually called Alexander Pasha, the able and honourable man already mentioned. His influence at once began to tell. The even-handed justice which he dealt out to Moslem and Christian alike won the respect of all the European Consuls, and would have succeeded at another time in keeping Crete in loyal subjection to the Sultan. But Abdul Hamid was bent upon supporting the Moslem party in their efforts to regain an ascendancy which should place the Christians in the abject submission in which they had been a generation earlier. Caratheodori's proposals were regarded unfavourably at the Palace. The Sultan, known to be in communication with the disaffected leaders of the Moslem party, was found to be secretly encouraging them to resist the measures which the Governor was carrying out for the pacification of the island.

In 1896 the Sultan removed Caratheodori and replaced him by Turkasi Pasha. The Cretans soon learned that the measures of their late Governor were set aside. Preparations were made to overrun the country with troops and Bashi-Bazuks or volunteers. The latter expected to have as free a hand over the Christians as they had had over the Bulgarians in 1876. Thereupon the Christians broke out once more into open insurrection. Europe determined to intervene. All the Ambassadors in Constantinople united in endeavouring to persuade the Sultan to adopt measures to satisfy the just demands of the population. He gave promises to that effect. The general who had been sent with reinforcements against the insurgents issued a proclamation vaguely indicating a redress of grievances, but demanding first that the Christians should lay down their arms. The experience of centuries told them that they would be fools if they obeyed such an order. The Ambassadors at the desire of the Sultan tried to open negotiations with the leaders. Simultaneously they pointed out to the Sultan the unsatisfactory character of the general's proclamation. The islanders flatly refused to lay down their arms. At length Abdul Hamid on the renewed representations of the Powers, consented once more to appoint a Christian Governor, to allow the Cretan Assembly to meet, and to bring again into force an arrangement for the government of the island known as the "Pact of Halep." But the Cretans were suspicious.

In 1896 the Moslem inhabitants had been joined by the troops, all, of course, Moslems, and continued their attacks on the Christians. The Cretan, whether Christian or Moslem, is a man who refuses to submit to injustice, and the Christians not only appealed to the Powers for justice, but fought heroically during 1896 and 1897. They compelled the attention both of Turkey and the Powers.

The inhabitants of Greece were divided in opinion. All, without exception, sympathised with their co-religionists in the island, but the Government desired peace, because they were not ready for war and because, while they expressed sympathy with the victims of Turkish misrule, they feared internal troubles from the introduction of a large body of Cretan voters. Meantime, popular enthusiasm throughout Greece grew daily more intense. Before the year 1896 ended, the Ambassadors recognised that Abdul Hamid was once more acting in bad faith, and did not desire even-handed government in Crete. They remonstrated, pointed out once more that his action was increasing discontent and arousing a feeling in Greece hostile to his sovereignty. His reply was to issue a circular to Europe protesting against the attitude of Greece.

In February, 1897, Greece was unable to resist popular feeling, and sent troops to Crete to aid the Christians. Thereupon the Christian Governor left the island. In March, the Ambassadors of the six Powers informed the Sultan by a collective note, first, that Europe intended to make Crete autonomous, and, second, that Greek troops would be sent out of the island. They followed this up by informing Abdul Hamid that a large number of the Turkish troops must also be withdrawn.

While it was difficult not to sympathise with the Greeks in their desire to set their Cretan brethren free from the Turkish yoke, it must be admitted that many of the statements made by the orators and in the Athenian press during the agitation which prevailed in Athens were ludicrous. One may forgive the countless allusions to their glorious ancestors and to the deeds of Plataea and Marathon, because these deeds of the best time in Greek history had furnished for two thousand years an inspiration and quickening tradition, a tradition which every man, woman, and child seems to have inherited. The ludicrous aspect was seen in the imaginative interpretations both of ancient but especially of modern Greek history. The struggles for independence in the 'twenties of last century were of a very mixed character, for while they illustrate the vainglory and boastfulness of the race, great Englishmen and Frenchmen took a higher and truer view of the situation, a view which Lord Byron made known in his vigorous lines to the British public. There were wild statements in 1897 of the superiority of Greek soldiers and sailors over the Turks and versions of struggles during the War of Independence which were ridiculous or wildly exaggerated: but they roused the blood of the Greeks to fever heat. Outside observers who cared nothing for Greek traditions were aware that the army of Greece was ill-organised and ill-disciplined, and that her fleet was hardly in a better condition; that, on the other hand, Turkey, which had become alarmed by the long agitation in Athens, had carefully prepared under German officers an army of invasion which would be able to have an easy march to Athens.

Meantime popular sympathy in Greece with the Cretans raised a general clamour for war. The Powers gave notice both to Turkey and Greece that the State which commenced hostilities would be held responsible, and formally rebuked Greece for her action. The Greeks, however, moved their troops towards their frontier. This gave Abdul Hamid his chance, and Edhem Pasha, with the aid of a few German officers, was sent in command of an army against them. Greece, as its rulers knew, never had a chance of success. The country was not prepared for war and its Government had counted upon a European intervention, which, after the formal notification of war, was for a time clearly impossible.

The war declared in April, 1897, was curious. The population of Athens had become so inebriated by the speeches of the orators in Constitution Square and the Omonia that an attempt to prevent it would have brought about a Revolution which would have inevitably led to the expulsion of the Royal Family. In such case Greece would have been without a friend. Hence, it had been decided by the Greek Government that the war must go on, and the secret influence of the Powers must be brought to bear in order to obtain the best terms. A short but disastrous struggle commenced. The Greeks were everywhere defeated. But at the demand of the Ministers, the Powers intervened to prevent its continuance.

The Sultan demanded the cession of Thessaly and an indemnity of £10,000,000 sterling. The Powers vetoed this demand, but the negotiations for peace were prolonged until September. Finally, the Emperor of Austria, with the approval of the other European Powers, decided that two small strips of territory should be ceded to Turkey, and that Greece should pay an indemnity of £3,600,000. The Turks returned triumphantly to their homes and the Greek dynasty was saved. The war was concluded May 18, 1897.

Meantime the struggle in Crete continued. Even during the war it had not ceased. It went on during 1898. The European fleets which had been sent to the island did what they could to prevent disorder, but all foreigners now openly expressed their sympathy with the Cretans. Angry negotiations went on with Jevad, the Turkish Governor, acting on instructions from his Sovereign. The European admirals in command found their action constantly thwarted by him and declared their position to be intolerable. During the negotiations Russia suggested that Prince George, the second son of the King of Greece, should be appointed Governor of the island. The Sultan objected. Germany and Austria withdrew from the negotiations and left them to England, France, Russia and Italy. In a disturbance which was believed to have been instigated by the Governor, a few British soldiers, who had landed from the fleet, were killed by Turkish troops. The Allied Powers then gave notice to Abdul Hamid that all Turkish troops must leave the island, and after the usual excuses for delay the Porte gave the necessary orders, and by the end of November, 1898, the evacuation was complete. Prince George was formally appointed Governor and remained in office till 1906. Abdul Hamid had lost Crete—lost it in spite of the efforts of the Powers to induce him to deal justly with the Christian population, to respect his own promises, and thus preserve it in the Empire.[1]

[1] In October, 1912, Crete was formally declared to be a part of the Hellenic Kingdom.

CHAPTER XI—*continued*

ABDUL HAMID'S TREATMENT OF SUBJECT RACES—*continued*

PART II.—IN ARMENIA.

Article 16 of San Stefano Treaty replaced by Article 61 of Treaty of Berlin; Mr. Goschen's attempt at reforms for Armenia; Consular reports; impudent despatch by Porte; reply by British Consuls; Collective Note of Powers, 1880; Great Britain alone in pressing for reform; Abdul Hamid has his own way for ten years; Armenians themselves submit project based on Article 61; relations of Armenians and Kurds; Abdul Hamid sends agents to arouse fanaticism; endeavours to conceal facts; correspondent *Daily Telegraph* reports situation; outcry in Europe; Mr. Gordon Bennett, of the *New York Herald*, authorised to send Commissioner; Mr. Hepworth accompanies him; his impartial account; Mr. Fitzmaurice sent; his report of story of account of conversion at Berijik, of holocaust of refugees in Cathedral of Urfa and murder of 2,500 people; disturbances in Constantinople; Fuad Pasha defends Armenians; attack on Ottoman Bank; telegraphic menace to Abdul Hamid by representatives of all the Powers; Collective Note; disturbance of trade; Armenian massacres conclusive evidence of want of statesmanship in Abdul Hamid.

Abdul Hamid's Treatment of Armenians.

ABDUL HAMID had so treated his Christian subjects in Crete as not only to have alienated their sympathy, but to have forced all Europe to interfere. Even Germany and Austria, though they had already formed designs which urged them to cultivate the favour and support of the Sultan, joined with the other European

Powers in pressing him to accept reforms which would have preserved peace in the island. We have seen with what result.

The condition of his Christian subjects in Armenia had always occupied the attention of Abdul Hamid, and the story of their treatment requires a fuller notice.

The reforms commenced by the Hatti-hu-mayun, and followed with steady though an-all-too-gentle pressure by the British and French Embassies, had their effect. Turkey was progressing towards civilised government. If Midhat's Constitution had not been suspended it would have been a valuable aid in the development of the reforms already initiated, and an effective arm for native workers and ambassadors for bringing about that reform which was more greatly needed in Turkey than any other, that, indeed, which in Turkey is the necessary preliminary of all reforms, religious equality between Moslems and Christians. Unfortunately, the Moslem population generally opposed equality, and failed to realise that its adoption would have been for the prosperity of the Empire. Nevertheless, when Abdul Hamid came to the throne, the tendency was in favour of an expansion of religious liberty, which would probably have largely developed had not the Sultan been its constant opponent.

The granting of such liberty, while important to all the populations of the Empire, would have been of special value to the Armenians, since they suffered more than any other race from Moslem intolerance. They have hitherto proved an indestructible race. Belonging to the Indo-European division of the human family, they held their own against successive attacks by members of the Semitic and Turanian races, and in spite of invasions, conquests and massacres, they lived on with unbroken national spirit for upwards of two thousand years.

In the six provinces of Turkey most largely occupied by Armenians, they numbered on the accession of Abdul Hamid about 1,200,000 out of a total population of 2,600,000. Both in those provinces and throughout the Empire they are a sober, thrifty, and intelligent people. Wherever they exist they are noted for their industry, their aptitude for business, and a certain obstinacy of character, which, while it has often brought them into trouble with the dominant power, has preserved their national sentiment. Throughout all the lifetime of New Rome they played an important part. Ten Armenian Emperors occupied the throne of Constantine, of whom Leo, the Great Basil, and John Zimisces are probably the best known. In modern times they have been the pioneers of commerce and industry in the Near East, and have occupied high positions in Turkey, Russia, Persia, and Egypt. In the Turco-Russian War of 1877-8, Loris Melikoff and other Armenian generals on the Russian side distinguished themselves. In Persia, Malkom Khan and others in recent times proved their ability. In Egypt, Lord Cromer points out that the Armenians "have attained the highest administrative rank," and mentions especially Nubar Pasha, Boghos Pasha, Jacub Artin Pasha, as men who have at times exercised a decisive influence on the conduct of public affairs in that country. In Turkey, many of the leading Ministers and administrators in the early part of Abdul Hamid's reign were Armenians. Dadian Effendi was an able Under Secretary of State for Foreign Affairs; Gabriel Effendi Nuradunghian, who is still living, was probably the ablest jurist, with the possible exception of the Greek Caratheodori, who served under Abdul Hamid. It would be easy to mention others who, like Dilber Effendi, had and have the respect of all classes of the community. In spite of a prejudice against the race entertained by Abdul Hamid, the Armenians held their own among the leading merchants of the capital. Those who lived in the north-east of Turkey, which is the home of the race, aided by their fellow religionists throughout the Empire, in spite of centuries of persecution, have never wavered in their attachment to their Nation, Church, and Language. When the great religious movement, known as the Reformation, occurred in

Western Europe, and ever since, their leaders have shown a desire to reap the benefits of European thought and of civilisation. They instinctively feel themselves to be Europeans. They welcomed amongst them the efforts of Roman Catholic missionaries, and at a later period those of Protestants from America. The Greeks in Turkey, who invariably confuse nationality with religion, will not willingly tolerate missions of any kind amongst them. To accept either the Roman Catholic faith or any form of Protestantism is treason to their race. Not so amongst the Armenians. The Roman Catholic missions have prospered, and the flourishing institutions in Vienna and at San Lazzaro in Venice, due largely to the generosity of an Armenian merchant, Mekitar, are evidences at once of their European tendencies and of their careful culture in arts and secular learning as well as in theology.

Men of this race have furnished useful citizens to Russia, England, France and America, and under a Turkish ruler possessed of insight would have been recognised as an invaluable element in the population. Under Abdul Hamid they became the special objects of his virulent hatred. They should have been cherished by him because their qualities of industry, thrift, and intelligence are precisely those in which the Turkish Moslem is lacking. Abdul Hamid could see nothing in them but the enemies of his person and government. He regarded them as ever ready to join with any foreigners in order to shake off his rule, whereas in truth long centuries of oppression had made them suspicious of foreigners, for those who came under their observation were usually under the special protection of the Turkish Government and were regarded as its spies. Nor did they wish to cease to be Turkish subjects, though they desired security for their lives, the honour of their women, and their property. They are hospitable to those whom they trust, but are shy of strangers, usually believed to be friendly with the oppressors.

The position of the Armenians in 1878 was already so

serious that a useful provision for reforms was inserted in the Treaty of San Stefano, and was to the following effect:—

"Article 16. As the evacuation by the Russian troops of the territory which they occupy in Armenia, and which is to be restored to Turkey, might give rise to conflicts and complications detrimental to the maintenance of good relations between the two countries" (Russia and Turkey), "the Sublime Porte engages to carry into effect without further delay the improvements and reforms demanded by local requirements in the provinces inhabited by the Armenians,[1] and to guarantee their security from Kurds and Circassians."

Unfortunately this was one of the articles mischievously tampered with at the Congress of Berlin. Instead of the San Stefano article, a modification of it took place which has already been given and became Article 61 [2] in the Berlin Treaty. A comparison of the two articles shows the important nature of the change. When the San Stefano Treaty was signed, the Russian troops were still in occupation of the Turkish territory inhabited by the Armenians which it had been agreed should be restored to Turkey. The presence of these troops constituted the best possible guarantee for the execution "of the improvements and reforms demanded by local requirements without further delay." It probably implied, or was at least taken to imply, that the Russians would not leave Turkish territory until they had seen the commencement of the execution of these reforms.

The provision was undoubtedly stringent, but it would at least have been effectual. Several members of the Congress at Berlin took it to imply that Russia might permanently occupy and take possession of the country, because, if such were her desire, it would have been easy to make the execution of the reforms difficult or even impossible. On the other hand, the feeling in Russia at that time was not favourable either to the

[1] The provinces inhabited by Armenians are Van, Bitlis, Erzerum, Diabekir, Kharput, and Sivas.

[2] For text, Article 61, see p. 81.

Armenians of Turkey or to the Armenians under Russian rule. The fanatical party under the Czar had tried hard, but in vain, to persuade the Armenians to accept the dogmas and discipline of the Holy Orthodox Church. In Russia the Armenians were persecuted because they would not sacrifice the traditions and beliefs of their race, and Russian sentiment did not show any special favour towards them.

It is interesting to note what took place at the Berlin Congress when Article 16 of the San Stefano Treaty came under discussion. Lord Salisbury proposed that the latter half of the article by which the Sublime Porte "engages to carry into effect without further delay" should stand, but that the first portion, in reference to the evacuation by the Russian troops, should be omitted. He did so on the express ground that the first half of the article appeared to render the evacuation by the Russian troops contingent on the concession of reforms by the Sublime Porte. When the Congress met two days later, the alterations came up for consideration, and the new article commenced with the words "The Sublime Porte engages itself," etc. Lord Salisbury had added "It will come to an understanding subsequently with the other signatory Powers respecting the extent of this engagement and the measures necessary for carrying it into effect." He appears to have been persuaded, probably by an important Armenian deputation which was in attendance at Berlin, that his condition was vague, and accordingly at the next meeting of the Congress a revised version appeared to the following effect: "The Sublime Porte must periodically make known the steps taken to this effect to the Powers, who will superintend their application." The evident weakness of Article 61, as Lord Salisbury must have recognised, was that no guarantee existed for the execution of the "amelioration and reforms demanded by local requirements." As a matter of fact, Abdul Hamid disregarded this clause entirely, never submitting any project for amelioration and reforms, and rejecting those suggested to him by the British Government through Sir Henry Layard and later ambassadors. So strenuous was the Sultan's opposition to any reform that apparently no Power cared to incur his displeasure by calling attention to the fact that he had promised to report the steps taken to effect reforms, and that the Powers had demanded and obtained the right to superintend their application. Article 61 consequently became almost entirely a dead letter.

Nevertheless both embassies and the Armenians themselves endeavoured to secure protection for life and property in Armenia.

We have seen how the efforts of Sir Henry Layard entirely failed to obtain reforms for the Armenians. Mr. Goschen during the short time when he was in Constantinople endeavoured to induce all the Powers to bring pressure to bear upon Abdul Hamid for the same purpose. He found on his arrival that one of the last acts of his predecessor was to protest against the promotion of Kiamil Pasha, who had been Governor of Aleppo. By the orders of Abdul Hamid he had encouraged, or at least had not tried to prevent, an attack upon the Armenians at Zeitun—the mountain fastness of Little Armenia which has always maintained a semi-independence. Moreover, he had been accused of taking bribes by the British consul at Aleppo, and, in consequence of the representations of Sir Henry Layard, had been dismissed. A few weeks afterwards he was appointed Under-Secretary in the Ministry of the Interior, and a little later was made Minister of the Evkaf (the Department of Pious Foundations) and decorated with the Order of Mejidie.[1]

The condition of Armenia grew steadily worse. Yet

[1] The appointment is a typical instance of what from that time onward Abdul Hamid almost invariably did. Whenever, by the efforts of ambassadors, an official was dismissed for his ill-treatment of the Armenians or for any other offence of which the Sultan did not disapprove, Abdul Hamid compensated him by giving him a more lucrative post. It would be easy to mention a score of such cases. A man of notoriously bad character was dismissed on the representation of the Turkish Debt Department for various reasons, one of which was that he was acting as a spy upon their proceedings and reporting on them constantly to the Sultan. The office he held was a low one; he was shortly afterwards promoted to be a Minister.

it is only just to say that independent and honest-minded Moslems protested against the ill-treatment of their Christian fellow-subjects, which they claimed was doing injury also to Moslems. One such Mahometan wrote to our consul, the present Sir Alfred Biliotti, that "it is impossible to give an idea of the state of things. Tyrannised over, robbed, and driven from their lands by Government officials and *agas*, Moslems as well as Christians shed tears of blood. The aspect of the country is desolate. No care is taken to preserve or restock the forests. The villages are only collections of mud huts in plains devoid of trees, water, gardens, or vegetables. The inhabitants are coarsely fed and coarsely clad. Neither roads nor bridges are in a serviceable state. There hardly remains a single public building whose interior or exterior is not partially in ruins. The nomad population is constantly entering the settled districts." A commission had been appointed to draw the boundaries between Russia and Turkey in Armenia, and the British vice-consul who accompanied the Commissioner compared the condition of two villages, one and a half hour's distance from each other, the one being under Turkish, the other under Russian, rule: "In the Turkish the people complained bitterly of the oppression of the soldiers, who took everything from them without payment, while the other, which had been ceded to Russia, was in a flourishing condition, and the Cossack troops who occupied it got on admirably with the people."

During the period between the Berlin Congress in 1878 and 1881 we have several volumes of consular reports relating to Turkey. They show constant anxiety both on the part of Earl Granville and of Lord Salisbury to point out to the Porte the danger to which perversity or inertia was exposing the Empire. The Turkish Minister Edhem Pasha, who succeeded Midhat, approved the reform project prepared by Great Britain.[1] His successor, Savas Pasha, in January, 1880, promised Sir Henry Layard his support in pressing for reforms.

[1] Despatch October 24, 1877.

But the Sultan would not accept any. Mr. Goschen reported "that the interest of Europe, as well as that of the Ottoman Empire, requires the execution of the 61st Article of the Treaty of Berlin, and that the joint and incessant action of the Powers can alone bring about this result." An identical note was issued by the Powers demanding "the complete and immediate execution of the article, and, in conformity therewith, called upon the Government of his Imperial Majesty to state explicitly what the steps are which have been taken in order to fulfil the provisions of that article." The Porte replied that, "in spite of difficulties, the execution of the article has always been present in the minds of the Ottoman Government, that it has sent competent officials into Kurdistan, that is the district in Armenia mainly occupied by the Kurds, and other provinces, to study the most efficient means of ensuring security to Armenians and other faithful subjects of the Sultan." The Porte claimed that it had already made reforms in the law courts, that it had tried various experiments for the creation of a new system of collecting taxes and tithes in order to secure peace and tranquillity, that it had begun to establish gendarmery and police in certain districts, that it found the establishment of courts of assize would be useful, and gave the division which the Porte proposed to make for judicial purposes. It added that the Government had already admitted to public employ capable and honest persons without distinction of creed; that it proposed to watch the progress of education and public works, "the principal cause of a country's happiness." The following significant paragraph concludes the Porte's despatch: "In bringing the foregoing to your notice, I regret to have to state that whenever misdemeanours—which naturally occur in every country of the world—happen to be committed in Armenia, some over-zealous people appear to take it upon themselves to invent imaginary crimes in addition to the real offences, and to represent them before the eyes of Europe and the consuls on the spot as having actually occurred." The despatch is a typical one as showing the effrontery of the Porte, and their determination to misrepresent the condition of Armenia. It shows also how completely Turkish officials had caught the knack of employing diplomatic phrases and of making much of little things.

The British consuls in Armenia were invited by Earl Granville to make their observations on this reply of the Porte and its significance. They affirm in their reply that (1) the reforms which the Porte asserts have been commenced are fallacious; (2) the commissions have done nothing; (3) the interference with the tribunals of law has only resulted in evil; (4) the asserted improvements in the system of collecting tithes and taxes, and in the organisation of the gendarmery, have not been made, and that Baker Pasha, the head of the gendarmery, which he is alleged to have visited and inspected, was a gendarmery which had no existence.

Mr. Goschen, writing to Earl Granville on August 30, 1880, states: "All the consular agents of her Majesty in Asia Minor repeat over and over again that nothing can be hoped for the provinces unless there is a real reform in Constantinople." For bold mendacity the Porte's note, doubtless drawn up at the instigation of, and approved by, Abdul Hamid, would be difficult to beat. The real reform wanted, as Mr. Goschen stated, was in Constantinople, meaning of course with the Sultan himself.

In consequence of this correspondence a collective note was sent on September 11, 1880, by the ambassadors of all the Great Powers. It is a complete answer to the equivocations of the Porte, and concludes with the following paragraphs:—

"It is absolutely necessary to carry out, without loss of time, the reforms intended to secure the life and property of the Armenians; to take immediate measures against the incursions of the Kurds; to carry out at once the proposed system of finance; to place the gendarmery provisionally on a more satisfactory footing; and, above all, to give to the governors-general greater security of office and a more extended responsibility.

"In conclusion, the Powers once more recall to the Sublime Porte the essential fact that the reforms to be introduced into the provinces inhabited by the Armenians are, by treaty engagements, to be adapted to local wants, and to be carried out under the supervision of the Powers."

The Porte replied to the collective note on October 3 without making the slightest reference to the censures which had been addressed to it. The reply was characterised by Mr. Goschen as "aggressive," and virtually stated that all that the Powers had to do with the matter in conformity with Article 61 was to thankfully rejoice at the promises which the Porte was pleased to make.

Europe did not protest against this violation of faith. Abdul Hamid was to have his own way. Mr. Goschen's hands were full, because it was at the time when, the Sultan having refused to cede Antivari, a naval demonstration was taking place before that town. The attitude amongst the other European Powers was one of hopelessness. Some seem to have been in favour of giving the Turks a respite, but Mr. Goschen notified his Government that if the Powers did not combine to ameliorate the situation in Armenia "dire results would ensue" and claimed that "the responsibility will not lie with her Majesty's Government."[1] The reports of our consuls showed that the so-called attempts at reform were, as one of them, Captain Clayton, said, "a perfect farce." The selection of Turkish administrators was absurd. In the district of Passin, for example, only one mudir out of seventeen could read and write. Another official stated that the condition of the country at the end of 1880 was worse than it was in 1879. "There is less security for life and property; poverty has increased, while crimes of oppression and corruption have increased proportionately with the impoverished state of the Empire." In January, 1881, Earl Granville instructed the British ambassadors in Paris, Berlin, Vienna, Petersburg, and Rome to call the attention of the Governments to which they were accredited to the state of affairs in Armenia. Russia's reply showed that she still resented the change of the article accepted at

[1] Blue Book 30, No. 6, 1881, p. 242.

San Stefano into that introduced at Berlin. She stated that she would join in the concert of Europe to make representations if the proposal met with the approval of the other Powers which had signed the Treaty of Berlin. Indeed, it is hardly too much to say that at this time England stood alone in pressing for better government in Armenia.

During the next ten years Abdul Hamid had his own way in reference to the provinces inhabited by the Armenians. He had defeated Europe, and continued to violate the promises which he had given in San Stefano and in Berlin. The Powers had indeed made a mistake when they allowed Article 16 of the Treaty of San Stefano to be replaced by Article 61 of the Treaty of Berlin.

When Lord Salisbury found that his labour to obtain reforms under the guarantee of Europe had failed miserably, he treated Abdul Hamid and his promises with the contempt which they deserved. He regretted that he "could not sail the fleet over the Taurus Mountains"; he was afraid that at that time Russia was not disposed to help the Armenians, and recognised that she could not overcome the aversion of the ecclesiastical leaders on both sides to accepting union with the Orthodox Church, implying indeed that without the co-operation of Russia his interference would be of no benefit to the sufferers, and in this he was right.

The Cyprus Convention and the indignant remarks of Lord Salisbury, at a later period, to the Turkish Ambassador in London, have already been mentioned. He expressed his indignation at the treatment of the Armenians and on a subsequent occasion his belief that in supporting the integrity and independence of Turkey at the Berlin Congress "England had put her money on the wrong horse."

The Russian delegates, who knew the Turks better, proved right in suggesting that without the presence of their troops, as provided for in the San Stefano Treaty, all other guarantees were illusory.

In fairness to Mr. Disraeli and Lord Salisbury, it

should be added that the distrust of Russia, especially in relation to her dealings in distant States, was great and not altogether without justification. Those who were in Turkey and could look on the question with detachment were of opinion that Russia at that time did not wish to increase the number of Armenians in her territory, nor to acquire new territory occupied partly by them and partly by Moslems.

Many attempts were made by the Armenians themselves, based upon Article 61, to obtain in a peaceful manner from the Sultan measures of reform. Their demands greatly irritated him. He came to loathe the mention of Armenia. Yet their leaders abroad and in Turkey, while always profoundly respectful, did not ask for autonomy, nor did they wish to be under Russian rule. They recognised that in none of the six provinces largely occupied by them were they in a numerical majority. All that they desired was security for life, honour, and property. They asked for administrative reforms and not political severance. The more advanced amongst them, residing outside Turkey, as well as their intelligent sympathisers in all parts of Europe, suggested a form of administration similar to that existing in the Lebanon, where the Sultan appoints a European governor with the assent of the Powers, who should be irremovable for a term of years. But the Armenians residing in the Empire never dared to submit such demands.

Differences in the first instance between the Kurds and the Armenians led to the outbreak of unusual massacres in Armenia.

It was in the autumn of 1889 that Lord Salisbury demanded a commission of inquiry to be sent into Armenia. The attacks by the Kurds, mostly a hill people, upon the Armenians in the plains, were led by a certain Mussa Bey, a Kurdish chief. By order of the Sultan, he was brought for trial to Constantinople. The accused was ostentatiously a braggart, boasted that Abdul Hamid would protect him, and that in robbing and killing Armenians he was acting under the Sultan's orders. Abdul Hamid himself at this time proclaimed his desire to do justice between the Armenians, "whom he loved as his own children," and the Kurds. Happily, the trial was public, and no one was surprised when, after the witnesses had been browbeaten and all sorts of irregularities in Turkish law had been permitted, Mussa was acquitted. The denial of justice was so flagrant that a new trial was ordered, and the accused was condemned, but notwithstanding the decision everybody recognised that Abdul Hamid was either afraid or unwilling to punish the culprit. The Sultan's mind was at that time full of the project, which shortly afterwards was carried into effect, of forming a regiment of Kurdish cavalry which was named after him, "Hamidiehs." Many of these were sent to Constantinople and swaggered through the streets in their gaudy uniforms, like red Indians, to the terror of peaceful inhabitants.

Kurds and Armenians.

Dispersed throughout all the six vilayets, or provinces, were about 190,000 Kurds. They were Moslems and warlike. In the provinces where the Kurds were most numerous, as indeed in all the "six provinces," the Christians had been disarmed. In the course of two centuries the Kurds had become a dominant class which occupied the hill country, while most of the Armenians lived on the plains. Disorder reigned during that period in all Armenia. In the course of years many Armenian villages submitted voluntarily to pay blackmail to certain Kurdish chieftains in order to be protected from depredations committed by other chieftains of their race or by Turks. A kind of feudal arrangement had indeed grown up between Kurdish freebooters and the peasant Armenians. The latter being more industrious than their Kurdish plunderers, had acquired comparative wealth. The result was that they were constantly pillaged by the Kurds. The amount of tribute was measured by the wealth of the subject Armenians. Their complaints to the local governors were not attended to. When in late years, after the Crimean War, these complaints were reported to Constantinople by European consuls, or by Protestant or Roman Catholic missionaries, they produced no redress. The condition of the Christian peasants gradually grew worse, and the attempts at reform made by the Powers did not improve matters. Those who complained were Christians; those of whom they complained were Moslems. The governors, who wished to stand well with Abdul Hamid, reported against the Christians and in favour of the Kurds, or at best tried to smooth over the difficulties between them. The difficulties arising from the constant pillage by the Kurds were greatly aggravated by the capture of Armenian women. The common answer to a complaint that a Kurdish tribe had violated or had captured the women of a village was that such women had desired to become Moslems and had accepted Islam. Everyone in the neighbourhood knew that the statement was false, but no redress was given. Indeed, the two constant complaints made by Armenians and by foreign consuls regarded the violation of wives and daughters and the pillage of Armenian property.

The half-savage Kurds being Moslems and lawless fighters, were rarely successfully attacked even by regular troops. On a few occasions troops were sent against them, but they usually attacked in half-hearted fashion and often joined with the robber tribes in their plunder of the Armenians. It was mainly the impossibility of putting an end to the anarchy which prevailed, and which his governors were unable to deal with, which led Abdul Hamid to try his own desperate remedy. For many reasons he had come to hate the very name of Armenia. He had long since given orders that it should never be employed in the newspapers, and the order had to be strictly obeyed. By an imperial decree Armenia ceased to exist. He carried his hostility even to an absurd degree, as, for example, when an Armenian who had regulated and attended to the clocks at Yildiz for years before Abdul Hamid's accession was dismissed peremptorily by Abdul, who declared that he would have no Armenian about his palace.

The persistency with which the claims of Armenia for better government continued to be urged by England, France, and in succeeding years by Russia, added to his irritation. The Armenian people, the great majority of whom remained attached to their national Church, and to the traditions especially of their national saint, Gregory the illuminator, had obtained for their Church a council which even Abdul Hamid hesitated to destroy.

The head of the Church for spiritual and doctrinal purposes was known as the Catholicos and resided in Etchmiadin, which was then, as now, in Russian territory. The temporal head of the Church in Turkey is the Armenian Patriarch, officially known as "Patriarch of the Armenians," who resides in Constantinople. A succession of Patriarchs since the Crimean War have shown a patriotism and devotion to their duties as heads of the Church in Armenia of quite a remarkable character. Ismirliam in particular will pass down into history as a man of unswerving devotion to the cause of his people. At the risk not only of his position, but of his life, he constantly urged intervention on the Sultan to protect the Armenian villagers against the Kurds. At first he, like other Armenian Patriarchs, was received with compliments, and fulsome promises of relief were made. Experience, however, soon showed him that the Sultan either could not or would not come to the assistance of his flock.

Massacres.

With the year 1894 began the great series of massacres in Armenia which will ever be memorable. The first of them occurred in the neighbourhood of Sassun. The exactions of the Kurds from their neighbours had become steadily worse. Most of the villages were paying blackmail to the chiefs of the tribes in order to secure protection. Of late years the Turkish authorities had abandoned all hope of receiving taxes from the Armenians, because they recognised that the exactions of the Kurds left them penniless, but in November, 1894, orders were given from Constantinople that Armenians must pay as they had done some years earlier, before the Kurds had instituted their regular system of levying blackmail. Turkish troops were sent to enforce payment. The peasants trusting apparently to their being defended by the Kurds, refused and claimed exemption. The officer commanding the Fourth Army Corps, whose headquarters were in Erzinghian, as well as troops from Bitlis and elsewhere, received orders to attack the Armenians. Without any sort of preliminary notice they opened fire on the unarmed population. Twenty-five villages were burnt and several thousand Armenians killed.

The massacre was somewhat of a surprise to the rest of the Empire and to the diplomats. The Porte judged it desirable to give its version of the affair. It was one so absurdly at variance with facts and with probabilities that it was regarded in the embassies at Constantinople with contempt. It put the movement down largely to bands of Armenian brigands furnished with foreign arms. It alleged that they had joined insurgent Kurds, and that the united bands had destroyed several of the Moslem villages. It pretended that regular troops had been sent with the object of protecting the peaceful population, that they had succeeded in accomplishing this object and had re-established order in the Sassun district to general satisfaction. It was not true, it continued, that Kurds had seized the cattle and effects of the Armenians. This Turkish circular was so absurdly false in its misstatements as to become the subject of general ridicule.

The perversity of the Sultan in rejecting the suggestions both of loyal Armenians and the Powers was noted by the best Moslems, as well as were the futile and farcical notifications of reform put forward by Abdul Hamid through the Porte. They were regarded simply as mockeries. Some of them indeed irritated the Moslems, though of no use to the Christians.

The hostility between the Kurds and the Christians became more pronounced. The Kurds, little better than savages, acted upon the belief that they had not only the right of dominancy over the Christians, but the approval of the Sultan. Abdul Hamid himself felt able to defy the Powers, and was determined to deal with the Armenians after his own methods, which implied the stimulation not only of the religious fanaticism of his Moslem subjects, but of their love for plunder.

The superior industry, thrift, and intelligence of the Christians had enabled them, amidst all their difficulties, to become comparatively prosperous. The efforts of the Protestant and Roman Catholic missions, and especially of their wealthier fellow-countrymen of the great towns, had produced a comparatively educated peasantry. The interest, not always friendly, which Russia and the Powers had taken in their progress, made the peasants less tolerant than they had formerly been of periodical robbery and outrages upon their wives and daughters. On the other hand, the impossibility of obtaining redress in the law courts, where indeed the Christian had no chance of justice against a Moslem, led the Kurds to constant encroachments upon the property of their neighbours. Lands were stolen, as all the inhabitants of a village knew, but the villagers were Christians, and their oaths were not admissible against Moslem testimony. The natural result ensued. Many peasants fled the country. Some found their way to America, where in the neighbourhood of Los Angeles there are three districts inhabited by comparatively large communities of Armenians, who have proved themselves industrious and good citizens. Emigration into Russia was still more easy. It was forbidden by the Turks and not welcomed by the Russians, who appear to have been afraid that the contiguous portion of their empire might become too largely Armenian. The refugees in Russia burning with a sense of injuries to which their relations remaining under Turkish rule were still subject, formed committees to work for redress in Turkey. It must never be forgotten that few among the great Armenian community in Turkey desired annexation by Russia. On many occasions they showed their belief that they would be better off in a reformed Turkey and had little sympathy with the extreme measures prosecuted by the refugees. Russia was still endeavouring to induce, or even to force, Armenians already in Russia to join the Orthodox Church. Moreover, there was the desire, always strong among a peasant community, to remain in the land of their fathers, to endure the ills to which they were liable rather than to fly to others in a distant and unknown country of which they knew nothing. It was only the persistent folly of Abdul Hamid which furnished members to the foreign revolutionary committees. Some of these committees, however, in despair, entertained the dangerous and foolish hope that by stirring up public disorders they would bring about massacres which would compel the intervention of Europe. The hope was foolish because the only country that could successfully intervene was Russia, and the sufferers themselves recognised that Russia's attitude at that time was not friendly. The result was that Abdul Hamid came to consider that he was allowed a free hand. Foreign Powers would not help, and he could deal with his own subjects. He had closed Armenian schools on the slightest pretext. His censorship had prohibited the entry into the Empire of any school books which even mentioned Armenia, or which in any way dealt with the history of the nation. As previously in Bulgaria, school teachers were regarded with suspicion and were constantly imprisoned without trial or any definite charge being brought against them. Wholesale arrests, imprisonment without trial, tortures of the most horrible character which the ingenuity of savages could devise in order to exact evidence or confession, murders committed in the prisons, misgovernment of every kind, all contributed to make a pandemonium of Armenia. Abdul Hamid knew of this condition and of the daily outrages and justified them. Sir Philip Currie told a story in 1894 which illustrates the Sultan's attitude

The Ambassador had received news from a consul in Armenia of the arrest, imprisonment and torture of sixty persons in a village where a Moslem had been killed. He went to see the Sultan and to ask that they should be released. Abdul Hamid replied, "But a Moslem has been killed," and this with an air of satisfaction, said Sir Philip, as if to say, "You can't object to imprisoning the whole lot when you remember that." Our Ambassador explained that in civilised countries the murderer would be sought out and punished. It was useless to try and persuade Abdul Hamid that order could be maintained by limiting the action of his servant in that fashion when Armenians were concerned.

Abdul Hamid recognised, however, that it was not expedient to arouse European attention to what was going on under his rule. He was carefully preparing for still more serious attacks upon the Armenians, and as far as possible determined to hinder tidings of what he was doing from reaching the West. Religious fanaticism was aroused by his agents. The Moslem cupidity was to be given a free hand, and the Faithful to be allowed to enrich themselves by robbing their neighbours, and in the case of resistance by killing them. A repetition took place of the worst features which had occurred in the Bulgarian massacres of 1876. Abdul Hamid sent his agents throughout Armenia with instructions as to their course of action. The manner of their proceeding was usually the following:—The Moslem population were collected in the largest mosque of the town, where of course no Christians were present. Abdul's agent declared that the Sultan had evidence that the Armenians generally were in revolt and that their principal aim was to strike at Islam. They were called upon as good Moslems to defend the faith and to give a lesson to intending rebels. He declared that according to the Sacred Law the property of rebels might be taken by Believers, and he invited his congregation on the morrow to loot their neighbours' possessions, informing them at the same time that if resistance were made, they would be justified in killing those who opposed. To appeal in this way to human cupidity in the name of religion naturally produced terrible results. It is to the eternal disgrace of Abdul Hamid that these appeals were made in his name, by his express orders, and in the name of the Islamic faith.

The outrages rendered some of the leading Armenians reckless, and this applied especially to the Russian refugees. A revolutionary society was formed amongst them, known as the "Henchak," and several of its members found their way into Turkey. The great majority of the Armenians regarded their proceedings with dislike. They recognised their patriotism, they shared their indignation against Abdul Hamid, but knew the spirit of fanaticism amongst the lower class too well not to understand that when measures were directed by Abdul Hamid, he would take advantage of them to excel himself in brutality.

Meantime, during the summer and autumn of 1894, and the first half of 1895, rumours of ugly outrages found their way to the Embassies in the capital and through Russia to Western Europe. Abdul Hamid had tried to stop all leakage of news. Every letter from the interior to the capital was delivered ostentatiously open. No correspondent or commercial or other traveller could obtain permission to enter any of the Armenian provinces.

But in spite of all his measures news leaked out. Abdul Hamid must do something. A scheme of reform had been prepared, and in October, 1895, he gave it his approval. He declared that his constant desire had been to carry out reforms adapted to the circumstances of the provinces, and calculated to secure the well-being of all his subjects. The reforms he had proposed were for the benefit of Moslems and Christians alike, but they would be first established in Anatolia. As usual, he was profuse in promises. He spoke of the great Hatti-hu-mayun, and of his intentions to settle the nomadic tribes (the Kurds) on lands belonging to the Government. Special regulations were to be made for the regiments of Hamidieh cavalry; and his proclamations became at once more boastful, bombastic and sickening than ever.

On the very day of the publication came the news of a massacre in Trebizond. One of the first accounts was given by the captain of an Austrian Lloyd's steamer. Every Christian had been killed. Those on board his steamer saw Armenians who were swimming out in hopes of escape knocked on the head by Moslem boatmen, or held under water until they drowned. There was some slight resistance, but while on the first day at least six hundred Armenians were killed, only five Moslems were slain. Men were burnt in their houses, and those who tried to escape were shot down. In reference to resistance in Trebizond, it is unfortunate that there and elsewhere the Armenians made little opposition. Their non-resistance is explained by the fact that on various occasions the whole Armenian population had been disarmed, were entirely unaccustomed to the use of arms, and probably believed that resistance would be worse than useless. The latter proposition may well be doubted. An Englishman, who was present in Trebizond and saw what went on, gave a vivid description of what he saw. The first idea that occurred to him was, that as the Sultan wished the Moslems to attack the Armenians, the lowest class of them thought only of plunder. Many of their companions anticipated resistance, and took no part in the first attack upon the shops, but when they saw that the Armenians were unarmed and did not intend to make a fight for their wives, children and property, joined in the fray and upon resistance being made had no hesitation in killing their opponents. The Englishman in question, who had travelled in the Western States of America and knew also the East End of London, declared that if there had been a dozen roughs from either of these parts who would have shown fight against the leaders of the mob, they would probably have been successful in preventing the great slaughter, for when the leaders found that they could take what property they liked without resistance, "the attack began of an ever increasing pack of wolves upon sheep." There are occasions when to turn the other cheek is neither good Christianity nor good policy.

Meantime word had passed round Armenia to Abdul Hamid's agents to make a general attack upon the Christians. The principal massacres in 1895 took place at Erzerum, Bitlis, Marash, Kharput and Zeitum. All the Powers in November demanded that they should cease. The Porte contemptuously replied that all the troops of the Reserves had been called out, the infamous suggestion being made that there was a general rising in Armenia, a statement which everybody in Turkey knew to be false.

While not afraid of the remonstrances of the Powers which had proposed, and had honestly endeavoured to obtain the reforms for Armenia, but had virtually done nothing, Abdul Hamid became greatly alarmed at the discontent among his own Moslem subjects. It was their discontent, coupled with the demands in November of the Powers, that alarmed the Sultan. The fantastical scheme of reform which had been put forward by the Porte remained a dead letter. Throughout the whole of Armenia there was wild disorder. Some of the American missions were looted. The property of American citizens, as well as of Italian, French and British subjects, was plundered or destroyed during the letting loose of the rabble upon the Armenian population.

The alarm in Constantinople was such that some of the Embassies in the capital requested Abdul Hamid to grant permission for them to have in the Bosporus a second despatch boat or "stationaire." Abdul Hamid hesitated and greatly disliked the proposal. After he learnt, however, that the whole of the Powers insisted upon his compliance, he consented. Everyone, Moslem or Christian, who had urged the Sultan, in his own interest or in that of the country, to effect reforms which would put an end to the massacres in Armenia, became an object of suspicion.

Said Pasha had ceased to be Grand Vizier because he had ventured to make such suggestions. He believed his life was in danger, and he probably was right, for he was followed by Abdul Hamid's spies whenever he left his house, and wherever he went. On December 9, he seems to have felt that he could stand it no longer. He entered a large shop in the Grande Rue de Pera, known as the Bon Marché. The spies remained at the door awaiting his exit. Accompanied by his young son, he went through the shop and out in another street two or three hundred yards from the British Embassy. He and his son hastened there and sought protection from Sir Philip Currie. He explained that he was being followed and believed his life to be in danger, and of course Sir Philip and Lady Currie gave him shelter. The anger of Abdul Hamid was known before the day was over to all in Pera. To the messenger sent to the Embassy Sir Philip replied that Said was his guest and would remain there. Then the Sultan requested a visit from Sir Philip on the following day. Our Ambassador gave the writer an interesting account of his interview. Abdul Hamid pretended that he bore no ill-will to Kutchuk Said, and that it was a mistake on the part of the refugee to imagine that he did. Thereupon he asked Sir Philip why he had taken him in, and why he did not give him up. Sir Philip's reply was characteristic of the man. In recounting his visit he said a happy thought occurred to him, and he replied "that according to English religion, and, as he believed, according to his Majesty's also, a refugee must be protected." Abdul smiled grimly and did not contradict the Ambassador. The Sultan declared that if Kutchuk Said would leave the Embassy he should not be followed by spies nor in any way molested. Sir Philip recognised that as the incident was already published in the local papers and was known fully to every Ambassador, its publicity was his safeguard, and accordingly Said left the Embassy.

In the last week of December an official report of the outrages was published. Its object was not intended to influence foreigners but Moslem subjects, and, like many similar reports, was a tissue of lies. It declared that the

Armenians had burnt mosques, had attacked Moslem women, and were the sole cause of the massacres which had taken place. The report did Abdul Hamid no good, because the statements themselves were not even ingenious. On every hand they were characterised as false. Meantime the year closed with massacres, of which that of Kara Hissar was typical. Every house was searched for Armenians, Moslems or Christians. When any fugitive was discovered in a Greek's house its inhabitants were at once butchered. Zeitum has already been mentioned as one of the places at which a massacre had taken place. Its inhabitants have for centuries occupied a place which in reference to Asia Minor corresponds generally to the condition of Montenegro. It was a mountainous region which was inhabited solely by Armenians. It once formed part of the kingdom of Little Armenia, which had been established by the Crusaders. Its mountains and defiles were easy of defence. When the Armenians were attacked they defended themselves bravely, but in presence of the enormous forces sent by Abdul against them, it was impossible that they could have held out. The Sultan was determined to destroy the whole of them. All the Powers took interest in their fate. Queen Victoria herself sent a letter to Abdul Hamid, beseeching him to spare its inhabitants. The intervention of the Powers, and especially of the British Queen, saved them.

It is satisfactory to record that some good Moslems revolted at the baseness of the advice given by Abdul Hamid's agents to Moslem subjects. One instance may be given where an Imam of a large mosque spoke up boldly in opposition to the advice of Abdul Hamid's emissary. He is described as a venerable old man with white hair and beard ; the mosque was full of Believers whom he had " led in prayer " for many years. When the emissary from Constantinople had finished speaking, he energetically replied in the following fashion :—" You have known me during all your lives as a good Moslem. I tell you that Islam teaches that Moslems are to respect the lives and property of ' the children of the books, ' (that is, Christians and Jews) unless they are in revolt against the Faithful. No man amongst you dare stand up and tell me that the Armenians in our town are, or have been, in revolt. They are quiet, peaceful people, and their lives and property are to be respected. This man from Constantinople states that he brings a message from the Padisha. I do not believe it, because the Sultan would never attempt to set aside the teachings of Mahomet. I tell you as a good Moslem that if any of you take part in pillaging or killing the Armenians, he is acting against the law of God and His Prophet, and he will have to answer for it in the Day of Judgment. In that great day I shall be ready to stand up before Allah Himself and bear witness that I uttered this warning. I will accuse any man who takes part in the action recommended by this emissary from Constantinople." Such utterances were probably not numerous, but there was hardly a town in which pious Mahometans did not shelter or seek to shelter Armenians during the massacres which commenced in 1894.

An abundance of evidence shows that massacres on a huge scale took place throughout all the Armenian provinces. The number of killed and of those who died from exposure and hardship consequent on the massacres will never be accurately known. The Armenians estimate it at 350,000. Few observers have put the number of victims lower than 100,000, but even they recognise that it is quite possible that they have underestimated them.

It may be admitted that the proscriptions, the arrests, the torturings, the murders, during the years preceding 1894 had driven many of the Armenians, who were residing outside the country, to something like madness. One may well excuse those who had had relations murdered from not looking calmly upon the pandemonium which existed.

While denouncing the utter and inexplicable stupidity and wickedness of Abdul Hamid's government of Armenia, many observers also denounced the sending of revolutionary Armenians from Russia to provoke insurrection. They urged, quite correctly, that the Armenians in the country would never have a chance of success in any rising.

Abdul Hamid never forgot the indignation in England and Russia consequent on the Press exposure of the Moslem outrages in Bulgaria, and was always keenly anxious to prevent the publication of his deeds in any section of the European Press. It was the knowledge of these facts which made the extremists among the Armenian exiles in Russia conclude that the only method of attracting the attention of Europe was to stir up agitation in Armenia itself and thereby provoke massacres.

One of the earliest notices that appeared of them in England was in the *Daily Telegraph* of April 2, 1895, sent by its special commissioner. In it he made the following statements :—" The Armenian population throughout the entire country are exhibiting a marvellous degree of patience under treatment which would rouse any other people to open rebellion. The mischievous remarks of people writing from Tiflis concerning the workings of a secret society, and so forth, are utterly devoid of truth. There is no secret society, worthy the name, in Armenia now. The Armenians are incapable of guarding secrets or of being welded into a powerful organisation ; and the revolutionary plans talked of are a mirage of the brain ; but the injustice and oppression of which the Armenian people are the victims would change the most loyal of Europeans into rebels. Women are being constantly insulted, assaulted, and dishonoured ; property is being seized by violence ; men, women, and children struck, wounded and killed ; and Christ's religion publicly reviled. Those who dare to complain are imprisoned, and the highest officials who enjoy the Sultan's confidence offer the very worst example. Every day I see property of Christian merchants publicly taken away by Mahometans, and when these helpless people kept their shops closed to avoid pillage the Governor-General himself ordered them to be opened.

" Two days ago, three Armenian ladies came to me

for protection. They did not fear death, they said, but only dishonour, and they had been told by Turkish officers that when the riot began each one of them would be handed to certain officers who had marked them for their own. The female teachers of an Armenian Protestant school at Erzeroum took refuge with the American missionary's family, as they were all too much alarmed to spend the night in the school-house."

"The collection of taxes offers opportunity for exaction and nameless injustice. I am enabled to state as an absolute fact that the governmental tax-gatherers are no longer satisfied with the money due to the Treasury, or the usual bribes for themselves, but indulge in wanton cruelties such as tying men to posts, flogging them, rubbing fresh manure into their eyes, nose, mouth and ears; slowly pouring cold water over them while they stand naked in snow; and forcing them to walk barefoot over sharp thorn bushes."

When the correspondent of the *Daily Telegraph* wrote, serious massacres had already taken place. Abdul Hamid had taken his measures carefully and had almost succeeded in keeping correspondents out of the country. Two, however, succeeded in reaching Armenia, one on the pretext that he was an engineer and was taking notes and drawings for a proposed railway, and the second as his dragoman, or interpreter. As, however, they were constantly liable to have their notes inspected, they had almost entirely to trust to their memories. Both were deeply impressed with what they saw and heard. Both recognised that the Turkish statement of a revolutionary movement due to committees which existed in Russia was greatly exaggerated, though they declared that the persecution to which the Armenians were subject would have justified much more serious movements than had actually taken place.

An outcry arose in Europe against the concealment of the news of what was going on; for the truth was gradually leaking out. Abdul Hamid, always sensitive to the influence of the foreign Press, was desirous of leading foreigners to believe that what he had done and was doing in Armenia was necessitated by revolutionary movements mainly due to the influence of Armenians in Russia instigated by Russian agents. The correspondents in Constantinople of every important European journal remained loyal to the truth. But very little news had been allowed to reach the capital. Instances of instigation or revolutionary movements of which they had obtained evidence were at once published, but they soon understood that events were happening of which they could obtain no trustworthy evidence. American and French missionaries, Protestant and Catholic, still remained in Armenia, and at the risk of their lives sent accounts to the United States Minister in Constantinople or to the British or French Ambassadors of what they saw. But the Turkish authorities exercised the most strict censorship of all letters, and refused to send telegrams the contents of which were suspected. One of the features to which foreign Consuls called attention was that the Armenians could save their lives if they became Moslems. To the honour of the race, they followed the example of their fathers, and, except in a few cases, refused to apostasize. The strength of will required to resist perversion to the religion of Islam was greater perhaps for the women than for the men. Some letters written by Armenians were smuggled into the capital. One, written by the wife of a poor Armenian—who, like so many of his countrymen, had come to Constantinople to take domestic service, remitting nearly the whole of his earnings to his family—explained to her husband that Moslems had come to the house, one of whom was armed with a long knife, and had offered her and other women the alternative of perversion or death. She mentioned that a bright boy of six or seven years of age was seized by the Turk with a knife, who threatened to cut his throat unless she would accept Mahometanism. She added in her letter, " You know what a dear chap he is, and, God forgive me, I changed and became Moslem. Many women in our town have done the same, and the Turks tell us that in the course of two or three years we shall be content with the change." Other letters containing similar testimony were smuggled into Constantinople by Europeans or kindly Moslems coming from Armenia, who hated the loathsome brutality of Abdul Hamid's treatment of peaceful peasants. The fullest source of information, however, was furnished by Consuls and missionaries.

As these and other communications, which escaped the vigilance of the Turkish censors and spies, were creating a strong hostile opinion in Europe and America, Abdul Hamid gladly availed himself of an opportunity, as he thought, of giving his version of the massacres through an important American newspaper. Mr. Gordon Bennett, of the *New York Herald*, had arrived in Constantinople, and was received by the Sultan as one of the princes of the Press. It is unimportant to know whether the suggestion of sending a special commissioner on behalf of his paper came from his Majesty or from Mr. Bennett, but each was willing that a commissioner should be sent: Mr. Bennett because it would enable his newspaper to be the first to give an account of the recent events and conditions in Armenia from actual observation; Abdul Hamid because he hoped and probably believed that his own version of the events could be imposed on the American people as a true one. In Constantinople the Gallios were amused, and remarked that the Sultan was at his old tricks; but those who desired that the world should learn the truth were alarmed. This alarm increased when the name of an extremely able man was mentioned as having been chosen by Mr. Bennett as his correspondent. As it was well known in the capital that the proposed correspondent's visit to the city had been for business where the support of Abdul Hamid was desired, it was judged by the leading Americans that he should be accompanied by another whose statements would be regarded as beyond suspicion. Mr. Bennett was therefore seen by Dr. Washburn, the President at that time of Robert College, who pointed out the unsuitability of having as a commissioner a man who was reputed, rightly or wrongly, to be seeking favours from the Sultan. Mr. Bennett received Dr. Washburn's representations with the independence which characterised him. He neither wished to give the Turkish nor the Armenian view. He wanted news for his paper, but it must be truth and not fiction. After considerable consultation, it was agreed that a literary man of high reputation in America should be joined as a second commissioner on behalf of the *New York Herald*. The commissioner named was the Rev. Geo. Hepworth, a Presbyterian clergyman, who had turned his attention largely to journalism. We have Mr. Hepworth's own account of his journey and of what he saw.[1] His book is itself a model of what such an account should be. He declares in his Preface that from the first he determined to be impartial. He kept his promise and his volume indicates a thoughtful and trustworthy man, with eyes to see and principles strong enough to resist the temptations thrown in his way to pervert truth. The accounts given on various occasions of efforts made to prevent him seeing persons other than those who were in the pay of Abdul Hamid are amusing and suggestive; but Mr. Hepworth was not a man to be deceived by Turkish cunning. The commissioners were accompanied by three of the Sultan's aides-de-camp and a secretary. The attempts made to prevent them from getting other information than from sources favourable to Abdul Hamid occur again and again. Mr. Hepworth says all that can legitimately be said against the Armenians. Yet he points out how some of them were worried into rebellion by attacks from the Kurds. He admits that the Russian Committee of revolutionary Armenians urged rebellion. He puts the matter however in its true light: "When I say that the Armenian massacres were caused by Armenian revolutionists, I tell a truth and a very important truth, but it is not the whole truth. It would be more correct to say that the presence of the revolutionists gave occasion and excuse for the

[1] "Through Armenia on Horseback," by the Rev. Geo. Hepworth. Isbister & Co., London, 1898.

massacres. That the Turks were looking for an occasion and an excuse, no one can doubt who has traversed that country." His testimony is valuable also in reference to the general relations between the Turks, in which are included the Kurds, and the Armenians. As already insisted upon, the economic question had much to do with hostilities between the respective adherents of the two faiths. But it is well to see what a keen-eyed observer says on the subject:

"Way down in the bottom of his heart, the Turk hates the Armenian. He will swear to the contrary, but I am convinced that the statement is true nevertheless. The reasons for this are abundant, as I have tried to show in other chapters of this book. The Turk is extremely jealous of the Armenian, jealous of his mental superiority, of his thrift and business enterprise. He has therefore resorted to oppression, and his steady purpose has been, and is now, to keep his victims poor. Equal opportunities for all are a delusion and a snare. They do not exist, and it is not intended that they shall exist. If the Turk could have his own way, unhampered by the public opinion of Europe, there would neither be an Armenian nor a missionary in Anatolia at the end of twenty years, for both are equally obnoxious."

"If you put an Armenian and a Turk side by side in a village it will hardly be twelve months before the Turk will retire impoverished because the Armenian has absorbed the business. The Turk has conquered the Armenian by force of arms, but the Armenian has the better of the Turk by force of brains. Up to the time of the recent massacres the Turk was continually losing money, while the Armenian grew richer every day."

The truth here stated by Mr. Hepworth that the Turks had conquered the Armenians by force of arms, but that the Armenians had the better of the Turks by force of brains, is one which should never be forgotten. Religious fanaticism had much to do with increasing the hostility between the two races. It has always been appealed to by tyrants like Abdul Hamid to stir up the disaffection of the Moslems against the Christians, but the groundwork of disaffection already existed in the jealousy of the superior intelligence and consequent prosperity of the Christians.

When the commissioners reached Armenia they saw, in spite of the attempts of the aides-de-camp and others to prevent them, that the evidence on the spot gave a very different impression from what they had received. "It is one thing," says Mr. Hepworth, "to read about the tragedy, the stupid blundering tragedy, when you are seated in your easy chair, thousands of miles away, but a very different thing to look into the wan and wrinkled faces of women whose homes have been broken up, and who were compelled to fly to the mountains amid the snows of winter in order to save themselves and their children while their husbands and fathers lay dead under the deserted roof."

The massacres commenced in 1894, and continued during three years. Mr. Hepworth says "it would be but a moderate estimate to say that 50,000 were killed. These victims were mostly heads of families," and takes no notice of those who perished from cold and exposure. Sir William Ramsay, who knows Asia Minor as well as any Englishman, says: "Abdul Hamid is responsible for half a million deaths, a still larger number who have suffered permanently from destitution, torture, mutilation, loss of property, of honour, etc., can vie with Mongols like Tamarlane. . . . Not one spark of any grand or great quality illumined his life or ennobled his fall."

The Armenians throughout the massacres mentioned gave many examples of heroism. Many cases were published in British newspapers and in the Blue-Books of men and women who refused to save their lives by the abandonment of their religion. They cannot justly be charged with cowardice. Though the people had been repeatedly disarmed they often made a bold stand.

Mr. Hepworth remarks on various occasions upon the dreadful alternative presented to the Armenians to "turn Moslems or be exterminated." . . . "The poor fellows at Birijik looked into the faces of their wives and children whose fate depended on their decision. It was a tragic scene, and tragic moment; their brethren in other parts were being murdered by hundreds. The cemeteries were glutted with victims. They surrendered and saved their lives. But the majority met their doom with the true and indomitable spirit of martyrdom and were as noble in their death as they were faithful in their lives."

Alluding to the abandonment of their faith by a few in Birijik, he adds: "Let those who think that they would prefer to have their skulls broken with a club blame the people of Birijik, if they choose to do so. I can only say that I myself dare not do it." "Think of women," says he, "holding their honour at such a price that they deliberately leaped from the bank of the Euphrates and sank beneath the raging torrent rather than submit to the lust of the Kurd. Can the old days of persecution furnish nobler examples of self-sacrifice than these?" He raised his hat to their honour as he passed the place from which they threw themselves.

From this account by an impartial American it is well to pass to one of equally unexceptionable authority furnished by a British official, Mr. Gerald Fitzmaurice, who was chief dragoman at the British Embassy until the declaration of war with Turkey in October, 1914, and who had already been many years in the employ of the British Government, for which he had done valuable work. He had acquired a reputation for his skilful knowledge of the various forms of Turkish, and had gained the confidence of Moslems and Christians alike. Sir Philip Currie, who in 1896 was our Ambassador to the Porte, had done his utmost, but in vain, to obtain the Sultan's consent to the amelioration of the Armenians. He probably knew more of what was going on in Armenia than the Ambassador in Constantinople of any other Power, but he regretted that his information was scanty. Abdul Hamid had dammed the supply of news. He succeeded, however, in 1896, in obtaining permission from the Sultan to send Mr. Fitzmaurice to Birijik. The special object assigned him, and on which Sir Philip had exacted permission, was to inquire on behalf of the British Government into the cases of conversion from Christianity to the Moslem faith which had taken place in that and neighbouring towns. Probably Abdul Hamid had not much objection to allow a British representative to make such inquiry because the majority of conversions were of women who had been taken into harems. Such women, to save their reputation, were often, perhaps even usually, ready to pretend that they had been voluntary converts. Birijik was specially mentioned because a number of women there were known to have accepted Mahometanism. Mr. Fitzmaurice's statement is contained in a report dated March 5, 1896.[1] His story of the conversions in Birijik is the following. The officer in command in the town asked the Christians to surrender their arms, otherwise he could not protect them. The Christians, believing that the implied offer was a genuine one, foolishly trusted in his word, and all the arms that had been left to them were sent to the Konak or Government House. The Kaimakan, or Assistant Governor, was one of the Moslems who loathed the task of carrying out Abdul's orders. As usual, religious fanaticism had been aroused, and the Moslem mob was eager for a conflict with the Christians and for the looting of their houses. The mob turned their wrath against the Kaimakan, and reproached him "as an uncircumcised infidel, with protecting Christians, and with concealing the Sultan's orders for their extermination." The story of such concealment was current in Armenia among Moslems and Christians alike ; for few of the Governors dared to contradict the statement that Abdul Hamid had signed such orders. On the Kaimakan remaining firm and expressing his determination to protect the Christians, the mob took the matter into their own hands. The officer at the head of the troops refused to keep his own promise to protect them. Thereupon

[1] Blue Book. Turkey No. 5, 1896.

there began a scene similar to what had taken place in many other towns. Every Armenian house, whether its occupants belonged to the National Church or were Roman Catholics or Protestants, was pillaged, ruined and desecrated.

Once more a kindly Moslem of good position tried to protect his Christian neighbours. He begged the officer in command "with tears in his eyes" to give him a few soldiers to go into the Armenian quarter and help to save what he could. His request was refused. The Christian quarter was surrounded. Many had taken refuge in a large building where they were menaced with death. Surrounded by a howling crowd, abandoned by the soldiers, their position was hopeless. A woman ascended the roof of the building and, showing a white flag, declared that all within it had become Mahometans. Mr. Fitzmaurice, speaking of what had happened, says: "They accepted Islam to save their lives, to save themselves from certain death."

An official report had been issued by Abdul Hamid's creatures which represented the conversions as voluntary. As usual in such cases, it was a huge lie. Even on the occasion of Mr. Fitzmaurice's visit the fanatical element, he declares, "was determined to kill any convert who renounced Islam."

Perhaps the most gruesome story, amid many horrors recounted by Mr. Fitzmaurice, relates to the City of Urfa, the ancient Edessa. He describes the massacre which took place in October preceding his visit and, especially, on December 28 and 29. Before it commenced the city contained 70,000 souls, of whom 30,000 were Armenians. The action of Abdul Hamid and the movements among the Armenians had created great tension between the two classes of the community, and little was required to bring about fighting between the troops, aided by the armed Moslem majority, and the Christians.

In the previous October an Armenian requested a Moslem to pay a debt. The Moslem saw an opportunity of escaping payment by appealing to the fanaticism of his co-religionists. His house was not in the Armenian quarter, but at some distance from it. He had the sympathy of his f iends in refusing to pay.

Mr. Fitzmaurice states that all the Armenians had been disarmed, and they, as well as the Moslems, believed that Abdul Hamid had sent orders for their extermination. The Moslems cut off the water supply to the Armenian quarter, and no person was permitted to carry food into it after the end of October. The Armenian bishop tried to telegraph to the Sultan, but failed. Amid the disturbances he had taken refuge in a monastery outside the town, and was there kept a prisoner. Neither he nor any other Armenian was allowed to telegraph or send letters by post. In the Armenian quarter was a brave American lady, a Miss Shattuck, who was greatly respected, not only by the Armenians of the town, but by all who knew her. As orders apparently had been sent from Constantinople to be careful not to allow any foreigner to be attacked, she was permitted to leave the town an hour before the great massacre of December 28 commenced.

In the interval between the end of October and the last days of December the Armenians assisted each other. They were now effectively in a state of siege. The water supply being cut off, they reopened old wells and carefully caught rain water. They managed also to obtain a scanty supply of food. Many messengers were sent out to take the news of their condition to other places, but all were caught and stripped. The mean trick of attempting to deceive the outside public was resorted to by compelling the Armenians to sign a telegram stating that tranquillity had been restored.

On December 28 the leading Armenians gathered in a great and ugly church, which was the cathedral. They drew up a statement of their fears and asked protection. The officer in charge of the troops promised that it should be given, but hardly had the promise been given before the massacre commenced. The cathedral, in which were the intended victims, was surrounded by a double ring of soldiers and mob. At the mid-day prayer a mollah waved a green flag, the emblem of the Moslem faith. Mr. Fitzmaurice states that thereupon "soldiers and mob rushed on the Armenian quarter and began a massacre of the males over a certain age." One of the ghastly incidents recorded is as follows: "A certain sheik ordered his followers to bring as many stalwart young Armenians as they could find. To the number of about 100 they were thrown on their backs and held down by their hands and feet, while the sheik, with a combination of fanaticism and cruelty, proceeded, while reciting verses of the Koran, to cut their throats after the Mecca rite of sacrificing sheep." Meantime, all the houses in the Armenian quarter were being plundered. Many women lost their lives in trying to protect their male relations.

The massacre on that day, which began by the waving of the green flag, ceased at sunset by trumpet sound. All outrages came to an end for that day. Here, as throughout the massacres, their organisation was carefully and officially complete. In some places they both commenced and ended with the sound of trumpet.

On the following day, Sunday, December 29, the trumpet sounded the signal for the attack to commence. Moslems who had not taken part in these on the previous day seemed to have been unwilling not to receive their share in the plunder of Christian houses, and on this day joined the Moslem mob. Savage butchery continued until noon, and "then culminated in an act," says Mr. Fitzmaurice, "which for fiendish barbarity is one to which history can furnish few, if any, parallels." The language of Mr. Fitzmaurice is exceptionally strong here, but it may safely be said that nothing, even in recent Turkish history, is on the whole more loathsomely brutal than the incident he relates. It was the deliberate sacrifice of a cathedral full of disarmed people at a time when it is not even alleged that there was rebellion, riot, or even resistance. The ugly, barn-like building will hold about 8,000 people, and on Saturday evening was crowded with refugees. A general belief existed there and elsewhere in Turkey, which was not without some foundation in fact, that unarmed people who took refuge within a church would not be molested. Even within the recollection of many in Constantinople the alarm of an anti-Christian or anti-Jewish riot caused the churches and synagogues to fill rapidly. Such buildings, indeed, erected during the last three centuries, always have the appearance of being built to support a siege.

On the Saturday night the Armenian priest in the cathedral entered a record upon one of the pillars of the church, which was read by Mr. Fitzmaurice, to the effect that he had administered a last communion to 1,800 members of his flock. All these persons remained all night in the church and were joined by several hundred more who believed that they were in a place of safety. When the church was attacked on the Sunday morning it is estimated that there were at least 3,000 people within it. The outside mob was well armed, the Christians within absolutely without arms. The attack commenced by firing in through the windows and by trying to break down the doors. After a short time the iron door was smashed in. The mob entered with a rush and killed all who were on the ground floor, all of whom were men, the women and children having gone into the gallery. The church treasures were at once rifled. The ornaments and shrines were torn down, amid cries from the mob of "Call on Christ to prove Himself a greater prophet than Mahomet."

The huge gallery was partly stone and partly wood, and was packed with a terrified and shrieking mass of women and children, with a few men. Some of the mob began picking off men with revolver shots, but this process of killing Christians was too tedious.

Churches and mosques in Turkey are usually covered with straw matting, often indeed several layers thick. Many of the refugees had taken into the church their yorghans, a kind of eiderdown, which may be used either as a bed or a covering. This mass of matting, and of yorghans, was collected together with other combustible materials, and arranged so that when set fire to they would burn the galleries. Then thirty tins of petroleum were poured over the mass and on the dead bodies of those lying about on the ground floor, and fire was set to the whole. The gallery beams and staircase soon caught fire, and then the mob left the mass of struggling human beings to become the prey of the flames.

Abdul Hamid had beaten the record even of massacres of Christians in Turkey. The slaughter at Urfa was sytematically conducted, like those of so many other places in Armenia. At half-past three on that terrible Sunday afternoon the trumpet once more sounded ; the mob withdrew, and the Mufti and other Moslem notables went round the Armenian quarter to proclaim that the slaughter was at an end.

Mr. Fitzmaurice reported that 126 families were so completely wiped out that not even a woman or a baby remained. No distinction was made in the slaughter between the various forms of Christianity which the victims professed. The majority were Gregorians, that is to say, professed the national religion of the race, but there were also Roman Catholics and Protestants. He estimates that on the two days December 28 and 29 nearly 8,000 persons perished, and of these, between 2,500 and 3,000 were killed in the cathedral. Between 400 and 500 persons, during the siege, became Moslems. Mr. Gladstone, speaking at the time of these outrages, declared that " the powers of language hardly suffice to describe what has been done and is being done in Armenia, and that exaggeration is almost beyond power."

Massacre in Constantinople.

The story of massacres of Armenians during the reign of Abdul Hamid does not end with the slaughter in the Armenian Provinces. A foolish demonstration made by Armenians took place in Constantinople itself in September, 1895. All the Powers remonstrated, but did nothing else. The Turks naturally knew what was being done and prepared to anticipate it by a Moslem onslaught of greatly superior force. The mob, consisting of the lowest of the Mahometans, largely enforced by the many Kurds who were then in Constantinople, were prepared with sticks, usually having a piece of angle-iron affixed at one end. Those so armed were spoken of as "sopajis," and on a given day the signal was given for attacking the Armenians in Stamboul, Galata, Pera, and in the villages on each side of the Bosporus. There were many thousands of them resident in these portions of the capital. It had long been the habit of members of families in Armenia to send the husbands, and after them the sons of the family, to Constantinople in order to earn their living. Most of the caretakers or guardians of khans, offices and shops belonged to this class. The great majority were honest and trustworthy servants, earned the respect of their employers, and did not meddle in politics. The proportion of wages which they remitted to their families was very large, often amounting to three-quarters of their earnings. In former times Moslems had usually been unwilling to take service under Christians, whether natives or foreigners, though during the first thirty years of last century they had begun to do so. They were then largely replaced by Armenians. The result was that the class of hamals or porters, the guardians, and messengers were nearly all Christians, without being willingly unfair to the poor Moslems, who are, to say the least, equally as trustworthy as the Armenians; most foreigners would agree that, on the whole, the Moslems showed less intelligence in the performance of their duties than did Armenians. Even the poorest Armenian could read and write his own language, and for all services mentioned such an acquisition was a great advantage. The result was that in the course of half a century Armenians from the provinces had largely replaced Moslems in these positions of trust. Thereby jealousy was created, and this, added to the great religious hostility, led to the massacre in the capital in 1895, the object of which, in popular opinion, was to clear out the whole of the poor Armenians in the capital and replace them by Moslems.

The attack upon them a year later was much more savage and equally unjustifiable. Had there been on this occasion also any decent police regulations, coupled with the will to preserve order without massacre, nothing serious would have happened. It was well understood, however, at the time that the Moslem mob was acting according to the will, and even by express orders from, Abdul Hamid. During two days in August, 1896, the Armenians were murdered in the streets of Constantinople itself wherever found. There was no resistance or attempt at resistance. There were, however, in the city a few Armenians of Russian nationality, some of whom were desperate men, prepared to resist and determined to make a demonstration against Abdul Hamid, but they were an insignificant portion of the number of Armenians in the capital. The sopajis went about in gangs and knocked every Armenian on the head whom they met. Every foreigner had a story to tell of some outrage of which he had heard or been a witness. The villages on the Bosporus in which isolated families of Armenians had been residing all their lives, men as little likely to take part in a public disturbance as the occupants of suburban dormitories around London would be, were hunted down relentlessly.

Many instances occurred in which Moslems of position, who loathed the outrages which were going on, did their utmost to save the Armenians. Amongst such men should be mentioned Marshal Fuad Pasha. He had been a friend, a generation earlier, of General Skobeleff. Both men at that time were young, and there was much in common between them. Both were daring and generous soldiers. Fuad in late years had come to be regarded with suspicion by Abdul Hamid on account of his out-spokenness. It was generally believed that the Sultan was responsible for several attempts upon his life, but he was surrounded by a body of faithful Croats and Albanians, each of whom was ready to shed his blood in his master's defence. When the order was given from the Palace, that is, from Abdul, to attack the Armenians, Fuad was residing on his farm immediately behind Kadikewi, the ancient Chalcedon, where he had a military command. When he learned what the orders were he immediately sent to the local authorities in the villages on the Asiatic side of the Bosporus to say that the Armenians were to be protected and that he would hold the officials personally responsible if any Armenian were killed or molested. His vigour and activity during the two days of massacre were remarkable. When he heard of the bloodshed on the opposite shore of the Bosporus he sent messengers in every direction to renew his orders, and in this way the lives of hundreds of Armenians were saved. Nor was he alone. An old Mollah, also residing on the Asiatic side, was acquainted with a British family living some eight miles from Constantinople in a purely Turkish village. The head of the household was a Scotchman, who, together with his family, had rendered generous and constant service to the poor Mahometans of the village, but the Imam appeared to resent the residence of foreigners in the village. The Mollah, who knew the village and the British family, was aware of the dangerous spirit aroused by religious fanaticism, and believed that the isolated houses would be attacked, possibly even by some of the villagers who had received favours from it. He therefore took down his old gun, seated himself on the doorstep of the Christian house, and let it be understood that he would shoot the first Moslem who attempted to enter it. Many similar incidents might be quoted.

The protection afforded by Fuad Pasha to the Armenians rendered him more than ever an object of hatred to the Sultan. Further attempts, which happily failed, were made upon his life, and even his sons were frequently harassed.

It was during these attacks that an incident occurred which deserves record of attacks by Kurds in the quarter of Constantinople, known as Kum Capu.[1] In that district there were a large number of resident Armenians, and in the midst of it is the cathedral church and the residence of the Armenian Patriarch. The British Society of Friends had gradually built up an Institution intended solely for the benefit of poor Armenians. Armenian women seem to have a transmitted faculty for needlework, and the founders of the establishment organised working parties of girls and women, where embroidery and other needlework was done which helped the workers to live. At the head of it was Miss Burgess, a lady of great energy and of fertile activity in all that related to the advancement of girls. The latter received instruction in their own language. The Institution became large and successful. It soon came to be understood in the neighbourhood that it was not established for the propagation of any form of Christian faith, but that its objects were humanitarian, and that there was no sort of gain sought or obtained by those who conducted it. During the earlier massacres the Institution had to pass through a troublesome time. The streets in the neighbourhood were patrolled by Turkish soldiers, as well as by a Turkish and Kurdish mob. When the agitation against the Armenians became exceptionally great, the British Consul sent a request, which almost amounted to an order, that Miss Burgess and the British teachers working with her should leave and go to Pera, the European quarter. Mis Burgess indignantly replied that she could not and would not desert her Armenian girls. Then came an order "Hoist the British flag." The ladies of the Society of Friends are probably not learned in the matter of flags, and as it was impossible to send a messenger from Stamboul to Galata to buy one, their only servants being Armenian, the ladies had to make one to answer the purpose. Woman's ingenuity was not at fault, and something like a Union Jack was

[1] It is worth noting that most of the great gates of Constantinople have names which, when translated, resemble those found in London or in other parts of England. Thus Kum Capu = Sandgate; Eski Capu, Oldgate; Yeni Capu, Newgate; Top Capu, Canongate; Egri Capu, Crooked Gate.

made which, sewn on to a piece of red cloth, answered the purpose. When Abdul Hamid's zaptiehs inquired angrily how it was that Armenians dared to hoist the British flag, the answer was a reference to the British Embassy. Happily the Institution escaped attack.[1]

The great slaughter of Armenians in Constantinople terminated with a daring but foolish attack made upon the Ottoman Bank. On August 26, 1896, half a dozen Russian Armenians with a few Turkish subjects took part in the attack. It was foolish, because it was unlikely to serve any useful purpose, the design of its perpetrators being to show how easily public buildings could be destroyed, and would be if redress were not granted to Armenia. The chief director of the Bank, Sir Edgar Vincent, now Lord D'Abernon, and the other officials were greatly alarmed for the safety of the interests with which they were charged. The evidence does not, however, point to any desire on the part of the leaders to do injury to property which belonged largely to foreigners. Hand grenades were thrown and a small bomb was dropped from the roof into the street, to which already soldiers had hurried. Sir Edgar and others wisely opposed any attack being made on the rioters while they were in possession of the Bank. With the consent of the Government the instigators were permitted to negotiate and were promised personal safety if they surrendered. This they did, and were allowed to take refuge on board Sir Edgar's yacht and, subsequently, to leave the country.

The massacre in Constantinople itself caused the Ambassadors to realise the horrors which had been committed in Armenia. Corpses lying in the road at Therapia and elsewhere before the Embassies compelled them to vigorous action. The first result was to lead to the sending of an open telegram to Abdul

[1] The Institution survived the storm until the Revolution in 1908, then it took new developments, greatly increased its number of scholars, and had the open approval of even its Moslem neighbours, as well as of every fair-minded man in the foreign communities It continued to do noble work for the elevation of the large Armenian population in the neighbourhood of Kum Capu until the declaration of war with England at the end of October, 1914.

Hamid, signed by the representatives of all the Powers, telling the Sultan that the massacre must cease immediately, and that its "continuance meant danger to his throne and dynasty." This startling message, sent open and in French in order that it might become publicly known, had an immediate effect.[1] The massacre ceased at once. A few days afterwards the following Collective Note was presented :—

"The representatives of the Great Powers believe it their duty to draw the attention of the Sublime Porte to an exceptionally serious side of the disorders which have recently stained with blood the capital and its environs.

"It is the declaration on positive data of the fact that the savage bands which murderously attacked the Armenians and pillaged the houses and shops, which they entered under the pretence of looking for agitators, were not accidental gatherings of fanatical people, but presented every indication of a special organisation known by certain agents of the authorities if not directed by them. This is proved by the following circumstances :—

"(1) The bands rose simultaneously at different points of the town at the first news of the occupation of the Bank by the Armenian revolutionaries, before even the police or an armed force had appeared on the scene of the disorder, while the Sublime Porte admits that information was received in advance by the police regarding the criminal designs of the agitators.

"(2) A great part of the people who composed these bands were dressed and armed in the same manner.

"(3) They were led or accompanied by softas, soldiers, or even police officers, who not only looked on unmoved at their excesses, but at times even took part in them.

[1] The telegram was drafted by Mr., afterwards Sir Michael Herbert, Chargé d'Affaires during the temporary absence of Sir Philip Currie, but signed by the representatives of all the Powers.

"(4) Several heads of the detective police were seen to distribute cudgels and knives among these Bashi-Bazuks, and point out to them the direction to take in search of victims.

"(5) They were able to move about freely, and accomplish their crimes with impunity, under the eyes of the troops and their officers, even in the vicinity of the imperial palace.

"(6) One of the assassins, arrested by the dragoman of one of the embassies, declared that the soldiers could not arrest him. On being taken to Yildiz Palace, he was received by the attendants as one of their acquaintances.

"(7) Two Turks, employed by Europeans, who disappeared during the two days' massacre, declared, on their return, that they had been requisitioned and armed with knives and cudgels in order to kill Armenians.

"These facts need no comment.

"The only remarks to be added are, that they recall what happened in Anatolia, and that such a force springing up under the eyes of the authorities, and with the co-operation of certain of the latter's agents, becomes an exceedingly dangerous weapon. Directed to-day against one nationality of the country, it may be employed to-morrow against the foreign colonies, or may even turn against those who tolerated its creation.

"The representatives of the Great Powers do not believe it right to conceal these facts from their Governments, and consider it their duty to demand of the Sublime Porte that the origin of this organisation should be sought out, and that the instigators and principal actors should be discovered and punished with the utmost rigour.

"They are ready, on their part, to facilitate the inquiry, which should be opened by making known all the facts brought to their notice by eye-witnesses, which they will take care to submit to a special investigation."

To this note, which, in diplomatic language, charged Abdul Hamid with being the author or instigator of the massacre, the Porte replied denying that the attacks on the Armenians by the Moslem mob had been instigated by Government agents, pointing out that among the dead there were many Mahometans who had been attacked by Armenians, and promising that the Mahometans as well as the Armenians who took a leading part in the riots would be tried by a special tribunal appointed for the purpose. No faith, however, was placed in these statements.

To appease the Ambassadors and to save his own reputation by throwing the blame on another, Abdul Hamid dismissed Kutchuk Said, though no one doubted that he was merely an instrument for carrying out the intentions of his master. Kiamil, his successor, recognised as far back as the beginning of 1895 the stupidity as well as the brutality of the massacres. He had endeavoured to persuade Abdul Hamid to accept a project of reforms for Armenia already submitted by the Powers, and especially a provision in it by which the Powers should have the right to appoint a foreign Commissioner to superintend their execution. Abdul Hamid refused to accept this provision or any modification of it. Kiamil tried his best to organise a Turkish Commission of Control which the Ambassadors accepted, hoping rather than expecting, in view of the rejection of their own proposals, that it would be effective. His efforts were fruitless. He tendered his resignation on two or three occasions, but the Sultan, knowing that he was respected by the Ambassadors, refused to accept it. The veteran Minister tried, and again failed, to persuade the Sultan to institute reforms for Armenia and resigned. Again the resignation was refused, but on November 6, 1895, the Sultan dismissed him, and sent him to be Governor of Aleppo as a punishment. He was ill at the time, was carried on board a steamer, and had to remain at Smyrna.

It need only be added here that Kiamil and the

best of the Moslems disapproved of the Armenian massacres.[1] These hideous deeds were done by order of the Sultan in spite of his Ministers. They were none of them at this time strong men, but they did their little best to be humane. In many cases Abdul Hamid sent *agents provocateurs* into the Armenian villages to incite the peasants to make foolish declarations against the Sultan, and then had them attacked for having made them.

Lord Salisbury, in 1897, in a public speech solemnly warned Abdul Hamid of the "ultimate fate of misgoverned countries," and expressed his opinion of the Sultan's conduct as strongly as one in his position could do.

The Armenian troubles, ranging as they did over four or five years, did great material injury to Turkey. They convinced all sections of the community that Abdul Hamid had either insufficient intelligence to see, or that his perversity of hatred towards Armenians made him unable to recognise that his action was not only ruining the credit of Turkey, but was destroying its industries and its commercial class. He never seems to have understood that internal peace and quiet were essentials to industrial prosperity. He took little interest in industries of any kind, because he knew nothing of them. It is therefore not surprising that he sanctioned methods which were ruinous to business enterprise. It was upon his suggestion that local passports were required to enable any person living in Turkey to pass from one town or village to another, that an examination took place of every passenger even who had obtained such a passport, an examination in which the reason for the journey was taken note of and any letters found on him were read. Travelling for business purposes was thus largely diminished; but while foreigners going about their lawful business were merely inconvenienced by these restrictions, native Christians, Greeks as well as Armenians, were practically con-

[1] See note 1 at end of this chapter.

demned to idleness. Many commercial houses had hitherto employed Armenian travellers or bagmen, on account of their acquaintance with the languages of the country, to visit various districts of the Empire to display samples of their merchandise and obtain orders. It was always found difficult, and in some cases impossible, to replace such men. Even flourishing industrial institutions belonging to Europeans suffered largely from the hindrances to business due to the difficulties imposed on travel.[1]

Meantime, petty persecutions of the Armenians existed throughout the country. The attacks and massacres in Constantinople itself were believed amongst all classes of the community to be intended to drive out all Armenians of the porter class from the capital, and to replace them by Kurds and other Moslems. In this respect the persecution largely succeeded. Hundreds of hamals or porters, guardians, cooks, and other Armenians, were replaced by Moslems. Villages in Armenia which had supplied such men for even centuries, fathers being succeeded by their sons, became impoverished. Indeed, the persecution of the Armenians was, from every point of view, sheer folly. When coupled with the inhuman treatment of thousands of industrious and peace-loving citizens, it places Abdul Hamid in the list of the enemies of the human race.

No other portion of the career of Abdul Hamid more fairly and fully illustrates his policy, the limitations of his ability, and his habit of mind. The

[1] One illustration may be given as typical. A flourishing business had an Armenian creditor who had never failed in his payments. He managed to get a letter smuggled through to the establishment in Constantinople, stating that if he could obtain permission to leave the town where he lived he would have no difficulty in collecting amounts due to him and consequently in paying what was asked of him from Constantinople, that his customers had been accustomed to pay him or his traveller, and would not make payments to others In spite of the employment of influence with the Government, the request was refused. In a hundred different ways business operations were impeded. It is true that the Turks generally, being unaccustomed to business, had very crude ideas of the elementary laws of economic science, and in this respect Abdul Hamid was a typical Turk. The result was that the revenues of the country diminished and many business houses were closed.

Armenians, when he was girt with the sword of Osman, though they had grievances, had not become troublesome subjects. The provinces mainly inhabited by them were remote from the capital, and Moslem opinion in Constantinople, which was practically all which Abdul Hamid respected, cared little about what was done to Christians in so distant a part of the Empire. At that time, had the Sultan been sensible or gracious enough to grant a few rudimentary reforms for the protection of life, honour and property, the Armenians would have been grateful. Rightly or wrongly they dreaded becoming subject to Russian rule. A wise ruler, even a Gallio, consulting only his own convenience and the interest of his country, could have flung them a few concessions which would have made him popular. Such an idea never seems to have occurred to him. He sent Governors who were notoriously robbing the people whom they ought to have protected. He protected the wrongdoers even after he had been informed by the Patriarch or the Foreign Embassies of the robberies committed by them. If the pressure from an Embassy became unusual, he removed the official and promoted him to a more lucrative post. This, indeed, was his way of showing Foreign Ambassadors and his Moslem subjects that he intended to govern Armenia as he liked. Year by year he neglected every suggestion made for the amelioration of the lot of the Armenians, even when made by his own Ministers. There was not a Consul belonging to any foreign State who did not report hideous cases of torture within his knowledge inflicted by Turkish officials of the baser sort in order to extort money from Armenian prisoners, their friends or relations, or to please their own superiors. The forms of torture were hideous and inhuman. Turkish women themselves complained of and, in some notable instances, were made ill by the terrible shrieks indicating sufferings endured by prisoners against whom there was no charge and who were never brought to trial. Even before the great massacres of 1894 had commenced, the pandemonium existing in the Armenian Provinces was the most damnable of which modern European history bears record. It is futile to suggest that Abdul Hamid was ignorant of these outrages. They were brought to his notice by several Ambassadors, and also by humane Moslem subjects. Such subjects, indeed, became notoriously marked men. During the whole period of the massacres, 1893-97, every European resident in Turkey heard stories of Moslems who had been persecuted because they had sheltered Armenians from the brutal cruelty of their Sovereign.

The only excuse that an advocate for Abdul Hamid could attempt to make for his conduct during this time was that there was a disposition to rebel amongst the Armenian people, and that he desired to prevent rebellion coming to a head ; but the excuse would have few facts to support it. Independent observers testified in the early years of Abdul's reign that the Armenians were loyal and, for various reasons, preferred to remain under Turkey's rule. The Armenians knew that, as there was no Province in which there were a majority of Christians, they had no chance of being formed into an autonomous Christian State. Such a proposal was never suggested in any newspaper either in Turkey, nor probably outside. The reforms suggested by the British Government and submitted by Sir Henry Layard and successive Ambassadors would have produced loyal and contented subjects. Abdul Hamid set himself from the first with such hostility towards every form of improvement in the position of his Armenian subjects as to lead to general belief in Turkey that his opposition was due to a personal sentiment of hatred towards them. Whether this was so or not it is impossible to say, but it is at least safe to declare that, until the period of the great massacres, he did nothing which indicated that he had the desire to do justice to them or possessed elementary ideas of statesmanship in regard to the rule of subject races.

When we remember his conduct in organising the massacres, in supporting every outrage committed upon his own subjects, we shall not be far wrong in comparing him, as Sir William Ramsay has done, with Tamerlane or Nero, or any other enemy of the human race. A recklessness of human suffering or life seems to have taken possession of him. Abdul Hamid's conduct as a statesman under such circumstances will ever be condemned. Assuming that the desire of a Sultan must be to preserve his territory intact, and to make the whole of his subjects loyal, Abdul Hamid took no measures in reference to Armenia which tended to achieve either of these results. His subjects were driven by him to look to Russia for deliverance, and the inevitable result followed, that they came to rejoice that the Provinces occupied by them should be under Russian rule. Whatever may be the result of the world-war which is now going on, we may take it as certain that such portion of the Armenian population as remains will be well content to be delivered from Turkish rule.

Note I.—NOTES ON VISIT TO ARMENIA, BY DR. RENDEL HARRIS.[1]

Professor Rendel Harris and his wife visited Armenia in 1896. The volume of the correspondence between husband and wife contains a most human account of the Armenian population after the massacres. Mrs. Harris was a woman of remarkable power, whose sympathy induced men and women, not only amongst the Armenians, but even Turkish women, to speak of what they had seen. Her letters are full of touches of pathos and of womanly insight into character, which make them specially valuable. Starting from Alexandretta she journeyed to Aintab and Urfa, where she visited the old Cathedral, the scene of the great slaughter more completely described by Mr. Fitzmaurice; passed on to Marden and then to Diarbekir, each of her letters from these places being full of interest. At Malatia she describes the act of a friendly Turkish Bey who helped the Armenians. She visited the harem of this man who had defended them at

[1] "Letters from the Scenes of the Recent Armenian Massacres," by J. Rendel Harris and Helen B. Harris. Published by James Nisbet & Co., Ltd., 1897.

the risk of his life and whose house at the time of the massacre was full of refugees. She saw a woman whose hand had been nearly severed by a sword, and whose wounds had been dressed by the Turkish ladies of the home In another place, she mentions a Kurdish village whose inhabitants had refused to help in the massacre of their Christian neighbours. She adds, however, that this was the only village out of a hundred which did refuse. In consequence of their refusal, Turkish troops were sent who destroyed and burnt the village as if it had been an Armenian one (p. 174). In many places she bears testimony to the humanitarian work of American missionaries, especially of two ladies, Miss Shattuck and Miss Bush, both of whom had devoted their lives to service amongst Armenian women. Both she and her husband speak of the devotion and veritable heroism of Dr. Gates, at that time the President of the (American) Euphrates College. Dr. Gates has been for the last seven years President of Robert College, the successor of Dr. Geo. Washburn. His work was highly appreciated in England, especially by the Committee in aid of Armenian distress presided over by the Duke of Westminster. The University of Edinburgh, in recognition of his services to education, conferred upon him the degree of Doctor of Laws. Mrs. Harris, writing from Harpoot on September 21st, 1896, alluding to the statements circulated in Constantinople and abroad that the Armenians themselves "always bring on these troubles," says (speaking for the localities she knows): "This is a falsehood patent to all who witness the events. The massacres are planned beforehand. The Armenians have been deprived long since of their arms; they are defenceless and cowed. Do the sheep attack the wolf? They have no recourse, no place to flee to. Abject submission is their attitude, and their only possible policy" (p. 207). Mrs. Harris's last letter is dated November 18th, 1896, and is from Marsovan. She speaks enthusiastically about the great American College, its large staff of teachers, and of the native professors, all of whom could converse fluently in English. The present writer may add that seventeen years afterwards, in 1913, he visited this college and can add his testimony to the useful work that it was then accomplishing. It was still in full vigour under a new Director, Dr. White, while the ladies mentioned by Mrs. Harris, namely, Miss Gage and Miss Willard, were still in the full vigour of active and useful lives.

Note 2.—SUMMARY OF MASSACRES IN ARMENIA.

The following is a summary (mainly from Blue Books) of the most important slaughters in Armenia during the great massacres :—

At the beginning of 1894, forty-one persons who had surrendered at Yuzgat were killed; thirty-two villages in the neighbourhood were burned in June and most of the inhabitants killed by order of the authorities. In consequence of these outrages a meeting was held in London in May, 1895, at which the Dukes of Argyll and Westminster—two men who were always prominent in doing what was possible to protect the Armenians —were the most distinguished speakers. The following months of the same year saw the worst of Abdul Hamid's doings; 2,000 persons were murdered at Baiburt, 1,000 in Erzinghian, the same number in Bitlis, 2,500 in Diabekir; all the above were in October. During November and December Harpoot, Sivas, Marash, Gurun, Arabkir, and Kaiserea each had upwards of 1,000, the last-mentioned having 2,000.

The massacres in Urfa, Zeitun, Mush, and other places were in 1896.

CHAPTER XI—*continued*

ABDUL HAMID'S TREATMENT OF SUBJECT RACES—*continued*

PART III.—IN MACEDONIA.

Want of statesmanship in dealing with Macedonia; all Powers desire to save it for Turkey; Abdul Hamid refuses to execute reforms promised at Berlin; position occasions anxiety to Bulgarians and Greeks; difficulties arising from uncertainty of Ferdinand's position; disputes between Orthodox and Bulgarian Churches; Germany supports demands for Bulgarian Bishops; Comitijis; Murzsteg Programme, 1903; its provisions; failure of; Austria's attitude doubtful; Hilmi Pasha's recommendations disregarded.

ABDUL HAMID's want of statesmanship was nowhere more conspicuous than in his treatment of Macedonia. He had witnessed the loss of Serbia and Bulgaria. In Macedonia, adjoining Greece and these liberated States, the people were mostly of the same race, religion, and language as those of these adjacent countries, and a ruler might have been expected to examine the circumstances under which they had been detached from the Empire, and to ask himself how far similar circumstances were likely to produce a similar result. Unhappily, his treatment of Macedonia showed that he had learned nothing. Every European State appeared, at least, to desire that it should remain under his rule. Its loss to the Empire was due to Abdul Hamid.

The Province had suffered previous to his accession from the same kind of mis-government which had led to aspirations in Bosnia, Herzegovina, Serbia, and Bulgaria, and then to the Russo-Turkish war. In the Treaties both of San Stefano and Berlin suggestions had been made for bettering the lot of Moslem and Christian inhabitants in order to remove legitimate discontent. While the usual evils attendant upon Turkish rule prevailed in Macedonia, such as the non-payment of the troops quartered upon the population, the lawless exactions of Moslems from the Christians, the want of protection for life, woman's honour, and property, Macedonia had its own special grievances. Non-government was a not less fertile ground of complaint than mis-government. The traditionally hostile elements of the population, Greeks, Bulgarians and Albanians, were left to fight out their own quarrels. Redress in the law courts could not be had. Corrupt as they were throughout the Empire, they were probably worse in Macedonia than elsewhere. Already a large portion of the country had been unjustly acquired by Moslems from the Christian peasants, and the disputes between the legal Moslem owners themselves, as well as between them and the peasants, had brought about something like anarchy. Abdul Hamid in the early years of his reign let things drift. He did nothing.

The Bulgarian element in the population was the most numerous, but in the southern portion of the Province there were districts where the Greeks predominated. Bulgars and Serbs—the two Slavic elements—made common cause. The Albanians were steadily encroaching on Serbian territory in Northern Macedonia. After Serbia had become a Kingdom in 1878 and Bulgaria a semi-independent State, the desire to get rid of the anarchy which prevailed became common to all the neighbouring States who were inconvenienced by immigrants of their own race. Abdul Hamid should have seen the need of sending his best men to check the encroachments of the Albanians, and to preside over courts where justice would have been administered. Had he done so he would have learned that the aspirations of the Christians had been increased by the liberation of their neighbours on all sides, but he would have learned also that the population had not yet conceived the idea of separation from his rule. Indeed, if he had possessed any gift of statesmanship he would have seen his chance of attaching Macedonia to it.

The Bulgarians and Greeks in their own countries naturally sympathised with men of their race who were still under the Turkish yoke, but they did not wish to be troubled by them. Abdul Hamid knew that Bulgaria, especially, was seriously harassed by the constantly increasing crowd of refugees who fled from Macedonian anarchy, and he could have worked to satisfy the desire of the people by establishing some form of autonomous government. Even short of that step, anarchy plus the street constable would have gone far to content them. Bulgaria would have aided him, for she feared danger from absorbing so many Macedonians. Greece would not have objected. But he did nothing.

During ten or twelve years after the conclusion of peace with Russia, all the old evils were allowed to continue. Gradually, however, Abdul Hamid formed the notion that his best policy was to encourage the Albanians. It is true that this highly interesting race were divided; but while there was a majority of Moslems, nearly half the population were Christians, those of the South belonging to the Orthodox Church, and those of the North to that of Rome; but the adherents of both Churches and, indeed, of both religions got on with each other better than in any other part of the Empire. That this statement is true is attested by a host of independent foreign witnesses. This happy result is due to various causes, one of the principal being that the Moslem Albanians were under the influence of the Becktashi sect of Dervishes, who have always been in favour of religious toleration. Members of the same family, some of whom were Christians and others Moslems, sat at the same table, partook of the same dishes, and often intermarried. Religious toleration was indeed their rule. Abdul Hamid had persuaded himself that his Albanian troops were the most loyal of his subjects, and so he gradually surrounded his palace with them. He gave them favours which were denied to other sections of his army. He promoted Albanians to high office, and this to such an extent, both in the Army and Civil Service, as to arouse a strong feeling of jealousy in both services. Their encroachments on the lands of Bulgarians, Serbians, and Greeks were encouraged. His policy of permitting the Albanians to capture the territory of their neighbours in Macedonia greatly increased the anarchy already existing.

During the years 1890–1900 the condition of Macedonia continued to cause anxiety to all the neighbouring States. Bulgaria, especially, desiring a peaceful neighbour and wishing to stop immigration, presented projects for its reform to the Porte. She did not ask for or desire its annexation, because, though the population of Southern Macedonia was largely Bulgarian, the people of the Principality did not wish their influence to be swamped by the union with the people of that Province. There was, indeed, considerable jealousy between the two populations, but Bulgaria suggested the establishment of an autonomous Government in Macedonia under the suzerainty of the Sultan. Thereupon the Albanians, probably at the instigation of the Sultan, put forth another project on different lines. Neither project was accepted by the Porte.

The anomalous position of Prince Ferdinand created additional difficulties in Macedonia. It was not recognised that he had the right to speak for his country. As the Powers refused officially to recognise him, the Sultan adopted the same policy. The Russians were constantly intriguing to regain their influence, so that the representatives of Bulgaria were unheeded. Stambuloff had his hands full, with struggles against the partisans of Russia, the influx of Macedonians, and plots against his own authority. One such plot may be mentioned. It was formed in 1889 under a certain Major Panitza to expel Ferdinand. Panitza visited the Commandant of the Army at Sofia by night and invited him to join the conspiracy. The Commandant refused and informed the Government. The leaders and the chiefs were arrested, and an examination of their papers showed that the conspiracy had many ramifications, some of the most serious of which were in Macedonia. Ten persons were tried, all found guilty, and Panitza was publicly shot on June 28, 1890, at Sofia. Stambuloff was convinced that his difficulties were largely increased by the non-recognition of the Prince, especially by Turkey. Ferdinand had humiliated himself before his own subjects by ostentatiously seeking Abdul Hamid's protection. But the Sultan would neither consent nor refuse to recognise him as Prince. Thereupon Ferdinand wrote in June, 1890, an unusual letter to the Sultan, in which the hand of Stambuloff is well seen. It declared that during five years the Porte had been hostile to Bulgaria; that in many ways the Prince had shown his desire to live on good terms with his Suzerain; that the plots against the Prince were instigated by foreign agents and backed by foreign money; and that they tended to weaken Bulgaria. The letter claimed that the Porte ought to try and strengthen the hands of the Prince. It finished with something like a menace, and was not without effect in leading to the recognition of Ferdinand.

A semi-religious element intensified the disputes between the Greeks and Bulgarians in Macedonia. They turned largely upon the claims of the supporters of the Patriarch against those of the Exarch for the possession of churches and schools. Disputes had already commenced between their respective followers, in other words, between Bulgars and Greeks. The latter, as far back as the formation of an autonomous Bulgarian Church in 1870, had been violently opposed to those whom it regarded as schismatic, because they had broken away from allegiance to the Patriarch. Nearly all the churches in the country were inscribed in the name of the Orthodox Patriarch until 1870 and this, according to Turkish law, implied ownership. But as some had been built solely by Bulgarians and many by both Greeks and Bulgars, the latter claimed, as was the fact, that the Patriarch held them in trust. The dispute as to possession led to fierce combats between the respective adherents of Patriarch and Exarch. The Bulgarians in Macedonia were left without bishops in sufficient number to meet the local requirements of their Church. When the proposal was made that the Porte should issue *berats*, that is, official permission for bishops to be appointed, Greece and the Greeks of Macedonia and the Empire made violent opposition, and the Bulgarian Note presented in June, 1890, aroused angry opposition against the Patriarch. He, indeed, tendered his resignation, when two bishops were appointed. It was seriously proposed to close the whole of the Greek churches in the Empire. No formal resolution to this effect was taken by the Patriarch and his Council. Indeed, some of the Greek bishops took a more sensible view of the matter and refused to give orders for closing the churches. Russia, Serbia, and Greece, all belonging to the Orthodox Church, supported the Patriarch in his opposition. The agitation became so serious that in the last days of October, 1890, the Porte made a compromise which, however, satisfied neither party. *Berats* were granted for Bulgarian bishops at Uskub and Ochrida, but refused for other places. In Bulgaria this was regarded as a triumph, and greatly strengthened the position of both Stambuloff and Prince Ferdinand. The triumph over Russian opposition was the more remarkable, since in previous years, when she was patronising Bulgaria, she had pressed the Porte to appoint Bulgarian bishops and had been refused. It is noteworthy that, in this semi-religious struggle, for the first time Germany supported the Bulgarian demands.

The anarchy which continued to reign in Macedonia was largely aggravated by the fact that the Turkish troops remained unpaid. They lived upon the Bulgarian and Greek villagers, taking, even in their religious quarrels, sometimes the side of one and sometimes of the other. In 1902 the dissatisfaction resulted in a serious insurrection in Macedonia, in which, though not always openly, all the Balkan States took sides. A large Macedonian Committee had been formed in Sofia, and bands of Bulgarians, locally known as "Comitajis," acting under their orders, attacked Turkish villages. The Greeks were not less active in opposing the Bulgarians. On each side bands of "Comitajis," made reckless attacks one against the other, the troops often assisting the villagers on whom they were living. An incident of no international importance, but illustrative of the condition of the country, created a certain excitement in 1901, when Miss Stone, an American missionary, was captured by a band of Bulgarian brigands. After long negotiations between the foreign offices of Sofia, Constantinople, and the brigands themselves, she was released. Large numbers, said to be 15,000, of Macedonian refugees in Sofia, were a costly, disturbing and dangerous element for the Principality. One section was in favour of diplomatic measures, but general opinion supported the brigands in the hopes of thereby driving the Powers to intervene and establish a Government which would preserve order. The moderate section which did not wish for annexation, put forward several attempts at reasonable reforms and submitted them to Abdul Hamid or his representatives in Sofia. All were peremptorily refused. The Turkish troops sent to suppress the insurrection, carried out their task with the usual unscrupulousness of an unpaid soldiery.

Nothing else was done to restore order, and during the years 1902-3 disturbances in Macedonia constituted its chief feature. Both Greek and Bulgarian bands were devastating the country. The Turkish troops, unpaid and undisciplined, were fighting for their own benefit, and perpetrating acts of cruelty now against one race, and now against the other. Sir Nicholas O'Conor in December, 1902, called special attention to these acts. The Greek community at Salonika complained "that they were scourged by the heavy oppression of brigand bands, aided by Bulgarian committees, who not only robbed the people, but did not stop at murder, rape, and arson." Revolutionary Committees now began to appear in various towns in Macedonia. They urged Sofia and the Powers to demand Macedonian autonomy from the Porte.

Indeed, the Powers had never ceased to press for reforms. As a result of negotiations between the Porte and the Powers, an Inspector-General of the gendarmery had been named, but with insufficient powers. The appointment itself, only accepted after long negotiations, marked the limit of the success of Europe.

The condition of the country became so serious that Austria and Russia, the two Powers after Turkey most interested in the pacification, took the matter in hand.

A meeting between the Austrian Emperor and the Czar was held at Murzsteg in the summer of 1903. It resulted in the drawing up of a programme of reforms which was presented to the Porte in October of that year. The important items in the Murzsteg programme were (1) that Austria and Russia should appoint Civil Agents to direct the Inspector-General of the gendarmery—the appointment of such an officer having been accepted by the Porte in principle. (2) That the gendarmery should be reorganised under foreign officers who should be subjects of one or other of the Great Powers. (3) That in order to meet local requirements, the existing territorial arrangements for the gendarmery officers should be changed (the intention being that the Bulgarians, Serbians, Greeks, Albanians, and Moslems should, as far as possible, be placed under separate local arrangements so as to avoid conflict between them). (4) That in each of the important towns of Macedonia there should be established a Mixed Commission formed of an equal number of Moslems and Christians to examine and decide upon local reforms. (5) That the Law Courts should be reformed. Lastly, it was stipulated that all these reforms should be put into force without delay.

In September Abdul Hamid expressed his regret to the two Powers that such demands were considered necessary, but, of course, left a further answer to be given by his Sublime Porte.

Instructions were sent by the Austrian and Russian Governments in October, 1903, to be ready to put them into execution. Great Britain, France, Germany, and Italy in November sent similar instructions to their Consuls, and the Porte was pressed to accept the proposals. So unanimous a demand could not be altogether disregarded. Moreover, Russia was now smarting under the murder in August (1903) of her Consul at Monastir, a crime which was attributed to orders from the capital. The Porte gave a general assent in January, 1904, to the demands of the Powers, but spoke of the necessity of guarding the sovereign right of the Sultan. During the next two years it made as many delays as possible in putting the reforms into execution. All the Powers agreed that a financial scheme for Macedonia was necessary and, therefore, contemporaneously with the endeavours to get the provisions mentioned into such a form as would be accepted by the Porte, a financial project was also under consideration. In all these negotiations the Porte endeavoured to whittle down the proposals of the Powers and to gain time.

In January, 1904, an Italian of experience in the organisation of gendarmery, General Di Giorgis, was appointed. But the Porte stipulated that he should not introduce any changes in the gendarmery unless they were sanctioned by it, and after he had received instructions from it. The project of having two Civil Agents, named by Austria and Russia respectively, was rejected by the Porte, unless it should be stipulated that they or their delegates when on inspection should be accompanied by Turkish officers. The proposed stipulation was at once refused by Austria and Russia. The suggestions in reference to both these articles were considered by all the Powers who, in this as in every other negotiation regarding Macedonia, were most anxious, while striving for reforms, to respect the Sultan's rights. A modified project was submitted to the Porte. It was rejected on March 2, 1904, as trespassing on his Majesty's sovereign rights.

Then the Porte grew bolder, and a fortnight later made a counter-proposal claiming that Turkish officers must retain actual control of the gendarmery, and that the number of foreign officers employed as inspectors and instructors must not exceed twenty-five.

The negotiations were long and ended in an unsatisfactory compromise. Austria, either because she was afraid that disorder in Macedonia might be too completely suppressed or was influenced by Germany not to push the Sultan too far, ceased to take an energetic part in pressing on the reforms. She and Germany now acted together, and it soon became the popular and not unfounded opinion that the districts for which they had the appointment of gendarmery officers saw little of the keen activity which those under British and French officers witnessed in the desire of the officers placed in charge to secure effective police. The stipulations which had been weakly accepted that the inspectors whose duty *inter alia* it was to report on murders or other outrages should only act on orders from Turkish officials proved useless. It was soon found that the great object of such officials was to conceal crime when committed by Turkish and other favoured bands, and their visits came to be regarded as worse than farce. Abdul Hamid was curiously persistent in his determination not to tolerate any reform initiated by the European Powers. He was equally minded not to allow any suggested by his own people.

During the years between 1904 and 1908, the Moslem population of Macedonia, as well as Bulgars and Greeks, again pressed Abdul Hamid to take measures to provide for the safety of life and property. The Murzsteg programme of the two Emperors had failed in producing useful results. Lord Lansdowne in February, 1905, informed the Balkan Committee that the British Government was "pressing the Porte for permanent and effective reforms." In November,

1905, England, France, and Italy sought to compel Abdul Hamid to carry financial reforms into execution. They asked that a budget of income and expenditure should be submitted to the two Civil Agents appointed under the Murzsteg programme. The Porte agreed, but objected to control by the Civil Agents, and asked to increase custom duties from 8 to 11 per cent. The Powers refused, but England proposed that the control should be international, and that a Council should be appointed. On July 11, the Porte refused, pleading the Sultan's sovereign rights. The Powers stuck to their proposal, and a fleet consisting of British, French, Russian, Italian, and Austrian ships made a demonstration. They seized the Custom houses of Mitylene and Lemnos, and held them until Abdul Hamid yielded (November, 1905). Germany had already begun to pose as the Sultan's friend, and would not name foreign gendarmery officers, or take any part in the naval demonstration. She was now the only great Power which declined to co-operate in securing order in Macedonia. No proposal for even the most limited form of autonomy was listened to.

Every year saw a larger amount of emigration from Macedonia to America, and other foreign countries. The best of the Moslem population, as well as the Christians, recognised that with an unpaid soldiery, disorder was certain to continue. Moslems and Christians came to believe that Abdul Hamid was the great hinderer of the execution of reform. He had refused to consider even the proposals made by his own subjects, just as he had cut out of the project presented by Austria and Russia the provisions which would have guaranteed the proposed reforms and would have contented the bulk of the inhabitants. All Europe insisted that reform was necessary; for during the years 1905 and 1906 the condition of Macedonia had become worse than ever, Greek and Bulgarian bands waged civil war against each other. Murders, theft, attacks upon villages by men of a hostile race; sometimes upon no pretext whatever, except, if by Greeks, that the village was Bulgarian, or *vice versâ;* at other times on the pretext that the villagers had given aid to rival bands: Turkish troops now joining one side, now another. Farms were deserted. Mines were abandoned. People of all races were seeking the means of getting out of the country.

In 1907 it was noted that in the small district southwest of Kastoria there were at least ten bands of Greek "Comitajis" plundering the country. They were notoriously paid in part by subscriptions from Greeks in the Kingdom or elsewhere, and their avowed object was to enlarge the ethnographic boundaries of a larger Greece by exterminating the Bulgarians. The latter had retaliated by driving Greeks out of Anchialos on the Black Sea. "Death to every Bulgar," was inscribed on a postcard which the Greek post-offices allowed to circulate. Macedonia had become a pandemonium. Independent observers as well as the European Powers called upon Abdul Hamid to do something to remedy an evil which had become a European scandal.

When the Balkan Committee in England suggested large measures of reform, the Sultan thought it desirable to do something to appease a European outcry which was becoming as loud as that which preceded the Russo-Turkish war. He had already sent in Hilmi Pasha, an agent whose reputation was high, in order to advise measures for pacification. Hilmi was respected by Ambassadors and by the best Moslem element in Turkey. Much was hoped from his appointment. But his failure was complete, and brought him under considerable obloquy. After the revolution it became known that he had sent various projects of reform of a practical and even of a drastic character, and such as would have been welcomed not only by the Christian but by the Moslem population. Abdul Hamid would not even consider them.

It deserves notice that a strong belief existed, both in the capital and Macedonia, that in the various negotiations Austria did not wish for reforms and was well content to see anarchy increasing. The belief in her double-dealing is not without evidence. That the Turks themselves suspected it was well known. One circumstance which probably pointed to such dealing was the following :—The Grand Vizier reported to Abdul Hamid a visit paid to him by Baron Calici, the Austrian Ambassador, who informed him that all the Ambassadors had adopted a note or resolution to be submitted to the Sultan condemning his inactivity, but that he, as representative of Austria, would indicate a way by which Turkey could save appearances. Let the Porte draw up a project of her own and have it shown at once to the Ambassadors and thus prevent the presentation of the objectionable note. The Grand Vizier declared in his report that he had been shown the original. By adopting his suggestion Turkey would save her face. A photograph of this report was published shortly after the death of the Grand Vizier and the authenticity of the fac-simile of his handwriting was not disputed. Though it was generally believed to mean that Austria wished to bar the reforms proposed by his colleagues, another explanation is possible. The Ambassador and the Grand Vizier, knowing Abdul Hamid's unwillingness to further any reform in Macedonia, may have concocted a harmless plot of a note as the only way to induce the Sultan to put forward a scheme which he would really support. The supineness of the Austrian Consuls and other officials in Macedonia was, however, generally put down to the desire of the Ballplatz to let things go from bad to worse, when possibly all Europe would agree to invite Austria to enter the province for the preservation of order. This was the view commonly expressed by the active spirits of the Moslem party in Macedonia.

Whether Austria was acting loyally or not, nothing can excuse Abdul Hamid's attitude. His own representative, Hilmi Pasha, indicated reforms as necessary. If Abdul believed that Austria was opposing them, as he probably did, he should have endeavoured to find out her motives for such opposition. Her attitude ought to have put him on his guard. The fact is that he rejected the suggestions of his own chosen and undoubtedly able agent with the same foolish obstinacy as he had done those of the Powers.

If there were no other complaints against Abdul Hamid than the treatment of his subject races in Macedonia, which led to the discontent of his Moslem subjects, he would pass down into history as having contributed largely to the disintegration of his Empire. His refusal to take any steps to introduce changes which would make an end of the existing anarchy alienated Moslems. They might have pardoned his indifference to the sufferings of the Christians, but they would not tolerate his neglect of the national interest.

The story of Abdul Hamid's treatment of subject races now becomes merged in the larger one which resulted in Revolution.

CHAPTER XII

COMMITTEE OF UNION AND PROGRESS. REVOLUTION. ABDUL HAMID DEPRIVED OF POLITICAL POWER

Formation of Committee of Union and Progress; Revolution; Abdul Hamid deprived of arbitrary power.

GRADUALLY there had been formed in Macedonia small bodies of disaffected Moslems who recognised that the Sultan was the great hindrance to any amelioration of the condition of the country and that he was a hindrance because all power was centred in his hands. Outside Turkey, in Paris and in Switzerland, especially, disaffected Turkish refugees had already gathered together and become the missionaries of revolution. Before long some of them agreed to common action with discontented fellow-subjects in Macedonia. As already mentioned, small groups of malcontents had been formed in many towns in Macedonia. In 1906 many of them united to form a Central Committee which met in Salonika. A similar Committee, under Ahmed Riza, was constituted in Paris in October, 1907. The two bodies decided to work for the establishment of constitutional government, by which was meant, after some hesitation, the demand for the putting into force of Midhat's Constitution, which had been in abeyance since 1877. Their members were at first almost exclusively Moslems with, possibly, the addition of four or five Jews, but, as many intelligent Christians, subjects of Turkey, were also exiles in France and Switzerland, some of these were taken into the French Committee. In Geneva also was a similar Committee. In all the Committees the Moslem element predominated. The members formed a body which took the name of the "Committee of Union and Progress."[1] By union, they meant that of all races and of all creeds in the Empire. The President of the Paris Committee, Ahmed Riza, was a Positivist, an honourable and greatly respected man. The two Committees formed one, but the more active portion held their meetings in Salonika. Thereupon the movement during 1906—1908 spread with remarkable rapidity. Discontent with the existing *régime* was widespread. It had now become organised.

It was impossible that some of the great army of spies in the pay of Abdul Hamid should not have known of the existence of the Committees before they adopted the now well-known name. His brother-in-law with two of his sons had fled from Constantinople in October, 1899, and were known to sympathise with them. Agencies of the Committee sprang up all over the country with wonderful celerity. Although in Constantinople men who were believed to belong to it would have been immediately arrested, and although some persons were arrested, yet its proceedings were conducted with such secrecy that it is doubtful whether the Sultan, or those of his agents who were faithful to him, ever realised that the Committee was formidable until it was too late to defeat its objects.

Two of the earliest and boldest adherents of the Committee, Niazi Bey and Enver Bey, now Enver Damat Pasha, deserve special notice. Niazi will always stand out as the typical missionary of revolution on behalf of the Committee of Union and Progress. He was a native of Resna in Macedonia. In 1897 he was a sub-lieutenant, took part in the Greek war, and distinguished himself as a brave soldier in the fight above the town of Volo. Sent to the capital in charge of Greek prisoners, he saw much of the *entourage* of Abdul Hamid, and was greatly impressed by the jobbery, favouritism, and injustice which existed in connection with promo-

[1] Before the formation of the Committee of Union and Progress the reformers were known by the old name of "Young Turks" They came prominently into notice under that name when in October, 1899, Mahmud Damat (the brother-in-law of the Sultan) fled with his two sons to Paris.

tion to places in the Army and Civil Service and in regard to the rewards bestowed on the soldiers. Then he was stationed in command over troops in the neighbourhood of his native hills. Their duty was to suppress the Bulgarian bands. But he was disgusted with what he saw. The commissariat officers enriched themselves at the expense of the troops. The latter were unpaid and lived on the peaceful peasants. Spies reported that Niazi had expressed his indignation at what he saw, and that he favoured reforms. He fled to avoid arrest and went to Paris. Thence he determined to return to Turkey and to work on behalf of the Committee. He landed in Greece, disguised himself in the fustanella, crossed the frontier and descended boldly to Salonika, where, if he had been recognised by Abdul Hamid's partisans, he would probably have been hung within twenty-four hours. As at that time, however, Abdul Hamid's agents were playing the game of supporting the Greek bands against the Bulgarian, as they had previously supported the Bulgars against the Greeks, the disguise was fairly safe. He met the Committee and was taken into their confidence. They fitted him up in Turkish costume as a hawker and saw him on board a steamer for Smyrna. There and at many other places in Asia Minor he went boldly amongst the soldiers and officers and, finding everywhere discontent with Abdul Hamid, induced many to join the Committee. He is stated to have travelled as a hodja or teacher, and in that character to have addressed Turks in the mosques; as a hawker and travelling merchant; as a begging dervish and in other disguises, everywhere spreading the new gospel of a Constitution. Every month the Committee of Union and Progress had new accessions. Some of its leading members in Salonika had joined a Lodge of Freemasons in order the more completely to keep their plans secret.

Enver Bey, now Enver Pasha, was almost an unknown man in either Macedonia or the capital. Little is known of his early history. He was a quiet, silent man, often regarded as surly. But from the first he was considered to be a daring soldier. He will always be memorable because he and Niazi were the first to raise the standard of revolt. In the first week of July, 1908, the two men took to the hills of Resna. From thence they issued an appeal to the army and the Empire. Each had a small but determined following.

Meantime the Paris and the Salonika Committees had decided to demand from Abdul Hamid the re-proclamation of Midhat's Constitution. They hesitated about fixing the time of a demonstration throughout Turkey in favour of their demand. They anticipated an angry refusal with the arrest of all suspects, and therefore increased their activity in gaining new adherents. Most of the leading employees of the railways in Macedonia, Christians as well as Moslems, were persuaded without much difficulty to become members. Each was sworn to obedience and secrecy. Each knew his own immediate superior in the conspiracy, but often knew no other confederate. A number, though not large, of the military officers and of others in the Civil Service, became members. Many Albanians sympathised with the Committee but did not show eagerness to join it.

But time was pressing. A meeting had taken place on June 9, 1908, at Reval, on the Russian Baltic, between Edward VII. and the Czar, and it was known that one of its objects was to agree upon measures for effecting reforms in Macedonia. The Russian newspapers announced that Sir Charles, now Lord, Hardinge and M. Isvolski, who had accompanied their respective Sovereigns, were near a complete agreement on a project of reforms necessary. The Young Turks, as the members of the Committee were still often called, recognised that the two Sovereigns would not be content to repeat the error of the Murzsteg programme which Abdul Hamid had emasculated, but feared that their decision would be to establish an autonomous government which would inevitably lead to the loss of the province by Turkey. What they wanted was to get rid of Absolutism and to establish representative government which would provide good government throughout the Empire. But they did not wish to diminish it. Hence the two Committees of Salonika and Paris decided that their demonstration should take place on September 1, 1908, the date of Abdul's accession.

An incident, however, occurred which brought about the demonstration at a still earlier period. The premature action of Niazi and Enver would probably have been without result but for the incident in question. Austria, which had many Consuls and other officials as well as a large number of subjects and "protected persons"[1] in Macedonia, appeared to be working for and confident of obtaining the annexation of the province. Of this the leaders of the Committee had no doubt. Throughout the Turkish Empire Austria was the Power which had the largest number of *cafés chantants* and registered brothels. In the neighbourhoods of Uskub and Kossova, which were largely inhabited by Albanians, the Albanian chiefs were greatly displeased with an Austrian Consul who sheltered under his flag gambling-houses, brothels, and other disorderly houses. The chiefs declared that their young men were robbed and demoralised by the debauchery protected under the Austrian flag. Under the Consul's auspices a great orgy, intended to last for a week, was arranged to take place at Fersovich, about halfway between the towns mentioned. Sheds and booths were erected for the purpose. Special trains were to run throughout the week when this great picnic was to be held. The Albanians collected on the neighbouring hills to the number of 20,000 and were determined to prevent the orgy. They set fire to the sheds and booths, and then, having prevented the contemplated meeting, decided to take the matter of public order into their own hands by attacking the Austrian Consulate. When the tidings of these events reached Salonika, the Committee of

[1] A protégé or "protected person" is one of another nationality who enjoys consular protection from a country of which he is not a subject. A Swiss, for example, is usually protected by Germany or France or Italy according to the canton from which he comes.

Union and Progress saw that any attempt on the part of the Albanians against the Austrian Consul would bring in the Austrian Army and certainly postpone if not definitely defeat their plans. Messengers were therefore sent in great haste to the Albanians to dissuade them from their proposed action. They met with such success that the Albanians forbore to attack the Consulate and consented to take part with the Committee in demanding a Constitution, provided that this should be done immediately. No time was lost. A formal demand was made and negotiations were pressed on between the Committee and Yildiz. When the Sultan heard of the Albanian meeting and of what they were proposing he at once sent orders to disperse them. Unhappily for him, the Committee had already amongst its members most of the telegraph and railway employees, and knew at once what orders were transmitted. Galib Bey himself, who received the order to disperse the Albanians, had become a member of the Committee. Abdul Hamid had heard the news from Paris both of the meeting and of what was proposed by the Committee. He at once promoted 2,000 officers in the navy and a great number of officers in the army. On July 19, 800 soldiers arrived at Monastir. Shemshi Pasha left Uskub with two battalions. Niazi and Enver were to be attacked; but the troops refused to fire on their comrades, and Shemshi himself was shot as he was about to lead them to the Resna Hills. The colonel in command at Seres shared the same fate. Everywhere in Macedonia the army showed themselves favourable to the Revolutionary party. The Sultan called upon Ferid Pasha, the Grand Vizier, to act as Seraskier or War Minister in order to punish the discontented. But Ferid, a cautious and able man, refused to interfere with the task of his colleague. Upon this Adbul Hamid, confident in the trustworthiness of his spies, took the matter into his own hands. He ordered forty of them to report upon the conduct of the troops and to send the names of the disloyal. But their mission became at once known and acted like a spark to a powder magazine. Those officers who had hitherto hesitated, declared for the Committee. Their declaration was due not so much to a fear of being reported as disloyal, as to the general loathing at the employment of spies against them. At the same time Abdul Hamid ordered the troops in Smyrna to be sent to Salonika. The army in Macedonia now followed up their telegram by another, demanding the Constitution or Abdication (July 21 or 22), and stating that the troops had sworn not to lay down their arms until the Constitution was proclaimed.[1]

Before the Sultan gave the order to the troops to attack the rebels, an incident occurred which enabled Abdul Hamid to learn that the disaffection in the highest sphere of the Moslem hierarchy was serious. According to Turkish custom, when Moslem is to be sent to fight Moslem the formal approval of the Sheik-ul-Islam is necessary. Abdul Hamid applied to the Highest Religious Court, or Fetva-hane, in which the Sheik presides, for an answer to the question "Is war justifiable against Moslem soldiers who rebel against the Padisha's authority?" The acute minds who preside in that Court asked for a statement of facts. Statements in detail had to be furnished which showed the whole case. The people of the capital, who learned that there was some kind of mutiny in Macedonia, waited anxiously for the decision. The president of the Court was a man greatly respected for his integrity, and all believed that his answer would be guided by his science and conscience. At length, and after he was known to have made a careful examination of the demands of the troops for reforms and redress of grievances, he declared that they were not contrary to the prescriptions of the Sacred Law. As a result the decision was taken to mean that if a Fetva were pressed for, it would not justify the war by Moslems against Moslems.

[1] The late General Von der Goltz, in a letter published in the *Neue Freie Presse*, declared a few weeks later that the system of espionage was the chief practical grievance of the Turkish soldier.

During the three or four days preceding July 22, similar telegrams were sent to Yildiz almost simultaneously from Salonika, Fersovich, and Uskub, in which the heads of the army joined, demanding a Constitution, and intimating that if it were not immediately granted "something very serious would happen to the Sultan himself."

The Sultan, in great alarm, called a Council of his Ministers. They sat at the palace on July 20, 21, and 22. The circumstances, but especially the demand and its menace, furnished a rude awakening. To acquiesce in the demand for the restoration of Midhat's Constitution was to admit the defeat of the policy which he had pursued unremittingly since he dismissed its author in February, 1877. To refuse it was to face the immediate opposition of his army in Macedonia. The position was exceedingly difficult. Could his Ministers help him out? Could he trust them? No published account has appeared of what passed in the momentous meeting. But some of those present did not hesitate after a few weeks to speak of it. The general impression left by their disclosures was that nearly, possibly all present, sympathised with the Macedonian demands. All recognised that if they were not conceded, civil war would at once ensue. After long discussion it was agreed at the third sitting that Abdul Hamid should be informed that they were unanimously of opinion that the Constitution should be proclaimed. Who was to be the messenger to inform him of so heart-breaking a decision? No one volunteered for the task. They knew the vindictive character of their Imperial master. They knew that he had opposed every reform, had persecuted Midhat to his death, and they naturally anticipated an outburst of anger when the decision should be communicated to him.

After long hesitation and considerable discussion, someone proposed that Abdul Huda, the Court Astrologer, should be asked to inform the Sultan of the result of their deliberations. Huda was known to be greatly favoured by his master, and that his utterances were regarded as inspired. He was therefore called into the Council Chamber, which he entered from a sick-bed, and informed of the decision which he was desired to communicate. A man of short stature, with a keen, intelligent and not unkindly face, he looked like one who feared no mortal. After fully discussing the situation he undertook the task. He saw that no plan could be suggested by which the demand coming from various parts of Macedonia and from the army could be successfully resisted.[1]

It was during the sitting of this memorable Council that news arrived that General Shemshi had been openly shot in the streets of Monastir. Other telegrams announced that all the troops in Macedonia were in favour of the telegraphic demands for the re-establishment of the Constitution. Abdul Hamid had tried the troops in Adrianople, but found they sided with those in Macedonia. It was in view of these facts that when the Sultan learned from his astrologer the unanimous advice of his Ministers he saw that he must yield. Accordingly, in the night of July 22-23, he sent telegrams to Macedonia, and before midnight the troops in Uskub, Monastir, and Salonika, saluted the proclamation of the Constitution. Eight hours afterwards, that is on the eve of July 24, the same news was published in the capital.

The proclamation of the Constitution was an epoch-making event. It signified to Abdul Hamid the entire failure of his plans. He had worked for thirty years to make himself absolute. He had exiled or killed the band of reformers who had worked for the establishment of the government of the Empire on constitutional lines. He had reduced government by Ministers by restricting their power and simply

[1] It was believed that he saw the important telegrams which arrived at Yildiz, and it was even reported that the favourite secretary of Abdul Hamid showed them to him before they were communicated to the Sultan, all of which would have given confidence to his predictions.

allowing them to put his personal edicts into decent legal form. He had chosen his Ministers for their subserviency or for their hostility towards their colleagues. By means of his army of spies he had debased the character of his Moslem subjects so that none dared openly speak of reforms. His arrangements for repressing any aspirations for liberty were elaborate, and those for his own personal defence were minute. Yet suddenly, with little warning, the storm burst over him, and all his preparations proved futile. To save himself he had to proclaim the re-establishment of Midhat's Constitution. It is difficult to imagine a more humiliating situation for a defeated Sovereign.

The proclamation of the Constitution, which was accompanied by notice that the Parliament would be summoned, had an electrical effect upon the population of the Empire. Constantinople went delirious with joy. Moslems, Christians and Jews were exultant. Rich and poor; merchants and labourers; imams, priests and rabbis, joined hands in congratulating each other that the arbitrary power of Abdul Hamid had for ever ceased. He had been like a dead weight on a powerful spring, which, when the weight was removed, at once acted powerfully. A wild cry of relief and delight burst from tens of thousands. Men and women alike shouted with joy. Even Turkish women, usually the most secluded and modest of their sex, shook hands and embraced their Christian sisters in the streets, and congratulated each other that liberty had dawned upon them. The newspapers, whether Moslem or Christian, gave expression to the public belief. Midhat's Constitution was not mentioned in the proclamation, but they assumed that that was what was meant, for it had been regarded for thirty years as the symbol of liberty. The special grievance of the newspapers was the presence in each office of a censor. The Constitution was assumed to imply liberty of the Press; and, on the day of its publication, the editors combined to bundle the censors out of their offices. The loudest cry of the public was " Down with the spies!" and before the day was over most of them had disappeared.

The public knew little of what had passed at the palace, and probably still less of the serious movements in Macedonia, and was in such good humour at the great news, that their cries of " Vive la Constitution " were scarcely more cordial than those of " Vive le Sultan." If Abdul Hamid had ventured into the streets of his capital he would have been received as a benefactor. When it was announced that, for the first time for a quarter of a century, he would visit St. Sophia, almost every house in Stamboul, Pera, and Galata was decorated spontaneously. An enormous crowd gathered before the gates of Yildiz, and kept up a continuous shout for him and the Constitution. On the following day when he went to the famous mosque, which embodies the history of the New Rome, he was everywhere cheered by crowds composed of all classes and faiths in the community. He was accompanied by Kutchuk Said, who had replaced Ferid. The Sultan showed himself to the multitude and declared that henceforth all his subjects would receive similar treatment. On Sunday, July 26, a crowd of Moslems, Mollahs, and Softas, made a demonstration before Yildiz in which cheers for Abdul Hamid were alternated with " Down with the spies!" The Sultan again showed himself to the crowd, and it was announced that he had sworn on the Koran that he would respect the Constitution.

After this demonstration, the crowd marched to the official residence of the Armenian Patriarch, thence to that of the Orthodox Church, and some to the residence of the Bulgarian Exarch. " No distinction between the subjects of the Sultan on account of differences in religion or race," was the general note of all the many speeches. The demonstrations which followed during the next week were unique. The street and private carriages in Constantinople are open, and processions passed daily through the streets, which had evidently been organised with great care. In the many carriages there was always some sign of fraternisation. Turkish Mollahs rode side by side with Orthodox Bishops, and many carriages were to be seen containing the representatives of apparently discordant creeds, Armenian priests with those of the Orthodox Church, or Chaldeans, or Jacobites, Jewish Rabbis with Christians, representatives of every Christian Church in Turkey, taking a part in the general rejoicing amid the plaudits of a dense crowd. It may well be doubted whether such a scene had ever been witnessed in the New Rome.

Two facts in the demonstration deserve special mention. The first—that in all prominent places the crowd halted while someone, usually a Mollah, though sometimes a Christian, stood upon a slight eminence in an attitude of prayer, with the palms of his hands held upwards and horizontally before him, and in a clear voice called upon Allah to preserve the Constitution, thanked Him for the blessings of liberty which had now been conferred upon the nation, and invoked the favour of Heaven upon the Sultan. Speeches were made in the mosques in which it was loudly proclaimed that Islam taught the doctrine of brotherly love to all "Children of the Books." Never was a crowd more reverent. Christians and Moslems fervently uttered their "Amens." The other noticeable fact was that no procession ever passed the British Embassy without giving a hearty cheer for the country which they recognised as the Mother of Free Parliaments. The new British Ambassador had not yet arrived in Constantinople, and the Embassy staff was at its country residence in Therapia. It seemed that with one accord the whole country recognised that the reign of Abdul Hamid as an absolute Sovereign was at an end. The popular instinct was right, for the revolution had triumphed and Constitutional Government had replaced absolutism.

CHAPTER XIII

DETHRONEMENT OF ABDUL HAMID

Popularity of Abdul Hamid after the re-establishment of Constitution; Kutchuk Said made Grand Vizier; his mistakes; "Atheists, Jews and Freemasons." Arrival of Sir G. Lowther; reaction begins; Mahometan Association; meeting of Turkish Parliament; visit of Balkan Committee; Kiamil defeated in Chamber; Nazim Pasha; growing disaffection; blunders by Chauvinist Party. Attempt at counter-revolution, April 13; Mahmud Muktar resists; Shevket in Macedonia; march on capital; Fetva obtained for deposition; delegates communicate news to Abdul Hamid; after deposition sent to Salonika.

THE Committee of Union and Progress had stripped Abdul Hamid of his arbitrary power. Many of its members realised that he was certain to give trouble if he had the chance. A minority of the Party would not have been unwilling to vote for his immediate dethronement or even death, but the majority wisely determined to keep him on the throne. The "Divinity which doth hedge in a King" applies with special force to a Sultan. Moreover, the outburst of enthusiasm which had welcomed the establishment of Constitutional Government caused the multitude to forget for the time Abdul Hamid's many misdeeds. The abolition of espionage and of the system of Yolteskeres, or local passports, the two most general grounds of complaint against his Government, were welcomed with gratitude as if they had been the free gifts of the Sultan. To have spoken publicly about the desirability of deposing him would have been generally resented. So long as he would consent to govern constitutionally through Ministers responsible to Parliament his subjects would have been content. They had seen little of him during his reign, and, if he had chosen to allow his Ministers to govern, discontent against the actions of the Government would have been directed against them and not against him.

On July 22, he had dismissed Ferid Pasha from his post as Grand Vizier. Ferid did not belong to the Committee, and probably by the majority of its members was looked on with a certain distrust. That however ceased when the Sultan dismissed him. Though he did not join the Committee, they recognised that in his refusal to take the place of the Minister of War when Abdul requested him to do so he sympathised with its action. Upon his dismissal Abdul Hamid sent for Kutchuk Said and Kiamil Pasha. To have done so must have been galling, because both these Ministers had fallen under his displeasure, and each of them had had to seek the intervention of Great Britain to ensure his personal safety. We have seen Kutchuk Said seeking shelter in the British Embassy in the time of Sir Philip Currie. Kiamil, a little later, had fled to the British Consulate at Smyrna, and did not venture to leave it until Sir Nicholas O'Conor had received assurances that if he came to Constantinople his person and property would be safe. The public demonstrations had shown Abdul Hamid that the Party in favour of Constitutional Government looked to England as their model, and inasmuch as both the men sent for were believed to be strongly in favour of British institutions, the Sultan rightly considered that the appointment of either would be popular. So far as Europe and the majority of his Turkish subjects could see, Abdul Hamid continued for several weeks after the revolution to be a simple passive spectator of what was going on.

The revolution had completely triumphed. It had been accomplished almost exclusively by his Moslem subjects; for although there were a few members of the

Committee who were Christians and a smaller number who were Jews, the authors of the revolution, the organisers of the Committee and its more active members, were Moslems. Abdul Hamid had done nothing consciously against the Moslems of Macedonia as distinct from the injury which his non-government and misgovernment had inflicted upon the inhabitants generally. On the contrary, he had encouraged the Moslem Albanians to encroach on the territory of Serbians, Bulgarians, and Greeks, and had allowed the Moslem overlords of Southern Macedonia to oppress their tenants. He had done nothing, however, to put an end to general disorder, or towards preventing the plunder of villages, now Greek, now Bulgarian, by his unpaid soldiery. But the result of his inaction, alternated with foolish action, had been to alienate the men who might have been ready to stand by him even when he allowed the Christians to be robbed or killed. They recognised that his rule tended to the disintegration of the Empire; and they saw in the Young Turk Party, with its new-fangled Committee of Union and Progress, the means of putting an end to his incompetent and destructive government.

Even the Albanian Moslems had failed him. He had entertained hopes of the attachment of his Albanian troops around Yildiz, but now at the moment of trial their loyalty was doubtful. He had favoured them during many years to such an extent that officers of high rank in his Turkish regiments declared that nothing would please their men better than to have the chance of attacking the encampment around Yildiz. Some of the Albanian officers, who had risen into positions solely through Abdul Hamid's favour, were ready, it was believed, to aid any rising in defence of the Sultan and against the Government of the Committee. But at the Revolution they made no sign. At a later period two such risings occurred in Constantinople. The Committee, however, had already many military officers of high rank in the Albanian regiments around the Palace, and these men made short work of the demonstrations in favour of the Padisha. It was astonishing to see how entirely friendless Abdul Hamid had become. Within a fortnight after the famous 24th July the Committee was recognised as the ruling body in the Turkish Empire.

Something must be said about the statement repeatedly put forward in Western Europe that the revolutionary party consisted of Atheists, Jews, and Freemasons. Ahmed Riza, the Chairman of the Paris Committee, already marked out as the President of the Senate, was a Positivist, and this was supposed to be the justification for employing the word "Atheist." An explanation is hardly needed, though a Positivist is not necessarily an Atheist. There is more sense in speaking of the Jews upon the Committee. It has often been pointed out that the Salonika Jews are the manliest set of Israelites to be found in the East. Nearly all of them are the descendants of exiles from Spain in the reign of Ferdinand and Isabella, and they still speak Spanish. Three prominent Salonika Jews were on the Committee, all of whom were respected amongst all classes of the community. There is a curious sect of Crypto-Jews in Salonika known as "Dunmays," whose history dates from the seventeenth century and is well known, but they are just as respectable a class as any other religious community in Turkey. It is commonly stated that Javid, who was appointed Minister of Finance, belonged to this sect. He proved himself an able financier. As for the charge that there were Freemasons among them, that, while admitted, does not require defence. It was necessary to have secret meetings, and as many of the inhabitants of Salonika were Italian subjects, it was not an unwise thing that the members should join an Italian lodge for their personal security. Those best acquainted with the facts, however, recognise that the revolution was the work in the main of the Moslem subjects of Abdul Hamid, and that they constituted the majority of the Committee.

The happy results of the revolution showed themselves at once. The Press for the first time during thirty years in Turkey became absolutely free. Public meetings were at once held which gave expression of popular satisfaction.

The outburst of delight on the part of the great majority of the population in the capital was remarkable and to all appearances unanimous. It was the apparent realisation of the great dream of Mr. Canning and of other Turkish reformers that throughout the Empire there should be complete religious equality. Justice was then tardily rendered to the memory of Midhat Pasha. He it was who had designed the Constitution. Assisted by the British Ambassador, he had chosen English institutions as the model for the regeneration of his country. He had been persecuted to his death by Abdul Hamid; but the great reformer had not lived in vain.

The many processions which perambulated the streets of the capital never failed to cheer lustily for England. A new Ambassador, Sir Gerard Lowther, appointed on the death of Sir Nicholas O'Conor, had not arrived when the Revolution occurred. When he did so on July 30, he was met, among others, by Mr. Leishman, the American Ambassador, and the representatives of the two great Constitutional countries received such a welcome as had never been previously accorded to the representatives of either of these States. British influence rose in Constantinople to boiling point; for it was hoped and believed that England, "the Mother of Free Parliaments," would rejoice in the establishment—as was fully believed—of a reformed Turkey, with institutions framed on British lines.

Mutual Suspicions and Distrust.

Meantime Abdul Hamid, who remained quiet, continued his weekly display known as the "Selamlik" with as much ostentation as in previous years. Gradually, however, public opinion began to distrust him and to suspect that, though silent, he was plotting to rid himself of the Committee which had brought about the revolution. Both he and the members of the Committee had troublous times before them, and before the popular demonstrations were over each saw dangers ahead. Abdul Hamid was not likely to part willingly with the absolute power for which he had been striving during thirty years. He probably regarded every Minister in office in July, 1908, as having betrayed him, and he was a man not likely to forgive. The leading members of the Committee knew that by their action they had become legally rebels and that the Sultan, should he regain power, would make short work of them and their reforms. He, nevertheless, put a good face on the matter.

Kutchuk Said was appointed Grand Vizier in succession to Ferid. But hardly had he taken office when he gave serious offence. The very proclamation which he had signed, declaring that the Constitution should be put into force, raised suspicion that Abdul Hamid had won him over; for the Constitution provided for the appointment of Ministers of State, but the proclamation reserved the appointment of the Ministers of War and Marine to the Sultan. The change pointed to Abdul Hamid's intention to keep all executive power in his own hands. Thereupon Kutchuk Said became suspect and had to resign. Hilmi Pasha was appointed in his stead. Hilmi's conduct entitled him to the confidence of the Committee. He was already experienced in government and had shown himself independent. When in the days immediately preceding the revolution he was nominally in command of the army in Salonika he steadily refused to join the Committee. When the latter on July 21 issued its manifesto he was informed that he must proclaim the Constitution within forty-eight hours or take the consequences. Hilmi met the order like a brave man. He had been appointed by the Sultan and would not sanction the proclamation without instructions from Yildiz. He telegraphed to the Sultan, who, happily for Hilmi, gave way.

Within three or four months after the revolution

the advocates of reaction began to raise their heads. They consisted mainly of employees who had been dismissed as useless from various public departments, the departments indeed being largely overstocked by orders from Abdul Hamid or some of his creatures, in order that they might be provided for at public expense. To them were added the great army of spies whose occupation was gone. Amongst the Ulema class there were a few, but apparently very few, who regretted the revolution which had been accomplished, and in addition there were naturally, as there would be in every country, a few opposed to any change. From these discordant elements a secret society called the Mahometan Association was formed. Its object was to oppose the Committee. It claimed to be working solely in view of preventing the government falling into the hands of the anti-Moslem elements. Some of its members declared that Abdul Hamid, in spite of his declaration, disapproved of the Constitution. But, so far as could be judged from the newspapers which were believed to be subsidised by Abdul Hamid, its main ambition was to establish the rule of the Sacred Law or Sheriat. Yet even that object could not be loudly proclaimed, for it would alienate all the non-Moslem elements of the population. The Association formed the nucleus round which the various elements of discontent gathered. The Kis-Agassi, or chief palace eunuch, together with the second eunuch, and at least one of Abdul Hamid's sons, were reputed to be its founders. We shall see that the Association played a serious part.

The Chamber of Representatives was convoked and met on December 17, 1908. Its place of meeting was one which had been adapted for such purpose as far back as 1876, and was situated in a building spoken of in Turkish as "The Fountain of Learning," at the south-east end of St. Sophia. The crowds in the streets on the occasion of its first meeting were unprecedented. Every Ambassador in the place attended in uniform. The cheers given for Sir Gerard

Lowther were undoubtedly more hearty than for any other. The Sheik-ul-Islam and the highest officials amongst the Ulema were present, but so also were the heads of all the Eastern Churches. The Committee was formally represented by Ahmed Riza and Enver Bey, and the Government, approved by the Committee, by Kiamil, now the Grand Vizier in succession to Hilmi. The Sultan, who had hardly been seen in the streets for thirty years, attended to take the most important part in the function and was accompanied by his five sons. It was noticed, moreover, as remarkable that Prince Jusuf Izzedin, the Crown Prince, was not present. Had he been there, his presence would have been regarded as an act of generosity on the part of Abdul Hamid, but it was openly asserted, and was probably true, that he had been requested not to attempt to go there. His Majesty's Speech was read for him and was hardly less truthful than such documents usually are, for in the course of it Abdul Hamid was made to say, "In spite of those who are of a contrary opinion, we have proclaimed anew the Constitution and have ordered new elections."

His appearance on this day did not create a favourable impression. As he stood up in the central box which had been fitted up for his use to salute his distinguished audience, they saw before them a weary-looking old man of short stature, whose pale and thin face made his large aquiline nose fully prominent. A quick, jerky habit of throwing his head round suggested a man full of apprehension, and when by a slight accident he dropped his handkerchief, his movement to one of his officers to pick it up indicated an impatient want of repose which is not a usual feature in reigning sovereigns. His bent figure and ashy face and the manner in which he shuffled rather than walked indicated a man a score of years older than the almanac declared him to be. His shrunken appearance was aided by his habit of wearing a fez and overcoat, each much too large for him. The

Ambassadors were nearly all men of distinguished appearance, and the noble figure of Ahmed Riza, the President of the Senate and ex-Chairman of the Committee of Union and Progress in Paris, caught the popular attention. The one important figure in the Chamber which did not even look dignified was that of Abdul Hamid.

After the friendly tumult which followed the reading of the Sultan's Speech, he was understood in presence of the Sheik-ul-Islam to have sworn fidelity to the Constitution. Whether he did so or not was doubtful, but to remove doubt he subsequently took an oath to this effect.

When the Chamber met for business there were a large number of proposals to be discussed. Naturally, also, there were many grievances to be exposed. Lively discussions of abuses commenced. Not only were the Ministers attacked, but several of the members boldly declared that the chief culprit was Abdul Hamid himself. A large sum of money collected for wounded soldiers in the Greek War in 1897 could not be accounted for. A suggestion was made and largely believed that it had gone into Abdul Hamid's private purse. The project to which Abdul Hamid had attached most importance as best pleasing to his Moslem subjects was the construction of the Hedjaz Railway. He boasted with truth that the money for its construction had been subscribed by Moslems all over the world, but it was asserted that, in addition to the money actually spent on the railway and a liberal allowance for it for unforeseen expenses, there was a sum of £700,000 over and above which had not been accounted for. Riza Tewfik, a fearless Deputy whom many will remember as having visited England on more than one occasion and who was known as the "philosopher," demanded explanations. That, however, which wounded Abdul Hamid more than these complaints of alleged delinquencies, was the vote in the Chamber to cut down the Civil List from £882,000 to £600,000. He was notoriously sore at the loss. Nevertheless, it was almost immediately after the vote that on

December 31 he invited all the Deputies to dine with him at Yildiz. He specially helped Ahmed Riza with water from his own decanter of Kiat Hané water, complimented the prominent men present, praised Jahid for his powerful advocacy of the Constitution in his newspaper, and delighted the simple representatives from the provinces, many of whom possibly believed in his statements. They heartily cheered him when he declared, "with a sob in his voice," that never in his life had he been so happy as at that moment. Even Ahmed Riza expressed his opinion that the Sultan honestly intended to become a Constitutional monarch. Many of his guests kissed his hand, while most shouted "Long life to the Padisha and to the Constitution!"

In spite of these demonstrations, dissension soon began to show itself both in the country and in the Parliament itself. The Turkish newspapers which were the organs of the Committee, and undoubtedly were better aware of what the Sultan was doing than the general public or the foreign Embassies, watched him with grave suspicion. Of the hundreds of spies in Constantinople there were many who sought to make their peace with the new Government. Still there was no talk of deposition. Foreigners and Turkish subjects generally were well satisfied with the change of government; trade began to flourish, and everything looked hopeful.

Yet neither the Sultan nor the leaders were contented with the other.

Hussein Jahid, a prominent member of the Committee, who perhaps saw more of him than any other public man, describes him as usually at this period looking cowed and anxious only to have his life spared and to be allowed to reign. Neither Jahid, however, nor any man who had had experience of Abdul Hamid, trusted either his looks or his word. They knew that duplicity had long been a confirmed attribute. Like all Oriental sovereigns, he had lived in an atmosphere of intrigue, and they continued to distrust him, as no doubt he distrusted them. It could not be otherwise. During many years a large portion of every day had been taken up in the perusal of the reports of his spies. The hundreds of such reports which are said to have reached him daily had obsessed him, and he daily continued to peruse them. Many thousands of them were subsequently found packed away at Yildiz, the enormous majority being not only worthless, but, as Dr. Shakir Bey, a trustworthy man charged to report on their contents, affirmed, contradictory and mischievous, explaining to some extent the Sultan's blundering in the two or three weeks which preceded the revolution, and especially how until within three or four days of the proclamation he appeared incapable of recognising that the revolutionary movement required more attention than the immediate arrest of a few individuals.

It was during the Vizierate of Kiamil that the British Balkan Committee sent out a deputation to congratulate the Committee on the happy revolution. As the Selamlik was undoubtedly one of the sights of the city, the members of the deputation, consisting of Mr. Noel E. Buxton, his brother Roden, Mr., now Sir Arthur Evans, and half a dozen others, went to see it. They were placed by prominent members of the Committee on a small covered terrace before which the Sultan passed in his short journey from the Palace gates of Yildiz to the Hamidieh Mosque, where he attended for the Friday midday prayers. The ceremony was not a specially interesting one; the feature in it which always jarred upon foreigners being that the Sultan, on his return up a somewhat steep hill to the gates of Yildiz, was followed on foot by a number of Pashas, some of them very fat, who puffed and blew a good deal to keep pace with the Sovereign's carriage. The spectacle would have been ludicrous if it were not ridiculous. The Sultan expressed a desire to receive the members of the Balkan Committee. His reception of these men who for years had urged reforms has been described by Mr. Roden Buxton. Kiamil Pasha, as well as the Young Turk Party, welcomed the British visitors as representing the opinion of a country with which constitutional government is always associated.

Kiamil Pasha continued in office as Grand Vizier until February, 1909. He, however, lost the confidence of the Young Turk Party and was only retained in his post because he was known to be favourably regarded by Great Britain. Though he was amongst those who at the great Palace meeting on July 23 had advised Abdul Hamid to give way, he was not and never became a member of the Committee. Indeed it may be said that he never worked cordially with it. He was an old man, already past eighty, and his ideal of Turkish government was that of the notable Viziers who had held office previous to Abdul Hamid's accession. He wanted a strong Government and did not believe that the Turks were fit for representative institutions; he wanted a just Government such as Ali, Fuad, and Reshid had attempted to form, in order that he might attack the abuses in the administration of justice. The special fault which the Committee found with him was that he had driven the Minister of War, Riza Pasha, and that of Marine out of office, and had appointed Nazim in place of Riza without consulting the Committee. A vote in the Chamber of 198 against and only 8 for him led to his resignation.

Whatever were the motives of Kiamil, there was a general feeling of satisfaction at Nazim's appointment, and especially among foreign military experts. The Second Army Corps, of which he had been placed in command, was lax in discipline when he took charge. The soldiers were discussing politics, asking whether it was best in their interest to support the Committee, or whether the Committee were working in the interest of the Giaours. They understood liberty and equality, as most of the uneducated Turks did, to mean that one man was as good as another, and that the soldier ought to have equal authority with his officer. They had to be coaxed to go to drill. They were disrespectful to their officers. Nazim Pasha soon changed all this. He told his officers that it was the business of a soldier to train himself for fighting, that political questions were not their business, and that the first duty of a soldier was to obey. According to all accounts he effected a quite remarkable improvement in discipline.[1]

The belief was generally expressed, when Kiamil appointed Nazim Minister of War, that what he had done for one army corps he would accomplish for the whole army. The Committee and the nation had full confidence in him. He had been kept in prison in Erzinghian by Abdul Hamid for seven years as a political suspect. During five of these years he had been confined in a room about ten feet square, but as a favour had been allowed access to military books. He was known as one of the best soldiers in the country when he was exiled and had added to his theoretical knowledge during his imprisonment. In June, 1908, he escaped from prison and made his way in various disguises during thirty-five days to Batum, where he learned that the revolution had occurred in Constantinople. He contrived to reach the capital, and was at once welcomed by the Committee and the army. He was heart and soul with their movement. But when Kiamil fell the Committee would not allow him to continue as Minister of War because he had been named by the fallen Minister. The previous Minister of War was placed again in office and the old system of letting every soldier do much as he liked took greater development than ever.

Observers other than the Turkish Ministers saw many other things than the lax discipline of the army, which led them to conclude that a cataclysm might ensue. There was a steadily growing dissatisfaction with the new *régime* because it did nothing. Regarding many matters this dissatisfaction was unjustifiable. In others, there was an impatience for results which was simply due to ignorance. Kiamil's Government had named Commissioners to

[1] Nazim had been trained at St. Cyr and approved of French rather than German methods of tactics and strategy.

frame Bills to present to the Chamber which would remedy many of the crying evils. Ignorant men, accustomed to absolute government, thought that the Sovereign's fiat could at once be used to put an end to the evils complained of. No such fiats were issued. It is true that the system of spies was abolished and that the abominations of torture had for a time come to an end; but disorder in the capital and the provinces seemed rather to increase. Liberty was taken to be licence. People saw no improvements in the administration of justice. The Law Courts remained unchanged. The beginning of an attempt to purify them had not even been made. The sensational trial of Nedjib Melhame, for alleged tortures which would have disgraced the Inquisition, had been dragging on for months. In popular belief the judges in this and similar criminal cases were seeking the means, at the instigation of the Palace, of postponing their decisions until the offences were forgotten and the prisoners could be released.

Then, too, the financial difficulties had not lessened. All the departments required money; the soldiers saw no advantages which they had gained by the revolution. The Ministry of Hilmi Pasha, which was purely and simply that of the Committee, showed a want of backbone. It gave orders which it had not the courage to carry out. There were even signs which were construed as an intention to interfere with the right of public meeting and with the liberty of the Press. Nor were matters improved under the rule of Kiamil. The Committee was discredited by the weakness of its nominees.

But the most ominous of the signs that a storm was likely to come was seen in the intolerance and narrowness of a small section of the Committee. People were asking whether it was worth while exchanging the tyranny of Abdul Hamid for that of this irresponsible body. The Committee felt that its rule was becoming unpopular and plunged. Everyone recognised that it had managed the revolution of July with skill and a moderation which deserved every praise, but with that admission admiration ceased.

A few days after the vote of want of confidence in Kiamil, in February, 1909, it was a matter of common talk that the officers of the fleet had declared that they would claim to elect their own Minister of Marine. A general uneasiness prevailed. Civilians became alarmed.

The manner in which Kiamil was dismissed did much to destroy public confidence in the Committee. He was contemptuously outvoted. Yet he was an old and trusty public servant who not only embodied the best traditions of the small party which during thirty years had opposed the tyranny of the Palace, but stood for the principle of liberty, of settled government, and of a school which was willing to grant equality within the limits of what was possible to all the non-Turkish elements of the Empire. He was not, therefore, a man to be lightly cast aside, though the opinion was quite fairly held that a younger man ought to be at the helm of State.

The downfall of Kiamil definitely marked the parting of the ways. The Committee of Union and Progress and the Chamber divided into sections. The first assumed the name of Achrars, or Liberals, and the other of Nationalists. Both sections were actuated by a common purpose to benefit the country. Both were passionately attached to constitutional government. Both considered themselves progressive, but one wished to go further or faster than the other. It had been said that the Liberals were in favour of "decentralisation," but the Nationalists made the same claim. What each agreed to understand by the term was that the local Governors should have power to take decisions in reference to public works and other matters of specially local interest without the necessity of referring every matter to the Ministers in the capital. The Liberals, however, preferred that there should be locally elected councils.

The parting of the ways was shown both in reference

to measures and to men. The extreme Nationalists showed an intolerance of all opinions contrary to their own and opposed all projects not previously sanctioned by them. Already some of them had insolently proclaimed that when liberty and equality were spoken of they meant only among Moslems. They wished to Turkify everything. Even Arabs and Albanians were to be forced to learn Turkish, which was to be the only official language used. The names of the streets, even in towns where Greek was the language of three-fourths of the inhabitants, were painted in Turkish characters which a very small proportion of the population could read. Old-fashioned Turks mocked at the absurdity. It was, however, a more serious question in Albania and Arabia. Among the Arabs, their language, that of the Koran, is regarded with a veneration which causes them to look upon Turkish as barbarous. To attempt to supersede the semi-sacred language increased the already growing hostility of the tribes towards the Committee. Already, before the revolution, in June, 1907, they had defeated the Turks near Sana, and the fear which the rebels, aided by the climate and lack of water, had aroused in the Turkish troops was so great that desertions were always frequent when troops were ordered to the Hedjaz. After the revolution, when at the end of October, 1908, the Seventh Regiment was ordered to Jeddah, they mutinied and declared against the Committee. The Hedjaz Railway, opened on September 1, enabled the troops on the side of the Government to effect their defeat, and Ratib Pasha, their commander, was captured. Nevertheless, the discontent among the tribes became so serious that Hilmi Pasha drew up a project of reforms with the Arab leaders which it was believed would satisfy them. When Kiamil came into power he gave it his entire approval. But it was not Turkish enough to satisfy the extremists and was set aside on the dismissal of Kiamil.

Upon Kiamil's dismissal, the Sheik-ul-Islam, Jemal-ed-din, resigned. The dominant section of the Committee begged him to remain in office. Hilmi Pasha joined in the request. But Hilmi's unexpected desertion of his chief on the Thursday preceding the Saturday of Kiamil's fall had created a bad impression in the minds of all who knew the circumstances. He had not played the game. The Sheik-ul-Islam refused. All that he would consent to was to recommend Zia-ed-din as his successor. The new Sheik-ul-Islam was greatly respected and it was hoped he would prove as able as his predecessor.

But the refusal of the Jemal-ed-din to continue in office was a significant sign that the Committee had forfeited the confidence of a man who carried great weight with the community, and especially with the Ulema, the most learned and highly placed of Moslems. No greater blunder could have been committed by the Nationalist Party than to alienate this class.

The position became threatening to Young Turkey. The Parliament which they had called together was working quite as well as could have been expected when it is remembered that nine out of ten members were absolutely inexperienced and unused to public life. Each one, however, recognised that the party was fighting for its life and believed that there was an unseen force, headed by Abdul Hamid, that was working for its ruin. Confident of their popularity in the country, they took few precautions, except that the larger part of the Albanian troops surrounding Yildiz were sent to other barracks and a few suspected employees were dismissed.

Suddenly, on Tuesday, April 13, 1909, a piece of news came as a bomb to Europe and even to the foreign Ministers in Constantinople. Yet there had been indications which ought to have put the latter on guard. The newspapers which spoke for the Mahometan Association, and even other local journals, had begun violently to attack the Committee. A public meeting was held in the first week of April to denounce changes in the Press Law. The employees of the only Turkish steamship company openly defied the orders of the

Government, that is, of the Committee. They retained possession of the steamers and ran them in defiance of the Committee's orders. It looked as if the Young Turks were losing all control. Then one of the editors, Hassan Fehmi, of a Mahometan Association newspaper called the *Serbesti*, was assassinated near Galata Bridge and his death was generally attributed to the Committee. Though the man had been of ill-repute, the assassination aroused such ill-feeling against the Committee that they obtained permission to bury him in the mausoleum of Mahmud the Reformer—in other words, to allege that they regretted his death. His funeral, designed to clear the Committee from suspicion, became a demonstration against it.

To return, however, to the events of April 13. What appeared like a general revolt of all the troops in the capital occurred. From the suburbs regiments marched towards the great courtyard of Saint Sophia and the large open space known in Byzantine days as the Augusteon, which lies to the south of the great church. All the soldiers carried rifles, and as they passed over the bridges across the Golden Horn hundreds of shots were fired into the air. The first impression was, and probably not an incorrect one, that the soldiers, who were mostly without officers, wished no harm to anybody, but were having an outing. The previous days had been Easter Sunday and Monday, feasts which all denominations of Eastern Christians celebrate by the indiscriminate discharge of rifles, pistols, and fireworks. They had had their turn and the Turkish soldier seemed to think that it was now his.

This was not, however, the view of the better informed. The garrison of the capital and the marines from the Arsenal had mutinied. Those who neared the converging places found that there were persons among the troops who raised the cry of "Down with the Constitution," "Down with the Committee," "Long live the Sheriat," the Sacred Law. It turned out afterwards that there were a number of men, disguised as mollahs, hojas, or softas, and wearing the white turban, who had been instructed to raise these shouts. The cry was a dangerous one because it tended to arouse religious fanaticism, and in former years and under different circumstances would have led to an attack upon the Christian population by the Moslem mob. That time, however, had gone past. It was not taken up largely, and the soldiers continued their demonstrations of joy. It was soon remarked that the regiments were mostly without officers. Then the news was spread that Nazim Pasha, the Minister of Justice, had been shot for refusing to give up his revolver; that a man had been killed under the belief that he was Jahid Bey, editor of the chief Committee newspaper; that Hilmi Pasha having refused to continue in office had been replaced as Grand Vizier by Tewfik Pasha, and that Abdul Hamid had promised pardon to all the mutineers. That it was an attempt at counter revolution became evident and cannot seriously be doubted. There was some religious feeling in the movement, but there was also a good deal of gold and silver. A great many of the noisy demonstrators subsequently arrested were found to possess considerable sums of money which they declared had been given to them that morning as recompense for raising cries against the Committee and in favour of the Sheriat. The mob evoked no enthusiasm and provoked little opposition. It wrecked the offices of the leading newspaper, the *Tanin*, the organ of the Committee. It destroyed those of the Committee, a Turkish ladies' club, and the property of another newspaper which supported the Committee.

In the afternoon all firing ceased until late in the evening. In the following day, April 14, the new Vizier formed a Ministry from which naturally Young Turks were excluded.

The most notable opposition had taken place at the barracks of the Seraskerat, which is situated on the highest ground in the eastern portion of Stambul. The troops there were in command of Mahmud Muktar, who subsequently gave a full history of what he did and saw on that day. He refused to admit the military mob into the barrack yard, not doubting that they were acting against the Sovereign's orders. Fighting took place between the men under his command and a portion of the military. During the struggle orders were brought to Muktar from the Palace that the mob was not to be resisted. He at once obeyed, but he knew that he had incurred the displeasure of the Sultan and of the party which was then in possession of the streets of Stambul. He therefore hastened away in disguise, crossed the Bosporus, and went to his house at Moda, at the extreme south-east end of that channel. After various remarkable adventures he got away from Constantinople on the following day by the help of the British and German Embassies to the Piræus, and three days later reached Salonika, where he joined Mahmud Shevket.[1]

The proceedings in Constantinople were concealed for many hours from the rest of the country, and especially from Salonika, where the silence of the telegraph wires occasioned great alarm amongst the Committee. The troops in that city and indeed in all Macedonia were under the command of Shevket Pasha, a brave soldier, respected by all who knew him. As soon as the news of what was immediately taken to be a serious revolt in favour of Abdul Hamid reached the city, Shevket was sent for by the Committee and asked what he proposed to do. He had only joined the Committee after considerable hesitation, but when the question was put to him his answer was worthy of his reputation. "I have sworn to defend the Committee of Union and Progress and shall respect my oath." As details of the rising reached Salonika he collected an army largely composed of Albanians and Christians in order to proceed to Constantinople. A detachment left for the capital on Friday, April 16.

In the eventful four days that followed the demonstration of April 13 all the prominent members of the Government and of the Committee went into hiding.

[1] Muktar declared "it would have been child's play to have put down the revolt." But on receipt of the Sultan's message he had to flee for his life.

Some sought refuge in one or other of the foreign Consulates, but most of them in friendly private houses. The storm had burst suddenly, and no one knew what would follow. When men found that the demonstration was entirely silly, futile, and without apparent guidance, they came out into daylight and, not altogether free from alarm, made San Stefano their headquarters. It was then found that the deaths during April 13 were less numerous than had been expected. The Minister of Justice and Arslan Bey were the only notables who had been killed. Eight officers also had been slain, but, excepting those who fell in attacking Mahmud Muktar at the Seraskerat, probably not more than a score perished.

At San Stefano most of the leading members of the Committee waited anxiously to see what the military party, and above all Shevket, would do. Many of the telegraph employees in the capital were members of the Committee and sent word to Salonika of what San Stefano thought and proposed. Abdul Hamid to the general surprise made no move. That the demonstration was intended to subvert the Constitution and bring back the personal government of Abdul Hamid was not doubted by most persons who witnessed it. That the demonstrators were supplied with money was proved by the confessions of men arrested even on April 13, upon whom considerable sums had been found. The question which everybody asked was to whom could a counter revolution be beneficial, and but one answer was given. Abdul Hamid, in his methods, always had a tendency to secret intrigue and cunning, and in none of his endeavours were these qualities displayed more conspicuously than in the way in which the demonstration of April 13 was organised.

Yet the question of the Sultan's share in it is not altogether free from doubt. Kiamil acquitted Abdul Hamid of any participation. The Sultan was "a broken-down man and went in fear of his life," according to him. It must be remembered, however, that Kiamil had been roughly treated by the Committee and his testimony may not be impartial. Shevket judged Abdul Hamid to be the instigator. The first and second eunuchs of the Palace were of the same opinion and gave curious details of Abdul's preparations. It was subsequently stated that the examination of the spies' reports are conclusive as to the Sultan's participation. It was remembered that Abdul Hamid had already destroyed one Parliament, and the belief was natural that the attempt on April 13 was another to accomplish a like object.

Shevket Pasha kept his word and did not lose a day in Salonika in preparing his army for a march and in pushing on to the capital. A National Convention consisting of members of both Houses met daily at San Stefano after April 16, and was not disturbed by the police or the troops who were still supposed to be acting on behalf of Abdul Hamid. The Army of Liberation, as those under Shevket were commonly called, made its appearance in the suburbs of the capital on April 22, 1909.

Everybody in the city expected a serious struggle. There was indeed opposition at two or three places, the first at Daoud barracks, about a mile outside the Adrianople Gate, and another outside San Stefano, but, gradually and skilfully, a semi-circle was drawn around the city having one end west of San Stefano and the other on the Bosporus, four or five miles northward of the city. The most serious fighting was expected in the neighbourhood of Yildiz; but on April 22, in the early morning, Shevket's army arrived in its neighbourhood and took possession of the outlying barracks around the Sultan's residence. They were attacked by some of the troops in the direction of the Taxim, and hundreds of shots were exchanged during two hours. About a score of soldiers and civilians were killed or wounded. Then opposition ceased until the afternoon, when again a few soldiers attached to Abdul Hamid's cause opened fire from the Tashkisla barracks. This was soon silenced, and at five o'clock in the afternoon hundreds of residents visited the neighbourhood of these barracks and found everything quiet. Yildiz had sent out spies to learn the whereabouts of the invaders, but they were captured. The Palace was soon to be in the possession of the deliverers. The semi-circle had converged. The Army of Deliverers were already in possession of the city. Their advance was so rapid that Abdul Hamid seems to have been unable to decide upon any action whatever. Fuad Pasha, an experienced soldier, maintained that with a small number of men he could have held the Deliverers at Chatalja for a period sufficiently long to have enabled the Sultan to bring up troops from many parts of Asia Minor. He did nothing; his enemies were already in possession. The Committee of Union and Progress had once more triumphed.

Thereupon, although not for the first time, a party in favour of deposing Abdul Hamid declared itself and became at once the majority. Some of the extremists would probably have voted for his death, but more moderate counsels again prevailed. He was to be allowed to live, but to be shorn of all power.

The population of the capital had believed that Abdul Hamid was a quiet spectator of what was being done. It was asserted that he was dazed, stricken with surprise and fear at the rapid progress which he was informed the troops marching to Constantinople were making; incredulous that his pampered Albanian troops should leave him defenceless; that among the thousands of his subjects who had lived at his charge none were forthcoming to organise a defence of the capital or even of Yildiz against the rebel army. What caused most astonishment during the army's advance was that no soldier was named to lead the defence. A few troops led only by officers of low rank made a show of fighting rather than a serious fight. In reality, however, Abdul was in a state of indecision. He could not make up his mind to play the man. Yet he was not altogether inactive. In his own unsoldierly way he had endeavoured to save himself. He had sent Yusuf Pasha into Albania to rouse a party in his favour. But

Shevket learned of the mission at Chatalja and sent two trustworthy men to watch the messenger. Yusuf was arrested and was found to have a large sum in gold packets in his luggage. Abdul counted for help upon the lower section of the Ulema, and it was claimed by the Committee that there was abundant evidence to show that he had expended money lavishly in bribing dozens of such men to arouse Moslem fanaticism in his favour. The Albanians who remained near the capital showed that they would not join in such a movement, and an eye-witness of what passed during the three or four days preceding the capture of Yildiz saw "Albanians marching hojas (Moslem teachers) to jail with as little ceremony as if these holy men were Pigs of Unbelievers."[1]

As soon as Yildiz was captured a Military Committee was appointed to preserve the lives of those within it and its contents. As already mentioned, the walls of the great park included many outbuildings and a large community. Every Turkish Pasha who can afford it has always a great number of servants and hangers-on, but in Yildiz there were an unusual number. There were said to be 370 ladies and their servants, together with the sons and daughters of the Sultan and their respective suites amounting to 160 persons. In addition were 350 persons who were chamberlains, body servants and aides-de-camp; 250 belonging to the kitchens; 350 stablemen, and body troops to the number of nearly 1,500.

The Saturday night after the capture must have been terrible at Yildiz. The Palace, which Abdul Hamid always had brilliantly lighted, was in complete darkness. The Sultan was not visible, and many believed that he was in a fit or already dead. Nothing but pity could be

[1] "The Fall of Abdul Hamid," p. 247, by Francis McCullagh. Abdul Hamid is said even in these the most critical days of his life to have believed that he, "the King of Kings, the Shadow of God, the Blood Drinker, the Hunkiar, the sole Arbiter of the World's destiny," was invulnerable. He still believed in the predictions already mentioned. When on the afternoon of Friday Yildiz was captured, he began to regard the situation as hopeless. It is right to add that trusted soldiers were placed around Yildiz and that his person and that of all in the great palace remained unmolested.

felt for the poor ladies who were alleged to have anticipated that they would be left to the mercy of the soldiers. The higher officials and functionaries were immediately taken away and placed under control. Many of them had gone into the harem, in which place also the eunuchs had taken refuge. Most of the ladies were conveyed to the Cheragan Palace which adjoins Yildiz or were taken quietly to imperial buildings at Seraglio Point. The citizens of Pera on the Monday saw a long procession of eunuchs, spies, slaves, and unarmed officers marched through the streets surrounded by a detachment of Macedonian soldiers.

Always careful to act so far as possible in conformity with the Sacred Law, the National Convention, which intended to depose Abdul Hamid, applied to the Sheik-ul-Islam for a *Fetva* authorising their proceedings. This was obtained without difficulty, and a deputation consisting of four persons was then appointed by the Convention to inform Abdul Hamid that he was deposed and to announce to Reshad Effendi, his younger brother, his accession to the throne.

Reshad had been living in retirement, carefully spied upon by the emissaries of Abdul Hamid, and could hardly believe the news when he received the deputation informing him that in accordance with the *Fetva* of the Highest Sacred Court Abdul Hamid was deposed and he had consequently become Sultan.

For our purpose it is more interesting to notice what was done by the Commission when charged to convey the news to Abdul Hamid. The most important member was General Essad Pasha, a man much respected and about fifty years of age. He gave an account of what happened at the interview to Mr. McCullagh.[1] The most prominent man after him was Carasso Effendi, a member of the Committee and a deputy from Salonika. He gave an account of the fulfilment of his mission to various persons, the present writer amongst the number. He is an advocate, an orthodox Jew, and is greatly respected on account of his character and ability. This

[1] "Fall of Abdul Hamid," p. 266.

was his second visit to Yildiz. Shortly before the revolution of July, 1908, he had been arrested while on his way home, and was taken in a steam launch across to Scutari and thence to Yildiz. He was severely interrogated, both in the launch and at the Palace. In the account of the interview at Yildiz, which the present writer entirely believes, he made up his mind that his only chance of getting away from the Palace was to present a bold front to the Sultan's agents. He admitted that he was a member of the Committee, and then told his questioners that they had ramifications in every part of the Empire, that the army was with them, and that there could be no chance whatever of successfully resisting it. In other words, he bluffed them to such an extent that after four hours' interrogation they let him out of the Palace at midnight, and to his great delight he was permitted to return to his family.

When on Tuesday, April 27, Carasso and his fellow Commissioners reached Yildiz, they informed the Sultan's secretary that they had a personal communication to make to his Majesty on behalf of the National Convention. The secretary warned them that his Majesty was in an excited condition and that he might draw his revolver on them. They were then surrounded by a party of about thirty black eunuchs and admitted into the room where they were to give their message. The most noticeable feature in the room was the number of mirrors which enabled the Sultan to see what persons entered, even from behind him. Abdul Hamid came in a few minutes after them, accompanied by his little son, Abdurrahman Effendi. The deputation advanced into the centre of the room and respectfully saluted. The eunuchs and secretaries remained near the door by which the deputies had entered. Abdul Hamid came in from behind a screen and asked why they had come, whereupon Essad Pasha saluted and replied that they were there by orders of the Chambers acting in conformity with a *Fetva* that had been pronounced by the Sacred Court and confirmed by the Sheik-ul-Islam, declaring that his Majesty Abdul Hamid could lawfully be deposed, and that in consequence Reshad would immediately be proclaimed Sultan. He added that the National Convention "charges itself with his Majesty's personal safety and that of his family." The Sultan replied in a state of great excitement that he was not guilty: "It is my Kismet," and then pressed them for an assurance that his life would be spared. He added, still speaking passionately, that it ought to be spared because he had spared the life not only of Murad, but of Reshad himself, who they stated had now become Sultan. Could they give an assurance that he would be safe? Both Essad and Carasso replied, in terms which they had previously agreed upon, that the Ottoman people were magnanimous and that the decision rested with them. They were then asked if they would guarantee that his life was safe. They declared that they were not charged to give any message regarding his personal safety, but their opinion was that his life would be safe. The Sultan burst out with the question "Will you swear to me that my life will be safe?" Essad expressed his opinion that the Assembly would not commit an act of injustice. Then Abdul asked if he might be permitted to occupy the Cheragan Palace. All that they could promise was that they would submit his wish to the National Convention, and would communicate its decision. Essad added that he personally thought such desire would be granted. Then Abdul Hamid whined out that he had conducted the war against Greece and had gained it, and that he had done many things in the interest of the nation, and that he did not deserve to be deposed. For a moment Abdul Hamid gave utterance to a cry of despair, finishing by calling upon Allah to punish the wrong-doers, a sentiment to which one of the deputation responded with a hearty "Amen." Towards the end of the interview Abdul Hamid passed from a state of excitement to one of collapse. The last three or four days had told heavily upon him. His beard had lost its dye, and the hair showed grey. The deputation then retired, and the last sound that they heard was the boyish voice of the little Prince, who was crying as if his heart would break.

On April 13 his mutinous army had cried out for the Sheriat; on April 27, according to the decree of the Sheriat, Abdul Hamid had ceased to reign. On the same day Reshad Effendi was proclaimed Sultan under the title of Mahomet V.

It is unnecessary for my purpose to record the punishment that was meted out to those who had taken the leading part in the attempted reaction on April 13.

On the evening of his dethronement, at about nine o'clock, two armed automobiles and two squadrons of cavalry with three Macedonian officers proceeded to Yildiz. They were under the command of Husni Pasha, with whom were Ghalib, Inspector-General of the Police and Gendarmery, and Ali Fatieh, who had been the Turkish Military Attaché at Paris. Husni Pasha, Commander of the First Division of the Macedonian Army, has given a full account of what happened. He saw Jevad Bey, the first secretary of the ex-Sultan, and requested him to announce his visit. Jevad Bey refused and said, "The Sultan is a good shot and never misses. You have no idea how well he aims." Husni replied, "I can kill you on the spot, go and do what I order; tell Abdul Hamid that I must speak to him on a question touching his life." He waited a quarter of an hour. Then Jevad Bey conducted him into the presence of Abdul Hamid, who appeared very much agitated, with his hands in his pockets, doubtless clutching two revolvers, and, adds Husni, "apparently convinced that the troops intended to kill him." Husni saluted the ex-Sultan with the greatest respect, and assured him that the nation did not wish to injure him, that he had nothing to fear, and swore to Abdul Hamid that his life was guaranteed. "Nevertheless," he said, "the decision is irrevocably taken that two Sultans ought not to remain in the same place."

Abdul Hamid answered, "I understand. What do you want?" "I wish to take you to Salonika." Abdul Hamid declared that he was ill and wished to pass his days at Cheragan, or to have his freedom and to be permitted to go to Europe.

Husni goes on to tell that he pleaded long with the ex-Sultan in order that he might yield. Abdul Hamid fainted. His women brought him water and wept bitterly. Finally he yielded to their urgent entreaties, and the carriages were ordered to get ready.

He was permitted to take with him three Sultanas, four concubines and a retinue, in all twenty-seven persons. He was only allowed to take a small portion of the luggage which he desired to take, but many boxes had been packed, and it was promised that these should be sent on by train, a promise which was kept. Abdul Hamid expressed a desire to take with him a favourite Angora cat, and this was also forwarded the next day. At midnight the automobiles, accompanied by a squadron of cavalry, started for the railway station. Abdul Hamid with two little Princes and three Sultanas was in a large landau; the rest were in automobiles.

It was noted that the ex-Sultan was pleased to see the railway station which he had never been in before. Probably he was now for the first time convinced that he was to be taken to Salonika, and that the representations of Husni were not part of a plot to kill him. At 2.30 a.m. the train for Salonika started on what is always a long and weary journey. Passing through Dedeagatch, it continued for about twenty hours, and at nine o'clock on the evening of the 28th reached its destination. There the deposed Sultan was lodged in the Villa Allatini, belonging to a well-known and highly respected Jewish family.

The story of Abdul Hamid as Sultan is finished. It only remains to add that he never appears to have recovered his spirits, but developed the distrust and querulousness which had always been marked features of his character. Had he wished to escape while in Salonika, he probably could have done so without much difficulty. The Villa Allatini was practically locked from the inside. From the time of his arrival there he entirely disappears from public view. It is, to say the least, curious that few persons, either in Turkey or out of it, cared to inquire what had become of him. Eleven of his suite, mostly ladies, desired after a few months to leave him and were permitted to do so. After about two years in Salonika the Committee considered it safer that he should be nearer the Capital, and he was brought to Constantinople and for a time lodged in a small palace on the Bosporus. It is said that he has again been removed to some place in the interior.

Note 1.—Full details of the visit of the Deputies to Yildiz to inform Abdul Hamid that he was deposed were given in the *Daily Telegraph*, the *Times*, and the *Daily News*. They agreed in giving credit to the delegates for correct and courteous treatment of the fallen Sovereign and in representing him as making piteous appeals for his life, amid passionate denunciations of his enemies. An excellent "Diary of Recent Events in Constantinople," by "One on the Spot," was given in *Blackwood's Magazine* for June, 1909, commencing with Tuesday, April 13.

A much fuller account and one picturesquely written is given by Mr. Francis McCullagh, who also was in Constantinople at that time (as was the present writer). Mr. McCullagh had the advantage of discussing events with, and of obtaining the versions of Shefket Pasha and several others of the prime actors in the events of April 13 and for a fortnight after the deposition of Abdul Hamid. (*"The Fall of Abdul Hamid," by Francis McCullagh, Methuen & Co.*)

Note 2.—FORTUNE OF ABDUL HAMID ON HIS DETHRONEMENT.

It has already been mentioned that Abdul Hamid was keen after money. A Commission appointed immediately after the deposition by the Chamber reported that on May 9, 1909, they had opened two of the safes in the secret portion of Yildiz, and found in gold and silver £T90,000, which were "placed in eleven sacks in one strong box." A further report declared that they found similar hoards in Yildiz of cash and notes amounting to £T480,000 and £T1,800,000 in securities. Abdul Hamid's private properties, many of which had been irregularly obtained, brought him in a large income, the mines alone producing annually from £T300,000 to £T350,000. These were transferred to the Government. It was never discovered what money he possessed in foreign banks, except his deposits in the Ottoman Bank, where he had £T50,000. He alleged that all his deposits abroad only amounted to £T1,080,000.

The same Commission reported that there were 300 cases of *Djournals* in the basement at Yildiz only.

NOTE ON THE YOUNG TURK PARTY, DIPLOMACY, AND THE ENTRY OF TURKEY INTO THE EUROPEAN WAR.

With the deposition of Abdul Hamid the story of the Committee of Union and Progress finishes so far as this book is concerned. But the writer may be allowed to add something to his story about them. That they were actuated when they made the Revolution of 1908 by praiseworthy motives is beyond reasonable doubt. No Englishman, knowing the condition to which Abdul Hamid had reduced his country, could fail to sympathise with their desire to establish Constitutional Government. Having accomplished that object by a union of all the elements in the country, internal dissensions were as inevitable as they were after the great English Convention which got rid of James II. Young Turkey began to blunder from the moment it had accomplished its principal object. But in the famous attempt at reaction on April 13, 1909, the Salonika branch of the Committee of Union and Progress gave orders, which were however not acquiesced in by the Constantinople section, for an attack on the Armenians in Cilicia, and a massacre followed which in wickedness equalled those in Armenia in 1894-7. This was the greatest initial blunder. Other blunders and shortcomings have been noted.

It is worth while to explain what was the attitude of Europe, and of Great Britain especially, towards the Young Turk Party. Many of the members of that party had been struggling for long years to remodel the Government on Constitutional, that is, British, lines. Many had been exiled for adherence or supposed adherence to such a project. Nearly all had risked their property and even their lives to realise a British ideal. When at length they compelled the Sultan to re-proclaim Midhat's Constitution, and eight months afterwards dethroned him, they counted upon, and had a right to expect, British sympathy. These events constituted together a Revolution which had been accomplished almost without bloodshed, and bore witness to the moderation of the counsels of the Young Turks. In spite of their many blunders, due to lack of experience and a too great fervency of zeal, their aspirations and general conduct would have met with the approval of Canning, of Russell, of Palmerston, and of the liberal men of both political parties in England who clung to the traditions in favour of struggling peoples. Young Turkey believed that while the rulers of other European States might look askance, it would at least obtain England's support.

When on July 30, 1908, Sir Gerard Lowther, her Ambassador, arrived in the capital, he was received with wild enthusiasm. British influence rose ; German fell. The occasion gave a unique opportunity for following the best British traditions. Unhappily it was not seized. Why ? It is difficult to give an entirely satisfactory answer. Professor Hobhouse is probably right in stating that the worst period of the Armenian massacres, 1894-6, "marks the moral bankruptcy of European statesmanship." Mr. Goschen when Ambassador to the Porte twenty years earlier expressed himself as disagreeably surprised at the indifference of the Powers to internal political development in Turkey, and even to human suffering. It became the fashion among the diplomatic class to be sceptical in all matters relating to the progress of the Turkish people, although, as already stated, Great Britain on several occasions took the lead and risked war in pressing for measures in Crete, Armenia, and Macedonia for the benefit of subject races. The selfishness and materialism of current philosophy—seen at its worst in Germany—had lowered the public opinion of Europe and had affected the tendencies of the governing class. The belief of our grandfathers in freedom, self-government, and constitutional liberty was a religious cult which the younger generation was gradually abandoning. In the Young Turk Party the latter saw a number of young, inexperienced and largely uneducated men striving to attain the ideals which Englishmen previous to 1870 had held up to the world. Having themselves lost sympathy with such ideals, they became contemptuous of those who followed them. A little kindly feeling towards inexperienced idealists, a little friendly guidance without any attempt at interference, would have stood England in good stead. British diplomacy looked on coldly, disdainfully, and did not rise to the occasion. The new Ambassador, Sir Gerard Lowther, had been many years absent from Turkey and could not be expected to have watched the growth of the Young Turk Party. He was an excellent Ambassador for all the matters with which he was acquainted. His great anxiety was to maintain the prestige of the Empire at the height to which it had ascended on his arrival. He successfully encouraged the Porte, that is the Committee, to ask for and obtain an English Naval Mission, a Mission which, under Admiral Gamble, then Admiral Williams, and subsequently under Admiral, now Sir Arthur, Limpus, was quite remarkably successful in reconstituting the Turkish Naval Service, in supporting the design of the Turks to obtain two Dreadnoughts, and to remodel their shipbuilding yards. In many other matters he showed his sympathy with the national aspirations. But Sir Gerard Lowther laboured under two great disadvantages, first, that he knew himself to be already struggling with the terrible malady which ultimately in the spring of 1916 brought his life to an untimely end. He manfully struggled on, especially in trying to relieve the terrible sufferings inflicted on Moslems and Christians alike by the two Balkan Wars in which Turkish military organisation completely collapsed, and in which he was aided by his wife's quite remarkable powers of organisation. His second disadvantage lay in the defects of our antiquated diplomatic system. Prince Bismarck once spoke of an Ambassador as in these latter days being a Foreign Office clerk at the end of a telegraphic wire. Such an arrangement works well if at one end of the wire the speaker is in touch with the sentiment of his country, and at the other the receiver knows the drift of feeling in the country to which he is accredited. But the statement indicates a change of circumstances from those of a previous generation. Lord Stratford de Redcliffe when a young man was for nearly two years unable to receive any communication from the Foreign Office, but he knew the general lines of the policy of which his country would approve, acted as if he were the Foreign Secretary for Great Britain, understood Turkey, and carried out British policy to a successful issue. History has shown that his judgment was usually right and, indeed, that the interference of his Government was sometimes mischievous.

Railway communication and the telegraph wire have considerably changed the situation. But the need for an efficient Ambassador is as great as ever, especially for one who, like Sir William White, knows the country well, or for one who is kept fully informed by a number of consuls who speak the language, are in touch with all classes, and can keep their chief fully informed. Great Britain was singularly fortunate during the reign of Abdul Hamid in her Ambassadors. Where she failed was in establishing satisfactory relations between her Embassy and her Consuls, the latter of whom are nearly all able men. But their duties and their relations with the Embassy are alike ill defined, and there has constantly existed jealousy between the diplomatic and the consular services. England did not make full use of her Consuls. Sir Gerard Lowther, returning to the country after twenty years' absence, had to depend largely for his information regarding Young Turkey and its aims upon inexperienced secretaries, and upon consuls who had not been expected or encouraged to watch political movements. The German Ambassador, the able Baron Marschall Von Bieberstein, had seen the reputation of

Germany fall on the success of the July Revolution of 1908. He recognised that the Committee was in power and was the only party in Turkey with vitality, and commenced at once to cultivate it. Within a year many of the leading Young Turks had become his friends. During that time it was a matter of public remark that nearly everyone at the British Embassy, except Sir Gerard himself, spoke disparagingly of Young Turkey. The only British newspaper published in the capital, and on that account supposed, quite incorrectly, to represent the opinions of the Embassy, was one of the most constant to join in denunciation of the Committee. Sir Gerard Lowther struggled on manfully and with success in achieving the objects mentioned in spite of the atmosphere by which he was surrounded. The system which made the Consuls a detached body gave him no aid.

The same general remarks apply to our diplomatic system both in Turkey and in all the Balkan States. The staffs of the diplomatic bodies in each capital belonging to various nations tend to constitute a clique closed to the outside world and knowing little of the people to whose Sovereign their chiefs are accredited. One heard almost everywhere in the Balkans of the arrogance and disdain of members of the diplomatic caste towards the governing classes of the small communities.

When the Great European War in August, 1914, commenced, the Turks were ultimately forced to join the Germans, Enver having gone over to their side. Sir Gerard had been replaced by Sir Louis Mallet, who from the first did much to show sympathy with the Young Turks. It has often been said that if the Committee had not been in power the adhesion of Turkey to the Central Powers would have been avoided. No valid reason exists to support this view. Abdul Hamid would have continued to be a pliant tool in their hands. It would be nearer the truth to say that if Sir Louis Mallet had not been known to be sympathetic, and in this to reflect the opinion of Sir Edward Grey, Turkey would have joined the Germans earlier than she did. Said Halim, the

Grand Vizier in 1914, and other members of the Committee were known to be favourable to France and England. Turkey was naturally greatly irritated when our Government pre-empted the two Dreadnoughts on which the Turks had built great hopes of defeating the Greeks ; but that act, though the Germans made the most of it in Turkey, would have been forgotten if a bolder statesmanship had been pursued. The present writer suggests that when the *Goeben* and the *Breslau* entered the Dardanelles they should have been followed by British ships and compelled to disarm. There was the error, in his opinion, of British statesmanship, for from that time the Germans became masters of the Dardanelles and of Constantinople. It is true that the two German ships were allowed to keep their crews on board out of consideration for Turkish susceptibility, but it was, nevertheless, a blunder ; they ought to have been compelled to disarm. Most of the Young Turkey Party would have been glad to see such energetic action at the crisis. It was these German ships, joined by others of the Turkish fleet and all under German leaders, which bombarded Odessa and at once brought Turkey into the war.

CHAPTER XIV

ESTIMATE OF THE CHARACTER OF ABDUL HAMID

It is fair in estimating the character of Abdul Hamid to consider his environment and the influence on him of the traditional treatment of possible or probable heirs to the throne. What Von Hammer calls "the legal justification of the slaughter of male children belonging to the Imperial family" has already been mentioned. The history of the Turkish Imperial family during the last four centuries points to the conclusion that such slaughter met with general approval. The inevitable result followed. There was constant rivalry or suspicion in the Imperial harem between the mothers of possible heirs and among the boys themselves. It was in such an atmosphere of rivalry and suspicion that Abdul Hamid was born and brought up.

As he had been treated, so he treated his younger brother, the present Sultan, Mahomet V., known before his accession as Reshad. Abdul Hamid kept him a prisoner in his house, with permission to walk or to drive within a radius of about a mile. Every visitor to his house was carefully watched. He never had a conversation with a foreign Ambassador, was never allowed to visit or be visited by the Turkish Ministers, or even to speak to them, unless they happened to ride or drive by chance across the area which was assigned to him.[1] No letters were permitted to enter his konak without the knowledge of their contents being communicated to an official who acted as Abdul's chief spy over his

[1] On one occasion, after Abdul Hamid had been for ten years on the throne, the Grand Vizier's carriage passed across the area and met that of Prince Reshad, as Mahomet V. was then called. The two men saluted each other and passed on, but an examination took place at Yildiz under the supervision of Abdul Hamid. The two coachmen and the outriders were summoned and examined separately in order to report precisely what had taken place.

brother.[1] When on April 27, 1909, the deputies appointed by the two Chambers were sent to communicate to Abdul Hamid the decision of the National Assembly to dethrone him, and, to Reshad, that he would be at once proclaimed Sultan, the latter was astounded at the news; for he had heard little of what was going on. Abdul Hamid, in the famous interview begging for his life, claimed merit for having permitted his brother to live. There were, indeed, many precedents for the killing of the heir to the throne, and in the eyes of the ordinary Turk such an act would not have been regarded as extraordinary.

The atmosphere of suspicion, always prevalent in the Palace, was fatal to the development of manliness and trustfulness. There is no evidence to show that in his youth the intelligence of Abdul Hamid was other than mediocre. Such virtues as he possessed were of the negative kind. He avoided the vices of his elder brother. He neither drank, nor was he a sensualist. He was not lazy nor invariably ill-tempered. But a despotic Sultan ought at least to possess virility, courage both physical and moral, and of neither of these did he give signs. He was self-willed and could be rash, could threaten heavily or promise freely; but his threats were often foolish and constantly disregarded. In the European sense of the term he had no literary education whatever, but he could write and read his own language, an accomplishment which of itself shows that he had had considerable application.

After he was girt with the sword of Osman his attitude of suspicion increased. From the first his fear of those about him led him to employ the suspicions of others to defeat the hostile designs he always suspected. That

[1] A lady doctor in the city, a German subject and possibly a German spy, had been in the habit of visiting the ladies in Reshad's harem, but she was suspected of or possibly detected in carrying some kind of communication. Abdul Hamid at once ordered her expulsion from the country, and though she was not unpopular with German ladies and with other Europeans, the German Ambassador was compelled to give way and to see that she left Turkey. Many stories were current in Constantinople which pointed to the strictness of the guard set over Reshad's movements.

a man was known to be the enemy of a Minister was a recommendation to the Sultan for his appointment to a post in which he could bring his enmity to play the spy upon him. It became a subject of common remark in case of a Ministerial vacancy that a successor would be appointed who was known to be hostile to some other Minister. It was Abdul Hamid's idea of statesmanship thus to play off one Minister against another. The Ministers themselves were often afraid to pay visits to their colleagues lest they should be suspected of being too friendly; for each one knew that any act that could be distorted to his disadvantage would be reported at Yildiz. But as suspicion breeds suspicion, Abdul became afraid of everybody. Many stories were told of Palace life which would be incredible but for his general distrust of everyone connected with it. One such will suffice: On one occasion two girls (of about nine or ten years of age) were in his room when the Sultan commenced his usual prayers. He had taken from his pocket a beautiful revolver which he generally carried, and laid it on the table, for a Moslem must divest himself of arms while at prayer. One of the girls took it up and with the dangerous curiosity of a child began to examine it. The Sultan saw the movement and motioned to her to put it down, which she did. When the prayers were finished he subjected the two girls to a cruel cross-examination in presence of a police officer. He wanted to know who had suggested that she should take up the revolver, and brought in another person to assist in the examination and to endeavour to make one of the children admit that she had been told to take it up in order to kill him. Suspicion was, in fact, depriving him of common sense.

If it be said that Abdul Hamid's suspicion was not entirely due to his environment but was largely attributable to an unhealthy trait of Orientalism, the answer is that many of his predecessors largely overcame it by a healthy out-of-door life. Abdul had never lived such a life; he took no interest in out-of-door sports; cared nothing for fishing, hunting, or other physical exercise.

He had ceased to ride on horseback and only took walking exercise in the restricted fashion already described. Yet it would not be just to say of him that he lived the luxurious, effeminate life of a typical Eastern despot, for in his own way he was far from being idle. He had spasmodic periods of energy, mostly, however, of the unwholesome indoor kind. His want of healthy companionship in his youth unfitted him for friendship. He retained his few youthful tastes, notably his love of carpentry and for animals and birds. But even to these he was inconstant. Having an almost unlimited supply of money, he would spend large sums in buying dumb creatures, of which pictures or descriptions had taken his fancy, but having seen them once, the whim to possess them passed, and he would cease to care what became of them. He was never self-restrained, and the stories told of him, both in his youth and later in life, reveal a character of impulses which he rarely made an effort to check.

The isolation of the period before his accession grew upon him and became habitual. It had kept him from the companionship of his superiors in knowledge, education, or natural shrewdness. If ever the desire for it existed he had outlived it. Never having mixed with such men, he never desired to understand them. Those, indeed, with whose company he seemed best pleased were of a lower order, good-natured sycophants who with mediocre intellect strove to obtain his patronage. But them also he usually suspected, and in a moment of temporary anger would banish them for ever from his presence.

Dr. Mavrogeni, his chief medical adviser and a trustworthy man to everyone else, fell into disgrace because he was reputed to be writing the secret history of Yildiz. Dussap Effendi, leader of his orchestra, was forbidden to show himself again at Yildiz because after the playing of the Hamidieh March an ass outside brayed loudly and set the audience laughing. A foreign conjurer noted for his skill in making up imitations of distinguished personages, including the Czar and the two Emperors, performed before the Sultan. When, however, Abdul learned that at an entertainment given in a Minister's house the conjurer had reproduced the Sultan, Abdul Hamid warned the Minister and at once sent a good sum of money to the performer on condition that he should immediately leave Turkey. Emin Bey was dismissed for mildly hinting that some measures of reform would increase his master's popularity.

As Abdul grew older his suspicion increased and his temper grew shorter. There was a good deal of Asiatic barbarism in him, which was especially shown in apparently uncontrollable outbursts of temper. The dangerous habit he had acquired of always carrying at least one revolver led to many tales of accidents which cannot all be inventions, and some of which are based on satisfactory evidence. He would never permit a man near him to attempt to take anything from his own pocket. Sadyk Pasha, a former Grand Vizier, was disgraced because he put his hand into his pocket to take out a document. His Ministers must stand in his presence in a humble attitude with their hands crossed before them and never touch their pockets. Abdul became so nervous that he was easily alarmed. One of his gardeners was trimming a bush when the Sultan passed, and the gardener immediately sprang to attention. Abdul Hamid saw him rise, fired at once and killed him. Examination showed that the gardener was without a weapon of any kind. Arminius Vambéry stated that while seated at table with him (for he was greatly favoured by the Sultan, who at that time addressed him as "Baba") he reached across to take a match. Abdul Hamid, startled with the movement, sprang up in an alarm which to his visitor was very painful. The ex-Chamberlain, who writes as Monsieur Dorys, tells the story of Arif Pasha, then President of the Council of State, that, feeling a draught, he stood up suddenly and asked leave to close the window. Abdul Hamid's hand at once went to his revolver pocket, and Arif hastened to reassure him. Adossides Pasha, Prince of Samos, on a visit to Yildiz, in backing out of the

Sultan's presence tripped up. The Sovereign plunged his hand into his terrible pocket and slipped out of the room. The same author gives other illustrations of this alarming nervousness of the Sultan and suggests that to its existence was largely due the fact that the number of his friends diminished, for they never went to the Palace without alarm.

To account for this nervousness allowance has to be made for his habit of seclusion and his ever-present suspicion; but something also should be put down to his chronic illness. Dyspepsia and some other malady known to his medical advisers account for much of the waywardness, want of self-control, ill-temper, and perhaps also for the erratic habits of life which at the end of the century had begun to display themselves. It was said that he would occasionally pass forty-eight hours without sleep. What is certain is that he lived in the midst of alarms, which were largely due to his own temperament. It was whispered at times that he suffered from some form of mental aberration, but no trustworthy evidence to this effect exists; that he doctored himself, taking ether and valerian; that he took such doses because he was suffering terribly, and that the crises which demanded remedies became more frequent. When Mahmud Damat, his brother-in-law, fled the country, taking with him his two sons, their uncle had a specially severe breakdown. He disliked darkness, and though he would never consent to electric light being installed in Constantinople (although he had permitted it in Smyrna and Salonika), his great park at Yildiz, with its many buildings, was brilliantly illuminated by its means.

As he grew older his vanity increased. Yet he found himself thwarted both by his own subjects and by the foreign Powers. The reports of his agents had a morbid fascination for him and could not have ministered to his vanity. The daily bundles of *djournals* worried his soul, increased his discontent, and made him more irritable. It was in vain that he told the Armenian Patriarch that he loved the Armenians as his own children, and that he would make no distinction between them and his Moslem subjects; for his spies told him that such statements were generally disbelieved, and undoubtedly angered him. He had no hesitation in slaughtering the Yezijis (or Devil-Worshippers) because they were neither Moslems nor "Children of the Books." None of those on whom he showered his flattery believed in him or loved him. The very Kurds, whom he had petted and allowed to do what they liked with the persons and territory of the Armenians, were not grateful. The Arabs were as unruly as ever. It was in vain that he sent regiment after regiment into the Hedjaz until the soldiers in Syria mutinied and refused to be sent to what they regarded as certain death. He had largely failed in trying to set one Power against another, and though newer hopes dawned upon him in consequence of visits from the German Emperor, he saw disorders increasing on every side. When Russian Armenians entered his territory his anger broke loose against his own subjects.

Before the century was five years old, Abdul Hamid had grown to be a wizened and weary-looking old man. He never went beyond his palace walls except to the weekly ceremony of the Selamlik, which by Moslem tradition he was bound to attend. Even in the performance of this duty he limited his exertions as far as possible; for, whereas on his accession he had followed the example of his predecessors and had said his Friday mid-day prayer in St. Sophia or in another of the stately mosques in Stamboul, in the last twenty years of his reign he never crossed the Golden Horn except on the annual occasion of the Hirkai Sherif, when tradition and Moslem opinion required him to venerate the sacred relics of the Prophet. Unlike his predecessors he would never be photographed, and persons found with kodaks on them at the Selamlik were arrested and their cameras confiscated. Did he fear the deadly accuracy of the camera, *kim belir?* Believing himself to be surrounded by enemies was he unwilling that his subjects should recognise him?

Probably this objection to being photographed, like that of being publicly seen, was due to care for his own safety. It was generally attributed to cowardice. The precautions which were taken when he went on his annual visit tended to confirm the popular impression. In his annual passage from his residence at Yildiz to Stamboul—a distance of about two miles—he had the choice of three routes. Two were by land and one by water. On the appointed day for the veneration of the relics, the 15th of the month of Ramazan, all three routes were carefully prepared for him. The roads were sanded; all objectionable houses examined; all places, behind which an enemy could hide, carefully guarded; soldiers lined the streets throughout the whole length of both roads. The sea route was between his palace at Dolma Bagshe, to which access could be gained through his garden at Yildiz, to Seraglio Point. There, in another of his own gardens he was conducted in state through lines of soldiers to the building, less than a quarter of a mile distant, where the relics are preserved. As he descended from his carriage an officer, following an ancient custom, recited the warning: "Humble thyself O Padisha, and remember that Allah is greater than thou." Did Abdul Hamid ever take the warning to heart?

Until Abdul Hamid was ready to start on this ceremonious visit, no one knew by which route he intended to go. It was an unkingly spectacle, unworthy of a man who claimed descent from Mahomet, the Conqueror. He knew or feared that men spoke of him as a coward, for in an interview with Dr. Engländer he smote his breast, and asked why should such a charge be made against one who had the blood of the Ghazi in his veins.

A French author[1] states, on the authority of one of his chamberlains, that Abdul Hamid had one of them to read to him before he went to sleep, and that his favourite books were those which related to assassinations and executions. "The successful issues of crimes prevented him from sleeping, but when it came to the shedding of blood, he became calm at once and slept." The statement

[1] G. Dorys; "Abdul Hamid, *Intime*," Paris, 1909.

is probably an exaggeration, but it is illustrative of the man's temperament. If the story be true that when Midhat Pasha was strangled, Abdul Hamid ordered the head to be embalmed and sent to Constantinople, the order was not a mere precaution to be certain that Midhat was dead, but because in popular belief he loved to gloat over his enemy's head. Another story from the same source is, that after the attempt by Ali-Suavi to dethrone him, Abdul Hamid called his first secretary and, pointing to the Sublime Porte, expressed his belief that there was at that moment a gathering in order to depose him. His secretary asked "Of whom?" The reply was: "My Ministers are plotting against me." Another time, upon seeing in the courts of the old Seraglio the portraits of Viziers whose heads had been cut off, because they had ceased to please his predecessors, Abdul Hamid remarked that they constituted useful warnings to their successors and regretted he could not get rid of them in the same fashion. In 1895, when the Armenian Patriarch, Ismirlian, was called to the Palace after an Armenian demonstration at the Porte which had taken place a short time before the massacre in Stamboul itself, "They wish perhaps," said he, "by this means to bring about European intervention. Foreign fleets may pass the Straits and European armies invade my capital, but before they will land, the waves of the Bosporus will be coloured red with the blood of every Armenian." The poor old Patriarch, greatly moved, threw himself on his knees and begged the Sultan to have pity on his people. Abdul Hamid, however, at once became impatient and peremptorily ordered him to get out.

It would be pleasant but is difficult to find anything to say in favour of Abdul Hamid. His most agreeable trait was his liking for a cat. When he was deported to Salonika, his great anxiety, as already stated, was that his favourite should be sent after him. It is pleasant to record that this was done. Even the pleasantest stories told of him usually speak of his vanity. He was invariably anxious to please European visitors. In talking with European Ambassadors he usually showed his best side, and was an adept in flattery. A lady of high rank who visited him was rather remarkable for a taciturnity which was regarded as obtuseness. He endeavoured to learn from the Ambassador of the country to which she belonged whether she took interest in anything. She knew and cared little for politics or music or literature. Someone, however, informed him that she was fond of birds. He at once led the conversation to this subject, and took her to see his collection, with the result that the lady became eloquent and astonished those who heard her into observing that never had she been heard to speak so freely. He prided himself upon influencing a man by what he said. He declared to some of the mediocre creatures who were around him that he could bring tears into the eyes of any listener. An old fellow was approaching, and he remarked to his hearers, "See, if I cannot do it." The experiment met with such success that the old Turk wept, and then his Sovereign turned round to his sycophants with the remark: "Did not I say that I could bring him to tears?" Illustrations of his smartness in repartees have been given; one here will suffice. After having entertained a foreign Minister at dinner, he with his guest witnessed a play in the little theatre within his grounds at Yildiz. In the interval between the acts, offering a cigarette to the Minister, he asked how he liked Turkish tobacco. The Minister, at Abdul Hamid's request, had furnished him a few days earlier with a stronger kind. Before replying he spat and asked his Majesty how he liked that which he had brought him. The reply came at once: "It is very good, but I keep it to smoke in the garden where I can spit."

During the last two or three years of his reign he looked weak in health, ashy-faced, with hair which, whatever its original colour, was dyed of that red-brown, with a suspicion of purple, which is so much beloved by Eastern peoples. His long, cadaverous face made him look unnaturally thin. He could never have possessed a stately figure nor have grown into a venerable one.

With a fez too large and clothes hanging loosely upon him, with a quick jerky movement and shuffling feet, there was nothing in his appearance either dignified or fatherly.

The life of Abdul Hamid will remain on record as an example of the mischievous and dangerous character of absolute government. An able man possessed of absolute authority may do much to enhance his reputation or add to his territory. An Alexander the Great or a Napoleon may emblazon the history of his country with military glory, but such success is never of advantage to the country unless accompanied by civil growth, and nations so glorified seldom gain more than transient victories. The danger in absolutism is that there is no certainty that the successor of an able occupant of the throne shall not be a fool. Such danger is greatly increased when the succession follows the Turkish rule, for under it, the heir, hidden away or more or less closely imprisoned, sees no men of eminence and, in all likelihood, becomes the more incompetent the longer he lives before being girt with the sword of Osman. But Abdul Hamid was not an able occupant of the throne, and his reign indicates the mischief which an incompetent ruler can do to his country.

The treatment of his brothers by Abdul Hamid throws light on his character; whether Murad continued mentally incapable or not, it is beyond doubt that he had alienated general Moslem sympathy by his intemperate habits. Whether he were living or dead mattered to nobody. He was closely guarded until his death. Murad was the elder brother, Reshad Effendi, the present occupant of the throne, was the younger, and received more attention from Abdul Hamid than did the elder, for he was a more dangerous competitor. He was closely watched. During the thirty years of his imprisonment Reshad never had any intercourse with any foreign Ambassador or with prominent Turks. Yet all reports spoke and still speak of him as a man of kindly disposition and fond of children. Ignorant of every language except Turkish, his opportunities of knowing what was going on in the political world were slight, and on the deposition of Abdul Hamid himself he was by no means anxious to ascend the throne. Since 1909, when he became Sultan, he has naturally been guided by his Ministers, and to his credit it must be said that he never attempted to treat the heir to the throne, Jusuf Izzedin Effendi, as Abdul had treated him.[1]

So far as one can penetrate the thick veil which concealed his private life, which is certainly not far, one sees in Abdul Hamid a singular absence of that geniality which goes far to make the average Turk a favourite. He was always vindictive, and never forgave a man who had offended him. The stories told of him usually turn either upon his cruelty, his distrust, or his bitterness of tongue. He was shrewd enough in repartee to have given a reply to his brother as Charles II. did to the Duke of York: "They will never kill me to put you on the throne," but there was nothing of the good nature which relieved the unpleasant record of the Merry Monarch.

One may hesitate to charge Abdul Hamid with physical cowardice, though the precautions he took to save himself point that way. His treatment of Ali Haidar Midhat, the son of the murdered Midhat, was curious. He became the recipient of the Sultan's many favours which were regarded generally as an indication of Abdul's cunning. The Revolution had marked the triumph of Midhat's projects, and it became desirable to placate the son of his old enemy.

A distinguished writer, who has travelled largely in the Near East and whose observations always deserve consideration,[2] suggests that Abdul Hamid designed to make of Turkey an Asiatic State, and that such an idea

[1] There came to England on the last day of January, 1916, the announcement that Izzedin had committed suicide by opening his veins, in other words, if the statement be true, by seeking to end his life in the same way as his father Abdul Aziz had done in 1876. Two days after the announcement the more probable statement came that the report of suicide was untrue and that he had been murdered. Whatever be the cause of death, it has not even been suggested that Mahomet or Mehmet V. could have had anything to do with it.

[2] Mr. D. G. Hogarth in "Oxford Essays," 1915.

was based on the logic of facts. That the Sultan may at various times have had such an idea is probable, but it never obsessed him. He was never long constant to any idea. He lived from hand to mouth. Just as he would send to England for beautiful dogs and a man to tend them, and when they were received would never again trouble to look at them, so with his ideas or notions or whims. Probably at one time he cherished visions of a Pan-Islamic movement, of which he should be the head. But they vanished in presence of new dreams. An English maker of machinery received large orders for elaborate and costly machines which were to be delivered in all haste. Three years later he went to Constantinople and found them lying unpacked and exposed to all weathers.

There is much to be said in favour of the statement that Abdul Hamid cared more for show than for substance. He obtained torpedo boats to let Europe know that he possessed them rather than for eventual fighting. He wanted gendarmery from Englard in order to persuade the Powers that Turkey had made reforms. The truer explanation of his conduct is to be found in the vacillation which was always a characteristic of his ill-balanced mind. Even in the army, where a Turkish Sultan would have been expected to prefer reality, he preferred show. While his weekly Selamlik made a brilliant display of men in new suits and with up-to-date arms, the great mass of his soldiers were ill-clothed, ill-shod, and always in arrears of pay.

When he was confronted with what he regarded as attacks upon his sovereign rights, he protested violently, but usually gave way. His record contains a long series of threats, protests, and absolute surrender. He was greedy of other people's property and a spendthrift of his own whenever he wanted to further any of his ignoble projects. He saw his country growing steadily poorer and yet, to all appearances, never had a notion of enriching it except by the levy of new taxes. He met men like Mr. Joseph Chamberlain, Mr. Shaw Lefevre, and other English and French statesmen and did all that he could to impress them with his determination to establish schools, to construct roads and railways, and to develop the industry and commerce of the Empire. But he never took a single step on his own initiative towards the accomplishment of any of these designs.

Abdul Hamid was delighted when he was spoken of in a newspaper as "Ghazi," or Conqueror, a title which was justly given to Mahomet II., after the capture of Constantinople. No title could be less appropriate to him. The term is applied by the Turks solely to military conquerors, and no Sultan ever showed less competence for the conduct of military affairs than did he. In 1885 he had a chance of proving his value as a military commander which he neglected to take. But neither then nor at any other time did he ever take or propose to take the field. Had he possessed the spirit of a Ghazi he would have recognised that he had European law on his side, and that England, France, Germany and Austria would not have interfered between him and his rebellious subjects in Eastern Rumelia. He lost much territory and virtually did not gain any. Bulgaria became detached from his rule as well as a large portion of Asia Minor including Batum and Kars; Crete was lost to Turkey through his incapacity in war and his inability to recognise that changes urged upon him by all the Powers of Europe were intended to preserve the integrity of his Empire. "We have tried to save the Empire," said Lord Salisbury, singing the Swan-song of Crimean War sentiment, but "Turkey," that is, Abdul Hamid, "refuses to accept salvation." The title of Great Assassin by which Mr. Gladstone denounced him has much more to be said in its favour than that of Ghazi. He ordered the massacre of Arabs in Arabia. He had at least 20,000 of the Yezides murdered in the region mostly to the east of the Tigris. He ordered the massacre of Greeks both in Crete and in Epirus. Albanians were ruthlessly slaughtered in Europe when they opposed him, and the Druses in Mount Lebanon without mercy. In all these cases there was no attempt to redress the grievances which had awakened discontent.

In his attack upon the Armenians in 1894-6 especially, he deliberately chose the method of carefully planned massacres by mobs rather than those which a military leader like Mahomet or any other Ghazi would have followed. So far from being entitled to the military epithet of Ghazi, he had none of the virtues which have often been possessed by soldiers even who behaved brutally. There is nothing military about the character of a man who carefully avoided the battlefield and cared nothing about his army so long as they could make a brave show at the Friday Selamlik and, as he believed, could and would defend him against his own subjects.

Enough has been said of Abdul Hamid to show that he has no title to be reckoned among the heroes. He must be classed as a Sovereign among the failures, as a selfish man among the mediocrities. A Turk may well ask the question, What did he do for Turkey? The answer should be that he helped to destroy it. Policy he had none, but his conduct of public affairs greatly weakened his government. He largely diminished the moral fibre of his people. The truthful, daring, and outspoken Turk whom our grandfathers admired became demoralised. A generation grew up under Abdul Hamid's sway which was the constant object of suspicion. Espionage is deadly, and creates a nation of liars and cowards. The presence of spies in the house, the mosque, the street, indeed everywhere, led to subterfuge and lying, to universal suspicion, and largely crushed out the manliness of the dominant race. It is never recorded of Abdul Hamid that he uttered a noble thought. He never touched the national imagination.

His long reign records a series of losses of territory, to which he largely contributed. Without military knowledge or experience, he became his own commander-in-chief in the Russo-Turkish War and by his incompetence and bad faith rendered the loss of Bulgaria certain. With preparations going on in Austria for mobilisation, with the presence of the British fleet, and with the assurances of Sir Henry Layard that Russia would not be allowed to enter Constantinople, this descendant of the great Ghazi was with difficulty prevented from leaving his capital. When the Bulgaria of the San Stefano Treaty had been largely reduced and Eastern Rumelia placed under his rule, with the right to re-enter the province in case of disorder, a right sanctioned by all Europe, his Ministers could not persuade him to exercise it. Though his representatives at Berlin had promised that he would introduce reforms into Armenia, he violated the promises given in his name. His violation of the Treaty in reference to Macedonia was not less flagrant. Every Power in Europe desired during several years to see reforms both in Armenia and in Macedonia. His own subjects, Moslems as well as Christians, desired them, not in the interest of Christians, but in that of Turkey. Abdul Hamid defied all Europe, though its central idea was to preserve general peace by preserving the integrity of the Empire. He rejected the elaborate schemes of reform prepared at the request of all Europe by Sir Drummond Wolff and Lord Fitzmaurice. It is true that at a later period of his reign Austria was not whole-hearted in her support, though she joined with the other Powers in regard to Armenia.

The Turk, considering his answer to the question what his Sultan had done for Turkey, might well ask, Did he know that the Powers were working in Turkey's interest? If the answer suggested is that they were also working in their own interest, then why, when trustworthy servants like Hilmi Pasha urged measures of reform, were they not listened to? Why, again, did he go out of his way to attack the ancient privileges of the Orthodox and other Christian Churches? They had been conceded by more convinced Moslems than he. Why should they be disturbed?

Abdul blundered badly when he refused to allow Turkish troops to enter Egypt with the British, for he was expressly warned that, with his consent or without it, the British would enter. His blundering in respect to the Wolff Convention was still worse. Sultans had hitherto kept their word. The tradition of the Treaty displayed at Varna is known to every educated Turk, and has done much to make them respecters of their signatures to such documents. Abdul violated his and lost Egypt. All the Great Powers wished the island of Crete to remain Ottoman. Greece herself did not desire to annex it. It is true that in 1897 Germany and Austria ceased to take part in a demonstration by the fleets, but they none the less wished the island to remain under the Sultan. But Abdul Hamid was found playing a foul game, supporting the Moslems against his own appointed Governor, and so the Sultan lost Crete. Abdul Hamid had sacrificed Tunis and Tripoli through his incompetence. A Turkish inquirer of an enlightened class would have nothing to say in defence of the massacres in Armenia, for those with experience of the country declare that no Moslem who followed what was done could speak otherwise than with loathing of Abdul's share in them.

There is nothing to be noted as compensation to the Empire for the loss of territory, of reputation, and of *moral*. Until the end of the century all Europe had worked with general accord to preserve the Empire intact. It was Abdul Hamid's perversity that hastened its disintegration. The Sultan had already been flattered by one visit from the Kaiser, and fell an easy victim to German flattery. Had he possessed the statesmanship with which he loved to be credited, he would have noted that Germany and Austria in his late years were working in accord, that they aided in increasing the discord in Macedonia, and that, as his spies doubtless informed him, they calculated upon the anarchy there existing as likely to lead to a European invitation to Austria to occupy the disaffected province. He would have recognised that Germany by taking over the railway to Ismidt and obtaining the extensions for Angora, Konia, and ultimately to Bagdad, and especially in seeking to obtain a monopoly of railways, was arranging for the economic annexation of Asia Minor, which would go dangerously near the political annexation of the whole Empire, and that, while such was the apparent design of the Central Powers, none of the other States appeared to desire a share in Turkish territory.

In home affairs Abdul Hamid's want of statesmanship is equally visible. It is sufficient in order to answer the question, What has Abdul Hamid done for Turkey ? to recall his suspension of Midhat's Constitution, entailing the silence of a Chamber of Representatives for thirty years, his treatment of its author, his rejection of every suggestion of reform in government, and the entire absence of ideas of his own to effect beneficial changes. He arrested the development of every race in the Empire. He never seems to have conceived the idea of welding them together, so that they should willingly accept his rule. He widened the breach between them. No step can be pointed to as taken by him which would indicate that he had a desire to make of his subjects one people.

He had many able subjects, but failed to make a confidant of any of them. He protected worthless fellows like his foster-brother Fehim, who, having notoriously committed in Constantinople every crime in the Decalogue, was, at the demand of Baron Marschall von Bieberstein and Sir Nicholas O'Conor, banished from Constantinople to Brussa, and upon his openly continuing his outrages on women and men was lynched by a long-suffering populace. He had alienated every supporter. He found the law courts on his accession treated with scant respect ; he left them with even less. He saw his army after his deposition driven before Bulgars and Serbs ; his fleet on his deposition was not able to face an enemy. He had taken all the moral stamina out of the nation. At the last stage of his career as Sultan he found himself friendless. None were sufficiently attached to him to regret his overthrow ; none so poor to do him reverence. He had become incapable of taking advantage of the movements either commenced by him or by some of those whose interest lay in keeping him on the throne. He remained passive in his palace while his adherents were being beaten. Though he had no reason to fear for his personal safety, this Ghazi seemed only anxious to save his life.

In his later years Abdul Hamid, prematurely old, fell a victim to his own machinations. His suspicion led to his being ill informed of what was going on around him. The *djournals* sent daily by his army of spies were so many that he could not find time to read them. He dared not entrust them to anyone else; and yet those which he did read were so contradictory that he ended, as was shown after his deposition, by leaving most of them unread. He was thus thrown back upon his own judgment, which was that of an ill-balanced and mediocre intelligence. For, whatever he had been in his youth, he had now become an essentially commonplace man, mean, sordid, and cunning. It may be doubted whether in the conduct of foreign affairs he ever tried to see any question from the point of view of the nation which it concerned. His conduct rather suggests that he held the opinion of the ignorant Turkish peasant that all other States ought to do the Padisha's bidding, and that imperial policy consisted mainly in playing off one country against another.

Long before the revolution of 1908 he had gathered all power into his own hands, and could have truthfully boasted, "*L'état, c'est moi.*" But in so doing he had made himself a terror. To those outside Yildiz he was a bogey; to those within the bogey resolved itself into a weak, ill-tempered, lonely old man, frightened at his own creation. It may be doubted whether he ever thought of the condition in which he would leave Turkey to his successor. If he did, he acted as if he would have added, "*Après moi le deluge.*" His favourites had been allowed to amass fortunes in the hope of binding them to his service. In the hour of need they deserted him. He had tolerated corruption in every branch of his service, and those who had profited by it were eager to denounce him when it became safe to do so.

His influence on his country and his race was pernicious. Without any lofty ideal of conduct, he blundered on in his old age in loneliness and in sickness, making every kind of progress impossible.

The Turkish population descended during his rule to a lower plane, to a less pure political and moral atmosphere. No ideals remained except among the handful of Young Turks whom he in vain tried to exterminate. Corruption and degeneracy had increased in every department of state.

Abdul Hamid when he was deposed had finished his life work. He had degraded Turkey; possibly he had destroyed her.

CHRONOLOGICAL TABLE

1842 (Sept. 22). Birth of Abdul Hamid.
1848. Revolutions in France and elsewhere.
1854–5. Crimean War.
1856. Treaty of Paris.
„ (July 18). Concession for Ottoman-Aidin Railway granted.
1857. Indian Mutiny.
1858 (Sept. 19). Railway opened, Smyrna to Aidin.
1861. American Civil War begins.
1866. Austro-Prussian War.
1867. Abdul Hamid visits Paris Exhibition and London with Sultan Abdul Aziz.
1869. Suez Canal opened.
1870 (March 10). Firman constituting Bulgarian Church.
„ Franco-Prussian War.
1873 (June 17). Railway between Constantinople and Adrianople opened.
1874. Disraeli Prime Minister of Great Britain.
1875. Insurrection in Herzegovina.
„ (Nov.). Great Britain buys Khedive's shares in Suez Canal.
1876 (March). Payment of interest on Turkish Debt suspended altogether.
„ (May). Abdul Aziz deposed and Murad proclaimed Sultan.
„ (May to Sept.). Massacre and horrors in Bulgaria.
„ (Aug. 31). Murad deposed and Abdul Hamid proclaimed; Murad commits suicide a few days afterwards
„ (Sept. 19). Baring's report on Bulgaria published; Gladstone's Bulgarian pamphlet.
„ (Sept. 27). Serbia, who had accepted an armistice, renews fighting.
„ (autumn). English officers engaged to form gendarmerie.
„ (Dec. 5). Conference at Constantinople.
1877 (Jan. 18). Turkish Great Council rejects proposals of Conference.
„ (Feb. 5). Midhat (Prime Minister) dismissed; succeeded by Edhem Pasha.
„ (March 19). First Turkish Parliament opened.
„ (April 24). Sir Henry A. Layard Ambassador at Constantinople.
„ „ War declared by Russia.

1877 (Dec. 10). Plevna surrenders to Russians.
1878 (Jan.). Battle of Shenova; capture of 60,000 Turkish troops.
„ (Feb. 13). British Fleet passes Dardanelles.
„ (March). San Stefano Treaty; Great Bulgaria created.
„ (May 20). Ali Suavi's attempt against Sultan.
„ (July 7). Cyprus Convention signed.
„ (July 13). Treaty of Berlin; Bulgaria autonomous; Eastern Rumelia under Sultan.
„ (Sept. 6). Murder of Mehmet Ali.
„ (Dec. 20). Decree of Muharem.
1879 (Feb. 8). Peace with Russia signed.
„ (April 29). Prince Alexander of Hesse elected Prince of Bulgaria.
„ (June). Deposition of Khedive Ismail.
1879-81. Great Britain's Afghan and South African Wars.
1880. Gladstone succeeds Beaconsfield.
„ (Sept.). Naval demonstration at Dulcigno.
„ (Nov.). German officers appointed to reorganise Turkish Army.
1881 (June). Trial and exile of Midhat Pasha.
„ Arabi made Minister of War in Egypt.
„ (Aug.). Arabi's revolt.
1882 (May). British and French Fleets arrive at Alexandria.
„ (June 11). Riot in Alexandria.
„ (July). Admiral Seymour bombards Alexandria; French Fleet withdraws.
„ (Aug.—Sept.). Battle of Tel-el-Kebir; surrender of Arabi; British enter Cairo.
1883 (Feb.). Anglo-French control in Egypt ends.
1884 (Jan.). Gordon sent to Khartoum.
„ (May). Midhat murdered in Arabia.
1885 (Jan.). Death of Gordon.
„ (Sept. 18). "Bloodless revolution" in Philippopolis.
„ (Nov.). Serbo-Bulgar War.
„ (Nov.). Massacres in Armenia.
1886 (Jan.). Collective note calls on Balkan States to disarm; Serbia and Greece refuse.
„ Gladstone's first Home Rule Bill.
„ (March 13). Peace between Bulgaria and Serbia.
„ (April 5). Alexander Governor of Eastern Rumelia.
„ (Aug.—Sept.). Alexander kidnapped; returns and abdicates.
„ (Sept.). General Kaulbars Russian agent in Bulgaria.
„ (Dec. 15). Ferdinand of Saxe-Coburg invited by Bulgaria.
„ Mahmud appointed Ottoman Commissioner in Crete.

1887 (July). Wolff's convention regarding departure of troops from Egypt.
„ (Aug. 14). Ferdinand becomes Prince of Bulgaria.
1888 (June). Accession of William II. as German Emperor.
„ (Aug. 12). Direct railway communication between Constantinople and London.
1889 (July). Cretan Assembly claims annexation to Greece; Greek Government refuses; insurrection breaks out in island.
„ (Aug.). Committee of inquiry sent to Armenia.
1890. Troubles in Armenia and Crete.
„ Haidarpasha line seized by Turks, and handed over to Germany; German ascendancy growing in Constantinople.
1894–1895. Great series of Armenian massacres.
1894. England, France, and Russia propose reforms in Armenia.
1895 (June). Jevad replaced as Grand Vizier by Kutchuk Said.
„ (July). Stambuloff murdered.
„ „ Massacres at Baiburt, Erzinghian, Bitlis, Diabekr, and other places.
„ (Nov.). All Powers protest against massacres in Armenia.
„ (Dec.). Abdul Hamid becomes alarmed, especially at the discontent of his Moslem subjects.
„ (Dec.). Massacres at Urfa.
1896. Rising at Zeitun.
„ (Aug.). Attack on Ottoman Bank in Constantinople, followed by massacres of Armenians in Constantinople; protests of Powers.
„ (Sept.). Cretan charter granted.
1897 (April 24). Sultan grants Berats for three new Bulgarian bishoprics.
„ (April—May). War between Turkey and Greece.
„ English and French garrisons occupy Candia.
„ Greece sends troops to Crete.
1898. Great Britain, France, Italy, and Russia constitute Crete an autonomous State; Prince George of Greece Governor-General.
„ (Sept.). Battle of Omdurman; conquest of Soudan.
„ (Oct. 18). First visit of Kaiser to Sultan.
„ Anatolian Railway concession granted to Germans.
1899–1902 Great Britain's South African War.
1899 (Nov.). Bagdad Railway concession granted to Germany.
1900 Hedjaz Railway commenced
1901 (Jan.). Queen Victoria dies; succeeded by Edward VII.

1901 (June). Cretan Assembly adopts a resolution in favour of union with Greece; the four protecting Powers refuse consent.

1902. Turks violate Aden frontier; Sir Nicholas O'Conor demands and obtains withdrawal of Turkish troops.

1903 (July). First section Bagdad Railway opened.

" (Sept.). Murzsteg programme of reforms for Macedonia; gendarmerie proposals

" Permission granted Russian Volunteer Fleet to pass Straits; Great Britain protests.

1904. Russo-Japanese War.

" Anglo-French Entente.

" (Aug. 31). Murad V., deposed Sultan, dies.

1905 (Feb.). Rising in Yemen; Turks defeated.

" German Emperor visits Jerusalem.

" (Dec.) Powers' proposals for Macedonia agreed to after naval demonstration at Mitylene and Lemnos.

1906 (Oct.). Extension Ottoman-Aidin Railway to Bulair and Eghidir.

" Central Committee of Union and Progress formed in Salonika.

1907. Central Committee of Union and Progress formed in Paris.

" Anglo-Russian agreement.

" Lord Cromer retires from Egypt.

1908. Crete's union with Greece proclaimed; disapproved by Powers.

" (June 9). Meeting of Edward VII. and Czar at Reval.

" (end June). Niazi Bey and Enver Bey take to the hills at Resna.

" (July 22). Army in Macedonia supports Committee of Union and Progress and demand constitution.

" (July 23). Sultan yields and proclaims constitution.

" (Sept. 1). Hedjaz Railway opened nearly to Medina.

" (Oct. 5). Ferdinand declares himself King of Bulgaria.

" (Dec.). Turkish Parliament meets.

1909 (April 13). Attempt at counter-revolution.

" (April 24). Arrival of "Army of Deliverers" under Shevket Pasha.

" (April 27). Abdul Hamid arrested in Yildiz; deposed.

" (April 29). Abdul taken to Salonika.

BIBLIOGRAPHY

I. *Relating to Topography.*—Excellent maps have been published during the last fifty years of Constantinople and its neighbourhood. Those of the city including Galata and Pera are fairly complete as published by several French houses. The Admiralty charts of the Bosporos and the Islands are, of course, as nearly perfect as possible. Of the environs of Constantinople, especially between the Black Sea and the Marmora, a map prepared and published by General Von der Goltz while in the Turkish service (Freiherr Colman v. der Goltz: "Karte der Umgegend von Constantinopel." 1898) is beautifully complete.

II. *For the Archæology of the City and Neighbourhood.*—The "Constantinoplis Christiana," of C. Du F. Du Cange (1680), cannot be neglected. It is found in all the three editions of the Byzantine authors.

The studies of the late Dr. Paspates, who resided in Constantinople till about 1884, are always valuable. Only one has been translated into English. "The Great Palace of Constantinople." Tr. by W. Metcalfe. Paisley. 1893. In Greek they are simply known as the *Meletai*.

Various studies of local topography were made by the members of the community of the Roman Catholic Assumptionists whose headquarters were at Chalcedon, the modern Kadikeui. In the transactions of both the Russian Institute in Constantinople and in that of the transactions Mitteilungen des Deutschen Exkursions-Klubs in Constantinopel are many valuable papers on the local topography and archæology.

To these may be added two valuable books by the late Dr. Alexander van Millingen, who was always a keen student of everything that related to the archæology of his native city, and whose books will preserve the plans and photographs of some of the ancient buildings that have stood for a thousand years but have been wantonly destroyed within the last four years. His principal books are :—

"Byzantine Churches in Constantinople." By A. v. M., assisted by R Traquair, W. S. George and A. E. Henderson. With Maps, Plans and Illustrations. Macmillan. 1912.

"Byzantine Constantinople. The Walls of the City and adjoining Historical Sites. . . ." With Maps, Plans and Illustrations. John Murray. 1899.

III. *Historical and Biographical*:—

H. A. Gibbons. "The Foundations of the Ottoman Empire." A History of the Osmanlis up to the Death of Bayezid I., 1300–1403. Oxford University Press. 1916.

Sir Paul Rycaut. "The Present State of the Ottoman Empire." 1668.

Sir James Porter. "Observations on the Religion, Law, Government and Manners of the Turks." 1768.

Rev. Robert Walsh. "Residence at Constantinople during the Greek and Turkish Revolutions." 2 vols. 1836. (Walsh was chaplain to the Embassy during the time of the hanging of the Patriarch and the brutalities inflicted upon the Greeks in the Greek Revolution, 1820–30.)

Charles White. "Three Years in Constantinople." 3 vols. Colburn. 1845. (The author, Colonel White, spent three years in Constantinople and wrote what Layard described as the best book ever written about the place. It is not only pleasant reading but full of valuable facts and observations.)

J. H. A. Ubicini. "Lettres." 2 vols. 1853–4. (English translation, 1856.)

William Miller. "The Ottoman Empire, 1801–1913." (Cambridge Historical Series, 1913.)

Stanley Lane-Poole. "The Life of Stratford de Redcliffe." 2 vols. 1888. (Popular edition, 1890.)

"*Odysseus*" (*Sir Charles N. E. Eliot*). "Turkey in Europe." 1900.

A. Gallenga. "Two Years of the Eastern Question." 2 vols. 1877. (Letters to *The Times*.)

"The War Correspondence of the *Daily News*, forming a continuous history of the War between Russia and Turkey." 1877–8.

Chas. S. Ryan. "Red Crescent." 1877–8, 1897. (Colonel Ryan was the only Englishman present with the Turks at the siege of Plevna.)

G. Dorys. "Abdul Hamid Intime." Paris. 6th edition. 1903.

Francis McCullagh. "The Fall of Abdul Hamid." 1910.

Sir E. Pears. "Turkey and its People." 1911.

An extremely valuable history of Turkey and the Balkan States was brought out in 1915 by the Carnegie Fund. A great number of books and pamphlets were published in Abdul Hamid's reign in Paris, Berlin, and Geneva; none of course in Turkey.

The above list covers the most important of the books relating to Constantinople and the Empire during the life of Abdul Hamid. The earlier ones mentioned, such as those by Rycaut, Sir James Porter and the invaluable Life of Lord Stratford de Redcliffe are of great importance, showing the steady decadence of Turkey, the causes which led thereto and the great attempts made to regenerate the Empire, especially by England and France.

INDEX

THE WHITEFRIARS PRESS, LTD. LONDON, AND TONBRIDGE

CPSIA information can be obtained
at www.ICGtesting.com
Printed in the USA
BVHW041705170419
545820BV00007B/30/P

9 780530 421636